Saints and Swordsmen.

Northumbrians in the Anglo-Saxon Age.

By Chris Kilkenny

The right of Chris Kilkenny to be identified as the author of this work has been asserted by him in accordance with the copyright, designs and patents act of 1988.

No part of this publication may be reproduced, stored in a retrieval system, or transmitted in any form or by any means, without the prior permission in writing of the author.

Dedication

For the Arkle family of Northumberland, and their descendants.

Northumbrians for over a thousand years.

Tarset burn and Tarret burn,

Yet, Yet, Yet.

Contents

INTRODUCTION 3
CHAPTER 1. 5
THE ORIGIN OF THE NORTHUMBRIANS, The Angles of the North. 5
   THE ANGLES IN NORTHUMBRIA. 7
CHAPTER 2. 14
AETHELFRITH-THE MAN WHO MADE NORTHUMBRIA 14
   THE MAKING OF NORTHUMBRIA 18
CHAPTER 3. 24
THE NORTHUMBRIAN PEOPLE 24
   THE LANGUAGE 39
   NORTHUMBRIAN PLACE NAMES 43
CHAPTER 4. 59
EDWIN-THE FIRST CHRISTIAN KING OF NORTHUMBRIA 59
   THE CONVERSION OF THE NORTHUMBRIANS 60
   THE DEATH OF EDWIN 67
CHAPTER 5. 69
OSWALD AND OSWIU-the sons of Aethelfrith 69
   OSWIU, Emperor of All Britain. 86
CHAPTER 6. 99
ECGFRITH and ALDFRITH. THE SONS OF OSWIU. 99
   ALDFRITH, THE MOST CIVILISED NORTHUMBRIAN KING. 118
CHAPTER 7. 122
8TH CENTURY NORTHUMBRIA. THE GOLDEN AGE 122
   THE NORTHUMBRIAN MISSIONARIES. 124
CHAPTER 8. 149
POLITICAL UNREST 149
CHAPTER 9. 152

THE COMING OF THE VIKINGS 152
   THE VIKING ATTACK ON NORTHUMBRIA.......................... 152
   THE JOURNEYS OF ST CUTHBERT`S BODY 160
CHAPTER 10 167
THE RISE OF WESSEX 167
   THE NEW DANISH ATTACK. 175
CHAPTER 10. 179
   ST CUTHBERT ARRIVES AT DURHAM 995 AD.................... 181
   UCHTRED OF BAMBURGH, EARL OF NORTHUMBRIA. 184
   THE LOSS OF LOTHIAN. 188
   THE NORTHUMBRIAN REBELLION 1065 AD. 196
CHAPTER 11. 198
THE ARRIVAL OF THE NORMANS 198
   THE BATTLE OF FULFORD GATE 1066 AD. 199
   THE BATTLE FOR NORTHUMBRIA 203
   THE LAST ENGLISH EARL OF NORTHUMBRIA 211
   NORMAN CONTROL OF THE CHURCH 213
   WILLIAM II, RUFUS, AND THE END OF NORTHUMBRIA . 218
BIBLIOGRAPHY.. 223
More Northumbrian Books from Chris Kilkenny, ... 226

INTRODUCTION

"I warmly welcome your eager desire to know something of the doings and sayings of great men of the past, and of your own nation in particular." Bede.

"Lo, it is nearly 350 years that we and our fathers have inhabited this most lovely land." The Northumbrian Scholar Alcuin in 793 AD.

This is about the people of Northumbria, their origins and achievements. It begins at the time of the migration of the tribes from the eastern North Sea lands and ends with their absorption into Norman England. It deals with those Swordsmen who created the successful Kingdom of Northumbria, who took tribute from all of Britain: with the Saints who converted the pagan Northumbrians then spread Christianity through England and the Continent: With those who created the first cultural achievements of the English, and with those who fought a three hundred year war to maintain their separate identity against Viking raider, Yorkshire Dane, Scot, Southern English Kings and Normans.

These are the people who made this land and named this land.

Northumbria is taken to be the boundaries of the kingdom, then the Earldom, which varied throughout this period, c.450AD to 1100AD, from comprising most of Northern England and Southern Scotland to being reduced to the bounds of the later counties of Northumberland and Durham.

As far as possible the story is in their own words. Luckily for the North East the main source for the 7th century was written at Jarrow on Tyne by the first English historian, Bede. His work was reinforced by later writers at Durham, such as the works attributed to Simeon. Bede of course was writing an Ecclesiastical history, he is less concerned with the warrior society, whose beliefs and swords provided the wealth to create the 600-man strong monastery where he wrote his book. For a glimpse of that society which was the foundation of later Northumbrian society we follow JRR Tolkein's dictum; "Beowulf is an historical document of the first order for the study of the mood and thought of the period, and one perhaps too little used by historians." So our story is reinforced by selections of Anglo-Saxon poetry,(mainly translated by RK Gordon.) shown in italics or **bold** throughout. The story is illustrated with maps and drawings produced by the author and numerous illustrations from the area and farther afield where relevant.

The original sources are acknowledged wherever possible.(abbreviation; RMS Royal Museum of Scotland. BM, British Museum. BL, British Library. NT, National Trust. BW Bede's World, Jarrow. EH , English Heritage. MoN Museum of the North, Newcastle. NCC, Northumberland County Council. YME, Yorkshire museum exhibition. York)

The main sources abbreviated in the text are as follows; Bede, (The Ecclesiastical history of the English Nation.) Bede Life, (The life and miracles of St Cuthbert.) NH, Northern History. AA, Archaeologia Aeliana. KNS, Kings of the North Sea, Exhibition and catalogue, (Esbjerg Museum, Tyne and Wear Museums et al.). Elsewhere an author's name is used and the book will be found in the bibliography at the end.

This is the first volume of a series covering the history of the Northumbrian people, The Angles of the North.

The Angles of Northumbria are to a percipient historian a people with marked and notable characteristics, (sufficient indeed to raise doubts as to whether the portmanteau term Anglo-Saxon possess any real validity.) If landscapes can mould peoples, the northern hills and valleys and wild grey coasts left their mark on the early Northumbrian's just as the industrial fields of this area have shaped their modern descendants."
Thomas.p.99.

CHAPTER 1.

THE ORIGIN OF THE NORTHUMBRIANS,
The Angles of the North.

The birth of the Nation

"I warmly welcome your eager desire to know something of the doings and sayings of great men of the past, and of your own nation in particular." Bede.

The first English historian, the Northumbrian monk Bede, invented the name *Northumbrians* to identify his people who settled in what is now North East England. He also stressed that they were Angles to differentiate them from the Saxons and Jutes and Frisians who also arrived about this time. The nation of the Northumbrians came from that piece of land which joins modern Germany to Denmark and which became known as Schleswig Holstein, the lands around the river Eider.

"those who came over were the three most powerful nations in Germany—Saxons, Angles and Jutes. From the Jutes were descended the people of Kent, and the isle of Wight...From the Saxons came the East-Saxons

(Essex),the South-Saxons,(Sussex) and the West-Saxons,(Wessex).From the Angles, that is the country called Anglia, and which it said from that time, to remain desert to this day, between the provinces of the Jutes and the Saxons, are descended the East-Angles,The Midland-Angles, Mercians, all the race of the Northumbrians, that is, of those nations that dwell on the north side of the river Humber, and the other nations of the English." Bede.

Other sources recall the Angles and their King Offa;

"*His ancestors sprang from the Myrgingas, and he had firstly gone with Ealhild, the beloved peace-weaver, out of Anglyn to the home of the king of the glorious Goths.*" Widsith

"***Offa ruled Angel, Alewih the Danes:***
he was bravest of all these men,
yet he did not perform mighty deeds beyond Offa;
but Offa, first of men,
while still a youth, gained the greatest of kingdoms;
no one of the same age achieved greater deeds of valour in battle:
with his single sword he fixed the boundary
against the Myrgings at Fifeldor.
Afterwards the Angles and Swabians held it as Offa had won it."
Widsith.

(Fifeldor is an island lying at the mouth of the Eider.)

This is a low-lying land of mud, bog and salt meadows, very susceptible to the flooding. This forced the inhabitants to build platforms called Wurten made from dung, turf and clay. The 5th century saw increased storm activity on the North Sea coast and these settlements were abandoned. It is quite possible that land shortage forced the Angles or English from their homeland. Bede said that the land was depopulated when they left, and there is archaeological evidence for this. (Resettlement occurred in the 8th century with improved tidal patterns.) Bede was writing 300 years after the migration period, but with knowledge of a strong oral tradition. Comparisons of brooches and pottery finds support Bede's statements about the distribution of tribes in Britain. Some historians find his division of tribes too neat, and state that no firm boundaries between the tribes can be made. Some claim that the invaders came from Frisia pointing out the closeness of their languages, and similarities of their burials and language;

"*Brod, butter en grene chiese, en wat dat net sayse ken, Is kin uprjuchte Friese.*"

(Bread, butter, and green cheese, and who cannot say that is no upright Frisian)

according to this test for Frisians, most Northumbrians would qualify. It is possible that English leaders picked up followers from other tribes, before they crossed the seas. It was common for young men to fight for a neighbouring tribe. The Angles had invaded Frisia in the first half of the 5th century so separating the tribes was made more difficult. The pagan Saxons encountered by Boniface, the English missionary, told him "we are one blood and one bone." Although this did not stop them from murdering him.

THE POST ROMAN TRIBES

Map showing: Picts, Scots, Jutes, Danes, Angles, Saxons, Britons, Frisians, Franks

THE ANGLES IN NORTHUMBRIA.

"As the rule of history requires, I have laboured sincerely to commit to writing such things as I could gather from common report, for the instruction of posterity." Bede.

Bede's methods were rigorous but his purpose was to write "An Ecclesiastical History of the English peoples" as an instruction for posterity, therefore he concentrated on matters of the church and religion, other areas were down played or ignored. He reached Chapter 25 before an Anglo-Saxon is named, Aethelbert of Kent, and this is in the context of Augustine's Christian mission from Rome. We reach Chapter 34 and the end of Book One before we have a Northumbrian, Aethelfrith, named. After another 9 Chapters Edwin arrives on the scene and Bede gets down to portraying the 7th century Christian king's as exemplars for his own time. The life of the pagan people is totally ignored. He wrote in Latin and he tried to show how the subjects of his history reflected the achievements of fathers of the Church and biblical characters.

Northumbrian Towns

Long before Bede there were Teutonic warriors in the north under the Roman Empire. The Romans used mercenaries from Northern Europe to defend their Empire, there were squadrons of Frisians stationed on the Roman Wall at Housesteads in the 3rd century. They were cavalry. There was also the Numerus Hnaudifridi or Notfried's unit of irregulars, who may well have been accompanied by their families. There were Anglo-Saxon graves in York, (Eboracum) the legionary fortress. The Romans brought in even more

Germanic tribesmen to deal with the growing threat from the Picts and Saxons at the end of the 4th century. Artillery was added to some forts and there was an increase in cavalry units. In 365 and 367AD, Picts and Saxons were uniting to attack Roman Britain. Roman defences increasingly concentrated on the coastline against raiders. Huge forts were built, and linked by watchtowers, such as that at Whitby, or as the English called it Streaneshalch, the Bay of the Lighthouse. As early as 325 AD Tigris boatmen from modern day Iraq, had been called in to Arbeia, the fort at South Shields. When later c.410 AD Rome called back the legions to defend herself against inroads from assorted "barbarians", she told the Britons to look to their own defences. It was natural for the post-Roman rulers of the country, like their forebears, to call in mercenaries from abroad, and it was equally predictable that these warriors would exploit the weaknesses of their hosts to seize what they could, be it plunder or land.

The ability of the Britons to defend themselves may also have been affected by widespread plague around 444 AD.

"on a sudden, a severe plague fell upon that corrupt generation, which soon destroyed such numbers of them, that the living were scarcely sufficient to bury the dead." Bede.

" *many a mead-hall was full of revels*
until mighty fate changed that, Wide walls fell
Days of pestilence came;
Death swept away the bravery of men
Their forts fell to waste" The Ruin.

There was another plague around 552AD according to Irish annals.

It seemed as if there was no love lost between the Britons who called themselves Cymru, the people, and the English who called the Britons, "Welsh", ie. foreigners. Bede held the Britons in contempt because they had not tried to convert the heathen English. Even when the English converted to Christianity, the Britons remained aloof;

"It being to this day the custom of the Britons not to pay any respect to the faith and religion of the English, nor to correspond with them any more than with pagans." Bede.

" They will neither eat nor pray with us, and they scour out our dishes with sand or fire." Aldhelm, complaining about British monks. (Roman writers at Vindolanda in the South Tyne valley had also referred to them as "wretched little Britons.")English riddles suggested their view of the Welsh,

"When breath is gone.I bind the hands. Of swart welsh; worthier men too."
Exeter 12. Ox hide. Alexander.

Of those English who settled in Britain, the wide expanses of the Humber estuary served as a border between the South and the North. The direct roman road between the roman towns of York to the north and Lincoln to the south is cut by a one mile ferry journey. The alternative road diverts far inland. This border may have been made wider by the widespread floods of the 4th and 5th Centuries AD.

Historians imply that the invaders followed a route that took them to the narrow sea crossings, so they landed in Kent and East Anglia. From there they moved into Lindsey, south of the Humber, then into Deira, north of the Humber. The English took over from the British Gaelic-speaking rulers in Deira, separating that province, (roughly Yorkshire, north of the Humber) from Bernicia. This was credited to Soemil, who is separated from the historical Aelle by 5 kings of Deira. Considering the fate of their homeland they wisely settled above the flood plain on the Yorkshire Wolds. The English leader Aelle was succeeded by Aethelfrith of Bernicia, the first King of all Northumbria, soon after 600AD.

From Deira, Higham suggests they moved into Cleveland, via Catterick and possibly to the Corbridge/Hexham area. The Ouse, the Tees, the Tyne and the long coast line made much of the area accessible to men in light craft. The interior was further opened up by the Roman roads or stanegates as the English called some of them. Myres suggests that the people of Lindsey gave their name to Lindisfarne. However there was a tradition among the Britons that the Angles moved directly from the Kent to Bernicia.

Those Angles to the North of the Humber were called Northanhymbre. It was,

" a little known country, wolf-slopes, windswept headlands, perilous paths across the boggy moors, where a mountain stream plunges under the mist-covered cliffs, rushes through a fissure." Beowulf.

"The land north of the wall is inhabited by snakes and wild beasts and travellers would be killed by the pestilent atmosphere" Procopius mid-6th century. (A view still held, some would say, by sections of the modern media and political establishment. Certainly the identification of "north of the wall with modern day Scotland, is a journalistic "howler" which continues to appear.)

THE ROCK FORTRESS OF BAMBURGH WITH A LATER MEDIAEVAL CASTLE.

The first named leader of the English Bernicians, was Ida and they gained a toehold at Bamburgh, (Dinas Guoroy) around 547 AD. The expansion of the English was checked by the Britons of Rheged (based around Carlisle) and of Manau Gododdin (based at Din Eidyn, Edinburgh.) and Strathclyde (based on Dumbarton.) Gaelic-speaking raiders from Ulster, the Scots, were at the same time gaining a foothold in Argyll at Dunadd. There was also still a small British kingdom Elmet in Yorkshire. According to Welsh sources a British King, Cunedda of Manau, had moved to North Wales and set up the kingdom of Gwynedd around the mid 5th century. This may have weakened those left behind. However some of these Britons were powerful warlords, (in the view of the Welsh sources.) in particular, Urien of Rheged who besieged Ida's son, Theoderic, for 3 days in Mercaut, (Lindisfarne). Urien was murdered by his fellow Briton ,Morcant. The siege failed. *"Theoderic used to fight bravely against Urbgen with his sons and yet at that time sometimes the enemy and sometimes the citizens used to be vanquished."*

The Britons were credited with a victory, of Owein of Rheged over the English;

The host of broad England sleeps,
With the light shining in their eyes,

And those who would not flee
Were bolder than they had need.
Owein punished them soundly
Like a pack of wolves after sheep. Tr. Bromwich in Hunter Blair,Northumbria.

THE POST ROMAN KINGDOMS OF THE NORTH

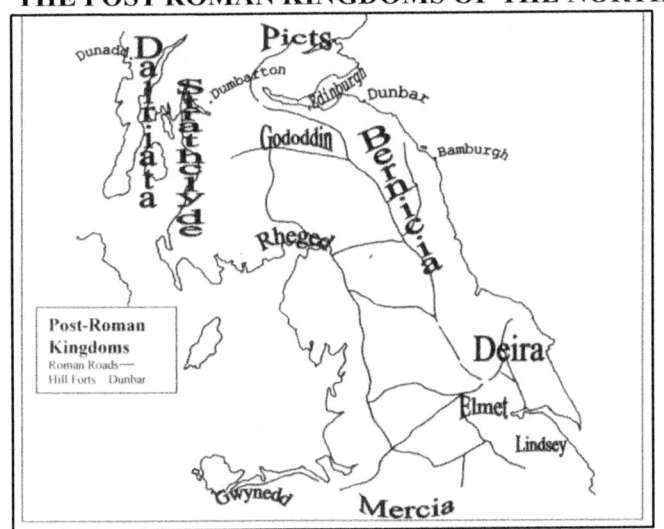

THE ROCK FORTRESS OF DUNADD, TODAY IN ARGYLL, SCOTLAND.

THE ROCK FORTRESS OF DIN EIDYN, EDINBURGH, now in Scotland.

THE ROCK FORTRESS OF ALT CLUT, DUMBARTON, SCOTLAND.

"In the meantime in Britain, there was some respite from foreign but not civil wars. There still remained the ruins of cities destroyed by the enemy, and abandoned, and the natives who had escaped the enemy, now fought against each other". Bede

The Angles fresh from their watery homeland across the North Sea were at home on water. Lindisfarne, half mainland, half island, was ideal for them.

Keel from *The Anglo Saxons. L. Turnbull.*

"Then the depths were troubled ,
The horn fish darted,
Gliding through ocean,
The grey gull wheeled
Searching for carrion.
The sun grew dark
A gale arose and great waves broke,
The sea streams were stirred,
Halyards were humming
Sails were drenched
Sea terror grew
In the welter of waves. Anon. St Andrew. Gordon.

CHAPTER 2.

AETHELFRITH-THE MAN WHO MADE NORTHUMBRIA.

" He often deprived his enemies, many tribes of men, of their mead benches, He terrified his foes; won praise and honour, until the men of every neighbouring tribe were obliged to obey him and pay him tribute. He was a good king." Beowulf.

The poet's definition of a good king is instructive of our ancestor's values.

BERNICIAN EXPANSION UNDER AETHELFRITH

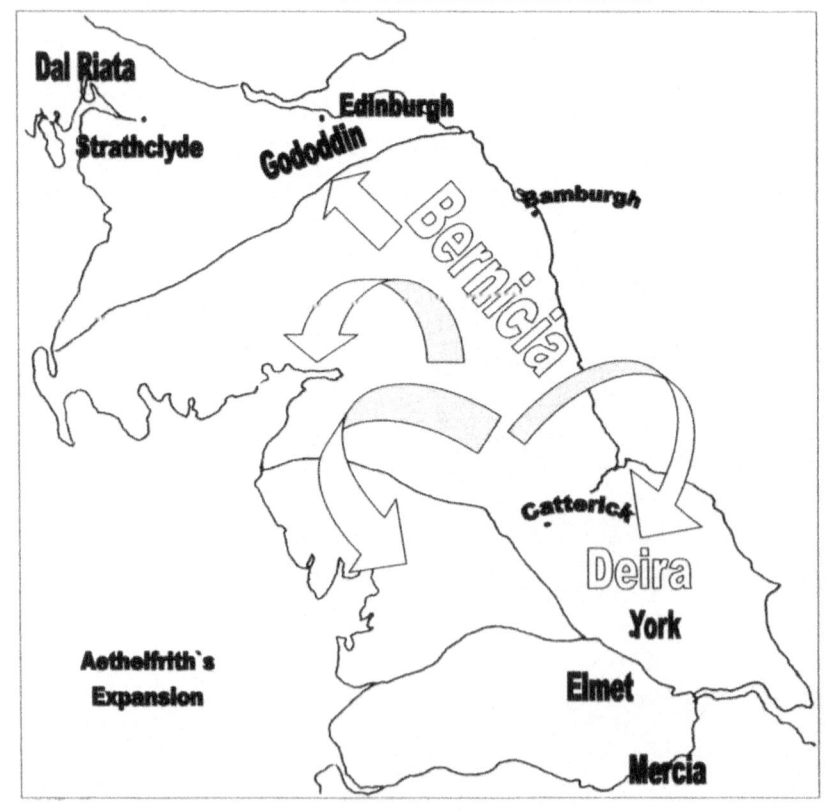

The first king of note in Bernicia was Aethelfrith. Called by his enemies "The Twister," "The Dodger" or perhaps more closely "The Fox." His deviousness might prove him to be a true descendant of Woden, as the God was noted for his disguises and trickery. His English name means "Noble-sword." Aethelfrith was son of Aethelric, who was son of Ida. He named Bamburgh after his first wife, Bebba, and he established the English as the dominant force in the North. He has claims to be the man who made Northumbria.

Aethelfrith was probably the victor at Catterick, where an army of Britons from Edinburgh with their allies were destroyed, as was commemorated in the poem of *The Gododdin* by Aneurin.

> *"the men went to Catraeth, swift was their army,*
> *the pale mead was their feast, and it was their poison;*
> *300 men battling according to plan,*
> *and after the glad war cry there was silence.*
> *Though they went to the churches to do penance,*
> *the inescapable meeting with death overtook them.*
> *The men went to Catraeth in column,*
> *raising the war-cry,*
> *a force with steeds and blue armour and shields,*
> *javelins aloft and keen lances,*
> *and bright mail coats and swords.*

The warriors arose together, together they met,
 together they attacked, with single purpose;
Short were their lives, long the mourning left to kinsmen.
 Seven times as many English they slew;
 in fight they made women widows and many a mother with tears at her eyelids.
Of 300 champions that set out for Catraeth alas, but for one man none came back."

Aethelfrith had broken the power of Gododdin. The mead drinking, treasure seeking, Gaelic speaking warriors belonged to the same Warrior society as the Northumbrians who defeated them.

"He ravaged the Britons more cruelly than all other English leaders, so that he might well be compared to Saul, king of Israel, except of course that he was ignorant of true religion. He overran a greater area than any other king or Ealdorman. Exterminating or enslaving the inhabitants, making their lands either tributary to the English or ready for English settlement. One might fairly apply to him the words of the patriach Jacobs blessing of his son, "Benjamin shall ravin as a wolf, in the morning he shall devour the prey and at night he shall dine on the spoil."" Bede.

WARRIORS ATTACKING A HALL from the Frank's casket. BM. BW. MoN.

Historians argue about whether there was a wholesale removal of the Britons, or whether an English aristocracy merely replaced a "Celtic" one. Bede's quotation suggests that both options occurred. D Whitelock sees a British strain in English personal names in Northumbria suggesting intermarriage. Myres suggests that there was a strong "Celtic" survival, which influenced the language and place names, but there are only a handful of British words in English Northumbria apart from a few river names The area of Bernicia, north of the wall, may have been fairly sparsely settled in any case, being a military and raiding zone. Lately prominence has been given to the effects of plague in the mid 6th century, which may have reduced the British population and their ability to resist the incomers. A bubonic plague, known as the Plague of Justinian, swept Europe from 540 to 590 AD. Perhaps the Britons in their hill forts were more susceptible to disease, or perhaps the English just recovered quicker. This imbalance may have been widened by the English habit of polygamy and the lack of shame in illegitimacy, compared to the Christian Britons, consequently the Angles had a rapidly replenished stock of young men.

"The roots from which they grow destroy them, their increase is too great, and leave no Englishman alive after you nor Englishwoman to tell the tale." Anon. Gaelic invocation against the English. 1513.AD. (CM.)

Bede writing in 734AD described the scattered nature of the English settlement, "many villages and hamlets of our people are situated in inaccessible mountains and dense woodlands." Which even allowing for hyperbole does not suggest that the English only took the best riverside land.

In 603.AD. Aethelfrith moved against Aidan mac Gabrann, who had been made king of the Dalraidan Scots by the blessed Columba (Colum Cille) at the fortress of Dunadd in Argyll. The Angles knew the Scots well. English troops had fought in Ireland against the U Neill clan. There is mention of two of Aidan's sons being assassinated by Englishmen. The Scots were defeated at Degsastan. In that fight Aethelfrith's brother Eanfrith, called Theobald by

Bede, was killed. The whereabouts of the battle, which was so well known to Bede's contemporaries that he didn't bother to explain where it was, has been a source of speculation by Historians, as have the sites of most Dark Age battles. Some say it was Dawston Rigg in Liddlesdale, but Addiston (at Aedan's stone) in Lauderdale lies on the Dere Street and within the Tweed basin and appears to have a good claim. It seems that a part of the Scots army was led by the son of a previous Bernician king, Hussa. So perhaps the Scots were backing a rival claimant against Aethelfrith.

"This year Aedan, King of the Scots, fought with the Dalreathians and with Ethelfrith, King of the Northumbrians, at Theakstone, where he lost most of his army. Theobald also, brother of Ethelfrith, with his whole armament, was slain. None of the Scottish kings durst afterwards bring an army against this nation. Hering, the son of Hussa, led the army thither." ASC

Despite the optimism of the Chronicles, war with the Scots was to last one thousand years. Defeating the Scots to the North, pushed Northumbrian influence to the Highland line and gave the English access to the rich lands of Lothian, Aethelfrith sealed an alliance with the Picts by marrying his son Eanfrid to a Pictish princess. This had unforeseen consequences for the future, the couple's son Talorcan became a king of the Picts. Their daughter married Beli of Strathclyde and her son Bruide mac Beli also became ruler of the Picts. (there is now doubt that the pictish succession was matrilinear, as elsewhere, an adult warrior from the ruling house was preferred.) It was Bruide who killed the Northumbrian king Ecgfrith, Aethelfrith's grandson, at the battle of Nectansmere in 685 AD and brought Northumbrian expansion to a halt.

Again Historians do not agree on the timing, speed or extent of Anglian penetration north of the Tweed. Some Scottish historians, one feels, would like to deny that there were any English north of the present Border at all. The grand Royal Museum of Scotland reduces English influence to one shelf of knickknacks. The survival of "eccles" names is usually taken to mean that there were British church sites which continued in use. It is suggested that "Celts" survived in the upland zones while the English took the more productive riverside sites. Initially the Lammermuirs provided the Northern border to English expansion and the Roman road the Dere Street the western border. This is supported by some place name evidence and backed by archaeology, in particular the existence of Grubenhauser, the sunken huts of the Northumbrian settlers, and the spread of Anglian sculpture. Sprouston, Simprin and the coast around Dunbar and Coldingham all appear to be early English sites. Nennius records that the first of the Celtic leader Arthur's battles was fought at the mouth of the Glen near Yeavering. But he also states that the sons of Hengist; Octha and Ebissa, settled as far as the borders of the Picts. This would place Anglo-Saxons north of the Tweed 125 years before Aethelfrith.

Reconstructed hut, Bede's World, Jarrow, South Tyneside.
THE MAKING OF NORTHUMBRIA

Aethelfrith then turned his attentions south and united Deira to his lands in Bernicia, he legitimised this move in the usual way, by marrying into the Deiran royal family, Acha daughter of Aelle, the king he had killed.

Acha's young brother Edwin, (or Eadwine), the Deiran claimant, fled into exile and was pursued by Aethelfrith's agents who were determined to dispose of this threat. Aethelfrith's attack on Mercia was in part because they harboured his rival who had married a Mercian princess, Cwenburgh. When Edwin fearing death fled to East Anglia, Aethelfrith attacked that country, but still failed to dispose of Edwin, which was to be his downfall.

A king and shieldman

In 616 AD Aethelfrith led an expedition against the Welsh and defeated and killed the king of Powys, at Carlegion or Chester, which battle also overthrew Cearl of Mercia who had harboured Edwin. Before the battle Aethelfrith ordered the butchering of the monks of Bangor. He showed an appreciation of the role of non-combatants and morale in warfare;

"Before battle was joined he noticed that their priests were assembled apart in a safer place to pray for their soldiers, and he enquired who they were and what they had come there to do. As soon as King Aethelfrith was informed of their purpose, he said, "If they are crying to their God against us, they are fighting against us even if they do not bear arms," He therefore directed his first attack against them, and then destroyed the rest of the accursed army, not without heavy loss to his own forces." Bede.

This defeat of the British had been prophesied by Augustine for the failure of the Britons to try and convert the English.

The death of Aethelfrith

Also in 616AD Aethelbert of Kent, the fourth Bretwalda, or over-ruler of Britain, had died. This led those kings subject to him to become more expansive, unluckily for Aethelfrith one of these was Raedwald of East Anglia who was harbouring the Twister's life-long enemy, Edwin. It is possible that Aethelfrith was returning home with just his household supporters when he was ambushed and killed by Raedwald and Edwin on the River Idle, where it is crossed by the Roman road. Welsh sources claim that he was killed by Ysgafnell, which may just be a welsh interpretation of an Anglo-Saxon name. Aethelfrith, went down fighting, Raedwald's son and his followers were also killed in the battle.

"Raedwald raised a mighty army to make war on Aethelfrith; who meeting him with much inferior forces (for Raedwald had not given him time to gather all his power),was slain on the borders of the kingdom of Mercia, on the east side of the river that is called the Idle." Bede

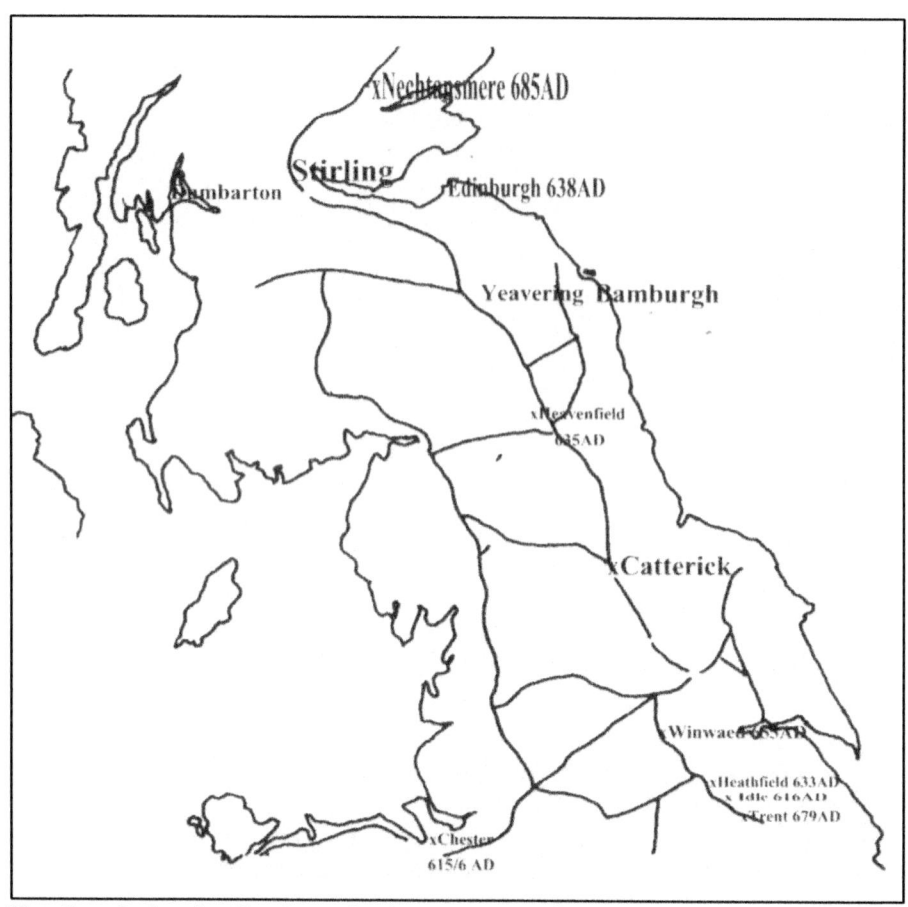

Northumbrian battle sites, the importance of roman roads is obvious, as is the Northumbrian-Mercian border lands. (Chester.615/6. River Idle 616. Heathfield.633. Heavenfield 635. Edinburgh 638. Winwaed 655. Trent 679. Nechtansmere 685.)

"Fetch this grey corslet from me, if you dare.
(this) heirloom covers these shoulders.
Well meshed and effective,
Enriched with gold it is glorious war-gear
altogether suited to a prince who must guard his lifehoard against enemies."
Waldere.

When Raedwald himself died a ship burial was made at Sutton Hoo, which yielded its treasures to archaeologists. Amongst them the king's sword. Is this the sword that killed the first King of Northumbria? And where does Aethelfrith himself lie?

Sutton Hoo swords. BM

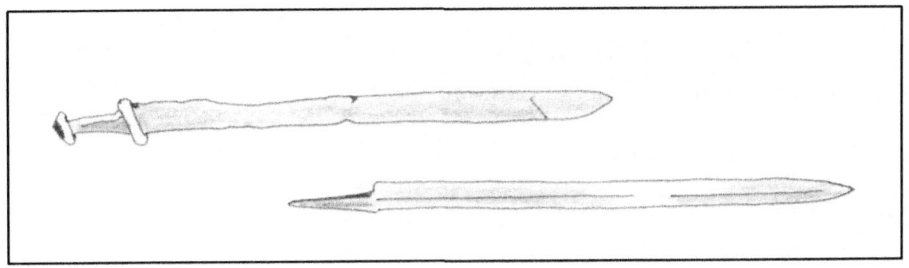

The poet describes what a pagan burial was like;
"Then the people of the Geats made ready for him a pyre firm on the ground,
hung round with helmets, battle targes, bright corslets, as he had craved;
then the sorrowing men laid in the midst the famous prince, their loved lord.
The warriors began to rouse on the barrow the greatest of funeral fires;
the wood-reek mounted up dark above the smoking glow,
the crackling flame, mingled with the cry of weeping
—the tumult of the winds ceased—until it had consumed the body,
hot to the heart.
Then the people of the Weders wrought a mound
which was lofty and broad, at the edge of the headland,
visible far and wide to seafarers;

They laid on the barrow rings and ornaments,
all such adornments as men, eager for combat, had erstwhile taken from the hoard;
they let the earth keep the treasure of earls, the gold in the ground,
where it yet lies, as useless to men as it was before.
"Let us not grudge gold
To melt with that bold man," **Beowulf** Gordon.

Would Edwin allow such a burial as a concession to his sister Acha, Aethelfrith's wife? Or would he humiliate the corpse as was to happen to Aethelfrith's son Oswald?

> *"(he) swore that in the morning he and his men would let*
> *their blood in streams with sharp-edged swords,*
> *and string some up on gallows-trees*
> *as sport for birds."*

Would Acha, who later entered a nunnery, seek a burial for her pagan husband? After Aethelfrith all the Northumbrian kings, bar the apostates, Osric and Eanfrith, were Christian and received a Christian burial. Many lie on the headland at Whitby, a place similar to the burial place described in Beowulf. There is still a chance that Aethelfrith or more likely his predecessors in Bernicia or Deira may have had a burial which could produce goods to rival Sutton Hoo. At Bowl Hole south of the rock of Bamburgh archaeologists have discovered a burial site which had been covered by the encroaching dunes. The graveyards would have been quite visible before the dunes began to be swept in around the Tudor period. Attempts to stabilize dunes which are now being eroded may be a misguided ploy. The site at Skarae Brae is an example of what may be revealed if nature is allowed to take its course.

Skeletons found at Bamburgh, Northumberland.

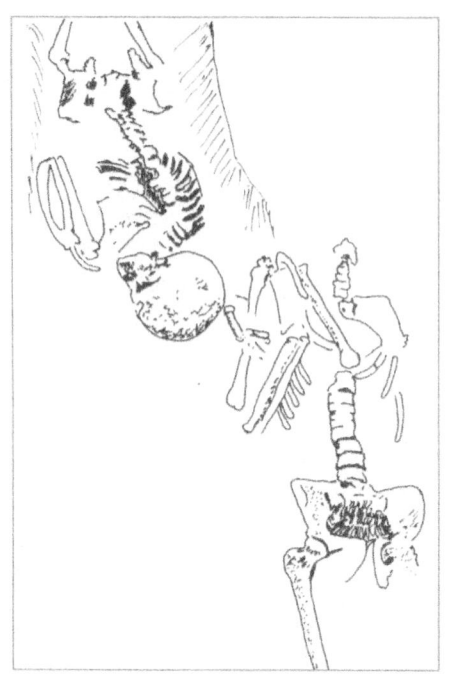

The burial mounds at Uppsala, Sweden.

22

Aethelfrith was the last of the line of pagan warrior kings of Northumbria. He had in fact created the kingdom by his victories. He deserves to be remembered.

"Aethelfrith could have ridden from the Solway to the Mersey through territory in occupation of his own people." Stenton

A view of the British isles from Bamburgh

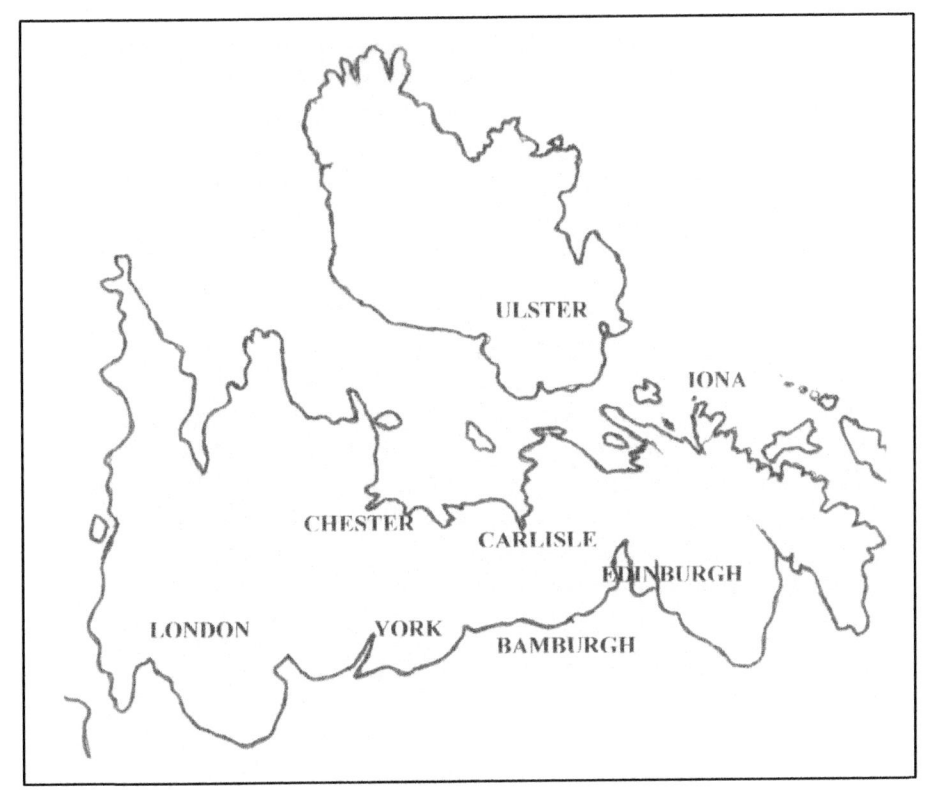

Northumbria was Britain's Middle kingdom.
From a base at Bamburgh it is only 80 miles to Edinburgh. Melrose 55. Dumbarton142. Carlisle and the Irish Sea are less than 100 miles. Less than the 120 to York the Deiran/Northumbrian capital. Ayr is 158 mile. Whithorn 200 mile. Chester is 235 miles.
London however is 334 miles. Winchester, the capital of Wessex, 359 miles, more than the far north of present day Scotland, John O Groats, at 355. Dover is 400.

CHAPTER 3.

THE NORTHUMBRIAN PEOPLE

The Northumbrians are descended from Gods. At least their Kings claimed that they were descended from Woden.

"AD 547 This year Ida began his reign; from whom first arose the royal kindred of the Northumbrians. Ida was the son of Eoppa, Eoppa of Esa"

Thereafter the line ran, Esa, Ingwy, Angenwit, Alloc, Bennoc, Brand, Balday, Woden. The English who descended on Deira and Bernicia, the two kingdoms that united to form Northumbria were pagans, worshipping a collection of Northern Gods. After their conversion to Christianity little of the old religion survived, although Pope Gregory wisely encouraged the Christian missionaries to use the pagan temples and adopt the pagan feast days into the Christian calendar. Christian churches were built on the hill top and wooded sites of pagan shrines. Others were built over the Headquarters buildings of Roman forts which had held altars and standards. Christian feasts replaced sacrifice of animals. Religion was built into the yearly cycle.

"For if those temples are well built they should be converted from the worship of devils to the service of the true God, that the nation may the more familiarly resort to the places to which they have been accustomed…and because they have been used to slaughter many oxen in the sacrifices to devils…they may build themselves huts about those churches…and celebrate the solemnity with religious feasting. For there is no doubt that it is impossible to efface everything at once from their obdurate minds." Gregory to Mellitus AD 601. Bede. The Anglo-Saxon year in both pagan and Christian times revolved around religious festivals and agricultural chores; a celebrated carving from the Anglian church font at Burnham Deepdale, Norfolk, shows the agricultural year;

The Year. from Burnham church font, Norfolk (Right to left) January. Drinking at home. February. Warming by the fire. March. Digging. April. Pruning (right to left) May.Beating bounds.June.Weeding. July. Scything. August.Binding a sheaf.

(Right to left) September. Flailing corn. October. Grinding with a quern. November. Killing a pig. December. Feasting.

It is good to see that from December our ancestors spent three months, feasting, drinking and keeping warm.

Anglo-Saxon Months
February , Sol monath; cakes offered to the Gods
March; To Hretha , a goddess .
April ;To Eostre , a goddess.
May, Thrimilic;When cows were milked 3 times a day.
Jun/Jul Litha , Moon month
Aug , Weod monath ,Weeding time
Sept; Halig monath, offerings for the harvest
Oct. Wintirfyllith, Winter`s full moon.
Nov. Blot monath, when cattle were slaughtered
Dec and Jan. included Feast of Yule.

Easter is still remembered as it coincides with the most important Christian festival, and Eostre's sacred Hare is remembered as the Easter Bunny. Yule and the ceremony of the Yule log is recalled and incorporated into Christmas.

Other Gods are remembered in the days of the week; Tuesday, Tiu was the God of war., Wednesday, Woden, the all-father, Thursday, Thor the thunder god, and Friday, Freya or Frig a fertility goddess. Freyr's boar emblems were seen as protective and therefore worn on helmets. There was also a goddess Erce who was invoked for a good harvest. "Erce, Erce, Erce, eorthan modor." Scyld the fertility god had a son called barley. Beer was central to English life.

Trees, wells and stones were also venerated. The church was still condemning that practice in the 11th Century, but people continued to touch wood for luck. Earlier when the church replaced cremation with inhumation it had condemned the practice of beheading the dead to prevent them walking after death.

Many charms and amulets and spells were used to ward off evil, this might come from God's shot, Elves shot and witches shot or from Goblins and monsters. Many English names included a reference to elves, eg. Alfred, elf counsel; Aelfric, elf ruler. Some of these charms involve the use of runes. Others were for good luck, **"Forth I go, may I meet with friends."** Journey charm

An interesting piece of skull found at Ribe, Denmark carries the inscription, "Ulf and Odin and high Tyr. Help against these pains is the drilling of a hole. And the goblin is defeated. Drill!." It is suggested that it may be a surgeon's amulet. (KNS) Other pieces of yew carry good luck messages, "Warrior always carry this piece of yew wood with you on your warpath." (Friesland. KNS), "May prosperity remain with the farm; at the yew may good fortune grow." (Groningen. Netherlands. KNS). Or the piece of wood may carry a message;

> *"hwaet!*
> *The carver of this token entreats a lady,*
> *Clad in clear stones to call to mind*
> *And hold in her wit words pledged*
> *Often between the two in earlier days."* The Husband's message. Alexander.

The folk tale of Weland Smith is commemorated on a number of surviving carvings, in particular the **Frank`s Casket** Weland made swords and other wonderful things in his forge but he was captured by king Nithhad .To ensure that Weland could only work for the king, Nithad had him crippled, by cutting his hamstrings. Weland`s terrible revenge was to murder the king`s sons and fashion goblets out of their skulls and give them to the king. He also raped his daughter, Beadohild and made her pregnant. Weland escaped on a pair of wings, which he had made for himself.

Old English society was a violent one, at its head was the king or lord and his gesithas, or companions. This was a society based on warfare; The Romans were well aware of the fighting capabilities of the Germanic tribes as Tacitus observed;

" Wild blue eyed, reddish hair and huge framed."

"the German tribes sing war songs and chant, the rhythmic rising and falling is made louder by placing their shields in front of their mouths."

Sidonius Apollinaris, Bishop and poet observed; "they outdo all others in brutality-ungovernable, entirely at home at sea, they attack unexpectedly. When they are ready to return home they drown or crucify 1 in 10 of their victims as a sacrifice-distributing the iniquity of death by the equity of lot" on Saxon raids on Aquitaine.

Individual bravery was highly prized. The elite were armed with a sword, which might well be highly decorated and an heirloom,

" the golden hilt, age-old work of Giants..
wrought by master-smiths,
the hilt, the ancient heirloom. On it was engraved
the origins of strife in time immemorial,
…on the sword guards of pure gold
it was recorded in runic letters, as is the custom,
for whom that sword, finest of blades,
with twisted hilt and serpentine patterning
had first been made." Beowulf.

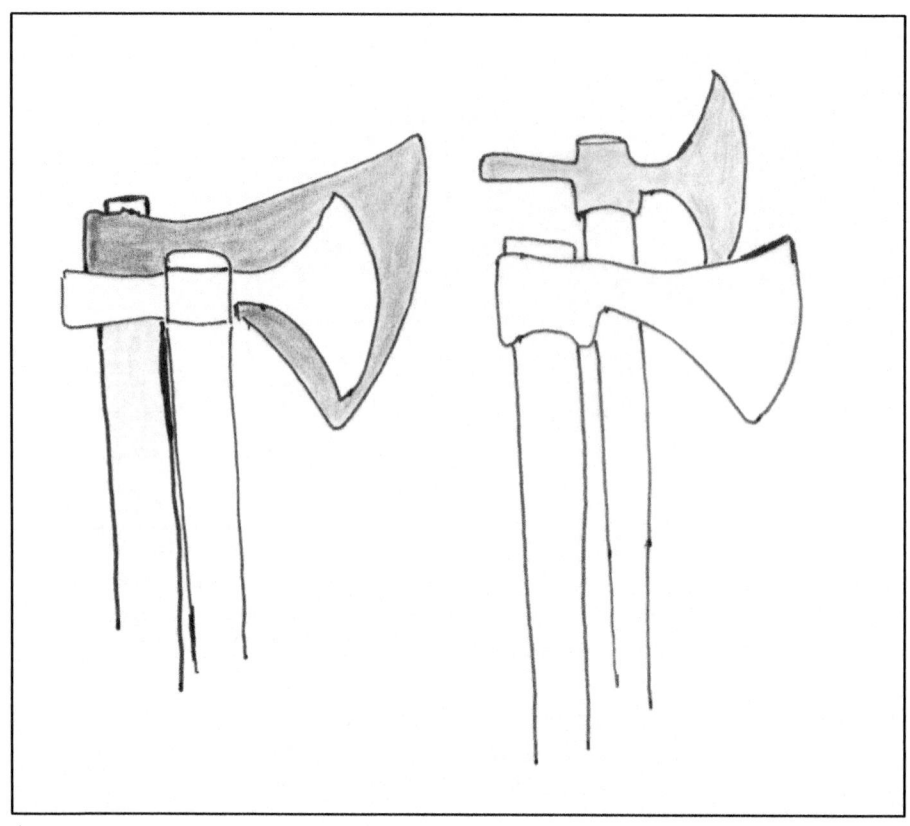

Axes. BM.

A rim of a scabbard found in Gelderland, Netherlands, bears an inscription in runes, "Property of Halehewas, he gives swords to the sword fighters."

They might also have the short one sided sword, the seax, which gave the Saxons their name, or the throwing axe which gave the Franks theirs. They also carried the ash spear, and the linden shield.

"The boss belongs on the shield, the finger`s safe protection." Maxims.
Poems mention the shield wall (the bordweall) which stood most memorably at Hastings. The most important men wore helmets,

The Coppergate helmet, York.

28

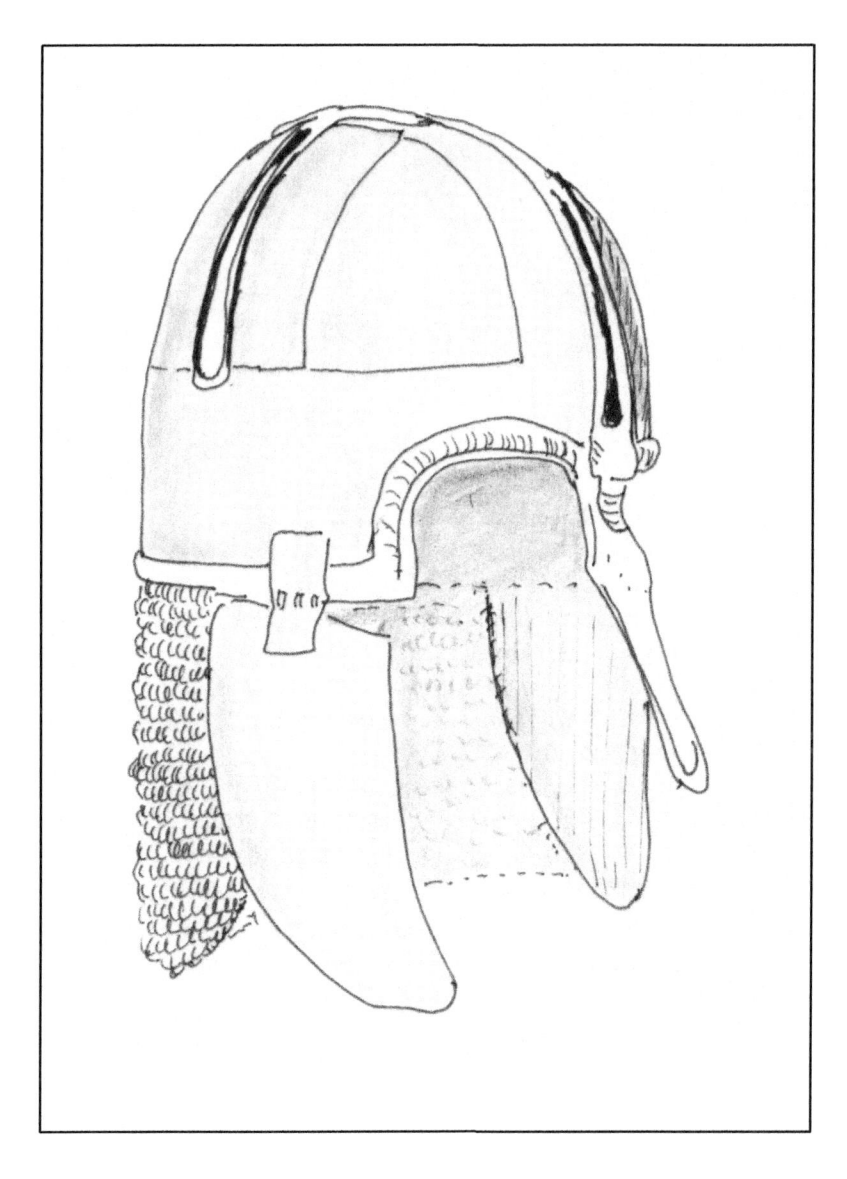

*" A jutting ridge, wound about with metal wires,
    ran over the helmet`s crown, protecting the skull,
    so that well-ground swords, proven in battle,
    could not injure the well-shielded warrior."* Beowulf.

Spear, Seaxes Swords and Shield boss. BM

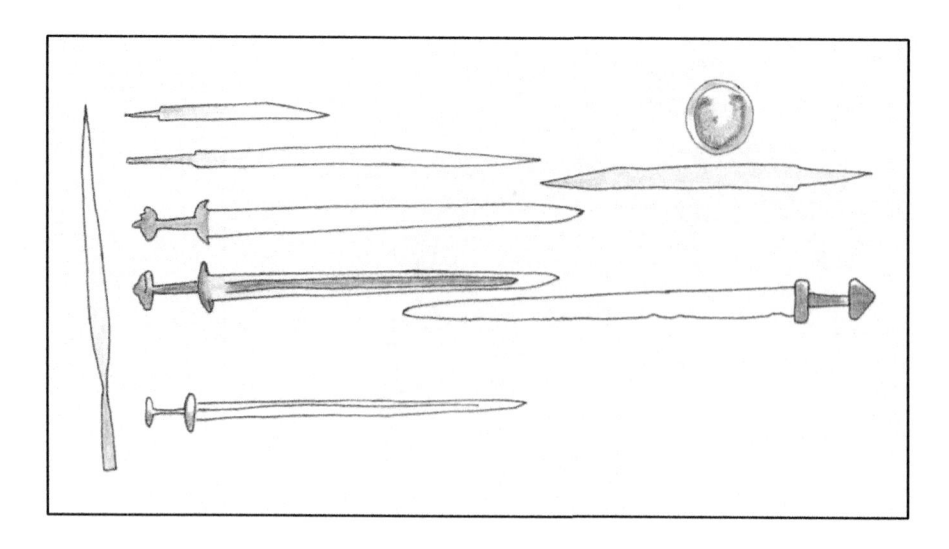

Horses were highly prized, they appear in graves, and their trappings appear as grave goods. The names of the earliest Anglo-Saxon invaders, Hengist and Horsa may be translated as Stallion and Horse.

> *" Now and then the brave men raced their horses,*
> *ate up the sandy tracks-and they were so absorbed*
> *that the hours passed easily."* Beowulf.

Kings gave horses to Bishops as a sign of respect, Aidan gave his away, the king asked if he could not have given away a poorer horse. Another bishop experienced the Englishmen's love of hoses; " the young men that were there with him, and particularly those of the laity, began to entreat the bishop, (John of Hexham) to give them leave to gallop and make trial of the goodness of their horses." Bede.

The Council of Clovesho in 747 proclaimed against horse racing on Religious festivals. The Northumbrian Alcuin wrote to his pupil Eanbald, Archbishop of York, "let not your companions gallop hallooing across the fields after foxes". Hindley.p.170. Papal Legates in 786 AD complained against men mutilating their horses to give them a more frightening appearance; "By a shameful custom you also mutilate your horses by slitting their nostrils and fastening their ears together. Indeed you also make them deaf and cut off their tails. Although you could have them uninjured you do not want this, but you make them repulsive to everybody." Hunter Blair.Northumbria.p.211.

Whether or not they fought on horseback has been a subject of debate.(see NH.1991.1993) most literature suggests not, but the Aberlemno stone(see below under Ecgfrith) suggest it may have happened on occasion. It also shows Northumbrian's with crop tailed horses.

The king in his hall feasted his followers and gave them gifts of rings and weapons.

> *" he would order men to make a hall building*

30

a mighty mead dwelling,
the greatest of hall dwellings,
he whose word held sway,
gave it the name of Heorot." Beowulf.

Reconstructed Hall at Bede's World, Jarrow, South Tyneside.
Fortunately archaeologists have given us a view of the Anglo-Saxon hall to match that of the poets. Hope Taylor excavated the site at Yeavering in North Northumberland and found evidence of a hall 80 foot by 40 foot built with 5.5 inch planks driven 8 feet into the ground. There was also a building named the grandstand not unlike a theatre's banking of seats. There is evidence that it was burned down in 639AD and 651AD. Eventually it was abandoned around 685AD, in favour of nearby Maelmin (Milfield.)

The mead Hall with its feasting was at the centre of Old English life. Drinking beer together,(gebeorscipe) was central to their lifestyle. Drunkenness was inevitable .

"No nation abandons itself more completely to banqueting than the German…drinking-bouts lasting a day and a night are considered in no way disgraceful." Tacitus.

St Boniface writing to the Archbishop of Cantebury complained about clerics not only getting drunk themselves but forcing others to get drunk as "neither the Franks, nor the Lombards, nor the Romans, nor the Greeks, but only the English do." Wormald .p.50. It appears that the English custom of drinking in rounds has an ancient pedigree.

"the sword's edge takes the life of one on the mead bench,
A drunkard in his wrath,
A man sated with wine;
Too hasty were his words before." Fates of Men. Gordon.

A Viking hall at Fyrkat, Denmark. Nearer Yeavering in size.

English feasting. BT
"The companions of the lord were well rewarded;
He broke not his pledge,
He bestowed bracelets at the banquet." Beowulf.
The English believed in wearing their wealth. They enjoyed rich and bright clothing, and rings, brooches and clasps. Gold and garnets were especially prized. *"These fitly belong, gold on a man's sword, jewelry on a woman,"* When the hero of *The Battle of Maldon,* Bryhtnoth, was only offered food for seven of his men at Ramsay, he replied, *"I will not dine alone without the men because I cannot fight alone without them."* The followers repaid the king by fighting in his battles, and if he died, falling with him. Loyalty was one of the

32

most important virtues of the English. It was the greatest dishonour to abandon your lord in life or death.

"Here our lord lies levelled in the dust,
the man all marred: he shall mourn to the end
who thinks to wend off from this war-play now." Battle of Maldon.

Then came vengeance and feud. An insult or injury had to be avenged in kind or bought off with a wergild or payment. *"feuding has existed amongst mankind ever since the earth swallowed the blood of Abel."*
Torhtmund, who avenged the death of his lord, Aethelred of Northumbria, was commended; **"King Aethelred's faithful servant, a brave man of proved loyalty who has valiantly avenged his lord's blood."** Alcuin to Charlemagne.

Since the followers were attracted by gifts which could only be provided by plunder, this warrior society depended on nearly constant war, and the eventual end of most rulers was a violent death. In the 7th century only one ruler of Northumbria, Oswiu, died in his bed.

"There are three things that, until one occurs, are always uncertain, illness or old age or the sword's edge can deprive a doomed man of his life."

If the local Lord could not provide opportunities for plunder, the young warrior's could look elsewhere:

"Nor is it in a man's own nation that he can win fame, but in neighbouring states as well." "many noble youths, deliberately seek out other tribes, where some war is afoot."

So the hero Beowulf, a Geat, fought for the Danes. Oswald and his Northumbrian brothers fought for the Dalriadian Scots, earlier Northern tribesmen had fought for the Romans.

Those not slain in battle were enslaved or driven into exile. Slavery was a fact of life in English, Celtic and Roman society. "as soon as Imma, was recovered from his wounds of the battle, his captor (a Mercian earl) sold him at London to a Frisian." Bede. Before 592 AD. Gregory (later Pope) could find Northumbrians from Aelle's Deira in a Roman slave market.

The ideals of this warrior society were adapted by the Christians, this is how they described Christ's 12 apostles to the Old English,

"Lo we have heard of 12 mighty heroes,
Honoured under heaven in days of old
Thanes of God. Their glory failed not
In the clash of banners. The brunt of war
After they were scattered and fled abroad
As their lots were cast by the lord of Heaven
Famous these heroes Foremost on Earth
Brave hearted leaders and bold in strife,
When hand and buckler defended the realm
On the plain of war on the field of fate." Andreas

This elite group of warriors were fed by the work of the **churls** whom they protected. Men like the **ploughman,** were portrayed by Aelfric.

"I work very hard. I go out at dawn, drive the oxen to the field and yoke them to the plough...there is no storm so severe that I dare to hide at home, for fear of my lord, but when the oxen are yoked, and the share and coulter have been fastened to the plough, I must plough a whole acre or more every day.'
"I have a boy to urge on the oxen with a goad, he is now hoarse on account of the cold and his shouting. I do a good deal more. I must fill the bins of the oxen with hay, water them and carry off their dung."
"It is great drudgery, because I am not free.

And **the King's hunter**, *"I weave my nets and put them in a suitable place and train my hounds to pursue the wild beasts until they come unexpectedly to the nets and are thus entrapped and then I slay them in the nets. I pursue wild beasts with swift hounds. I take Harts and Boars and Does and Goats and sometimes Hares. I catch Eels and Pike ,Minnows, Burbots, Trout and Lampreys and whatever swims in the rushing stream and Herrings, Salmon, Dolphins and Sturgeons, Oysters and Crabs, Mussels, Winkles, Cockles, Flounders, Soles and Lobsters.'* Aelfric.

And **the shepherd**,
"In the early morning I drive my sheep to their pasture, and in the heat and the cold I stand over them with dogs lest wolves devour them. And I lead them back to their fields, and milk them twice a day, besides this, I move their folds, and make cheese and butter, and I am faithful to my lord."
There was room for craftsmen like **the shoemaker,**
"I buy hides and skins, and prepare them by means of my art, making of them foot-wear of various kinds- slippers, shoes and gaiters; bottles, reins and trappings; flasks and leather vessels, spur-straps and halters, bags and purses; and not one of you could pass a winter except for my trade."
But the English were not just an agricultural society, they lived by the sea and rivers, they traded with the Mediterranean countries, with Rome and Byzantium and through them with places further east, all manner of sophisticated goods were available from **the merchant**;
"I go aboard my ship with my wares, and row over parts of the sea, selling my goods, and buying precious things which cannot be produced in this country. Then, with great peril on the sea, I bring them here to you. Sometimes I suffer shipwreck, and lose all my things, scarce escaping with my life...(I bring) Purple garments and silks, precious gems and gold; strange raiment and spice; wine and oil; ivory and brass; copper and tin; sulphur and glass, and many such things."

There was a position in society for all types of men;
> *"One he lends possessions here on earth, worldly treasures,*
> *One is unsuccessful, an ill fortuned man but yet he is skillful in the arts of mind."*
> *"One is knowledgeable in the tasting of wine, a good keeper of beer.*
> *One has ability to play the harp with his hands, he has the art of dexterous flourishes upon the singing wood."* The Gifts of Man

> *" The old man is the most knowing, the one grown wise through far off years who has already experienced much."*

The English were great craftsmen, as their respect for Weland suggests. They excelled at wood carving, metalwork and bone carving. The recent finds of the Staffordshire hoard demonstrated techniques in cutting garnets which modern jewelers would struggle to emulate. The English quickly adapted to stone work to make churches and crosses, their women were acknowledged as the finest embroiderers in Europe.(The oldest surviving example of their work lies in Durham Cathedral.)

The Old English poets also mention **women**, they are often called the peace weaver, as victories were very often followed by marrying the women of the defeated party. Other poems give a more stereotyped view;

> *"Woman belongs at her embroidery."* Maxim
> *"against a woman's chatter: eat a radish at night, while fasting; that day the chatter cannot harm you."* Charms
> *"A roving woman gives rise to talk she is often accused of sordid things men speak of her insultingly, and often her complexion will decay."*

The Frisian woman was held in high esteem:
> *"A king shall buy a queen with goods,*
> *with beakers and bracelets;*
> *both shall first be generous with gifts.*
> *Battle, warfare, shall be strong in the earl,*
> *and the woman shall thrive, beloved by her people,*
> *be cheerful of mind, keep counsel,*
> *be liberal with horses and treasures,*
> *everywhere at all times before the band of comrades*
> *greet first the protector of the nobles with mead,*
> *present straightway the first goblets to the prince's hand,*
> *and shall know wise counsel for them both together,*
> *the householders.*

*Dear is the welcome one to the Frisian wife
when the ship comes to rest.
His vessel has come, and her husband is at home,
her own provider; and she bids him come in,
washes his sea-stained garment and gives him fresh clothes.
Pleasant it is for him on land whom his love constrains.*
Gnomic verses .Gordon.

Women were however more independent than they were to be under the Normans. They could own and dispose of property, including slaves. The law said that "no woman shall ever be forced to marry one whom she dislikes, nor be sold for money."
Women were free to go on pilgrimage,

"there are indeed few cities in Lombardy or in France, or in Gaul in which there is not an adulteress or harlot of the English race." Boniface to Cuthbert.

The English were well aware of the transience of life, but were still optimistic, and acutely aware of the weather,

"grief is a strangely clinging thing, but clouds will glide by."
"frost freezes, fire crumbles wood."

The North East winter in the cold stone monastery on the Tyne was commented on in a famous letter;

"I have sent in accordance with your wishes the books about the man of God, Cuthbert, composed in verse and prose. And if I could have done more, I would gladly have done so. For the conditions of the past winter oppressed the island of our race very horribly with cold and ice and long and widespread storms of wind and rain, so that the hand of the scribe was hindered from producing a great number of books". Abbot Cuthbert (not saint) of Jarrow to Lul, Bishop of Mainz.

But as we know;

"Winter shall wane
Fair weather come again
The sun-warmed summer."

THE LANGUAGE

Arguably the finest weapon the English brought with them was their language. Their other weapons were overcome by Viking and Norman, but in the end their language was triumphant. The Danes were converted and French absorbed by English. The English revelled in words and word play, they loved puns and riddles, often coarse. Their style foreshadowed the banter of Shakespeare's characters and the not too subtle double meanings of the "Carry on" films and Benny Hill.

"A curiosity hangs by the thigh of a man, under its master's cloak. It is pierced through in the front; it is stiff and hard and it has a good standing place. When the man pulls up his own robe above the knee, he means to poke with the head of his hanging thing that familiar hole of matching length which he has often filled before."

The answer to this riddle was…a key.

The double meaning and deception was carried into art. The inscriptions on the Frank's casket read forward then backwards. In illuminated books animals and birds appear from abstract shapes then consume themselves. The first Northumbrian King was called "The Twister."

To be remembered for famous deeds was most important, esteem and the praise of one's peers was highly valued, what the neighbours thought was important;

"Holly has to be burnt and a dead man's legacy divided.
Good repute is the best thing."

"A good man belongs in his native land forging his reputation."
Those who recounted these deeds were well rewarded,

> '*One will delight a gathering, gladden men sitting at the mead-bench over their beer, the joy of the bibbers is redoubled here*
>
> ***One will settle beside his harp at his lords feet, be handed treasures and always quickly pluck the strings with a plectrum-with that hard hopping thing, He creates harmonies, harpist , heart's desire.*** ' The Fortunes of Men.

The deeds were handed down by word of mouth since the only writings were runes, (from *Run,* a secret, a mystery) and these have been found mainly in inscriptions on swords or cross; although finds in Scandinavia, where wood has been preserved, suggest that runes may have been much more widely used for everyday communications. A wooden sword from Friesland, Netherlands is engraved "Oath messenger," and may have been used to call warriors to an oath swearing or wapentake. Similarly a whale bone staff bears the inscription "Choose a witness Tuda."(KNS)

Rune stone, Sweden.
The poet was the scop, hence the word scoff. The first recorded English poet was the Northumbrian **Caedmon**, a brother in Hild's abbey at Whitby;
"*having lived in a secular habit till he was well advanced in years, he had never learned anything of versifying; for which reason being sometimes at entertainments, when it was agreed for the sake of mirth that all present should sing in their turns, when he saw the instrument come towards him, he rose up from the table and returned home.*"

Following a vision he was able to, *"make pious and religious verses, so that whatever was interpreted to him out of Scripture, he soon after put the same into poetical expressions of sweetness and humility, in English, which was his native language. Others after him, in the English nation attempted to compose religious poems, but none could ever compare with him."*

"Now we must laud the heavenly-kingdom's keeper,
the Ordainer's might and his mind's intent,
the work of the father of glory: in that he the Lord everlasting,
appointed of each wondrous thing the beginning; he the holy Creator,
at the first created heaven for a roof to the children of men;
He, mankind's Keeper, Lord everlasting, almighty Ruler,
afterwards fashioned for mortals the middle-earth, the world." Caedmon's Hymn.

(this may be seen engraved in stone in the Basil Hume garden, St Mary's Cathedral, Newcastle, opposite the Central station.) Scholars dispute the authorship of this verse.

Northumbrian remains the language with the highest percentage of words deriving from Old English (82%) R.Bibby. Northumbria. Discovery Guide.

Caedmon's poem, Basil Hume Garden, St Mary's RC Cathedral, Newcastle.

NORTHUMBRIAN PLACE NAMES

Aethelfrith's people used the word ingas or ing to represent themselves, and they attached it to their chief's name, Ida, Wudhere, Wulfrige, Elli, Offa ,Cedd , Eadmund etc.

To that they would add their name for Homestead,(tun or ton,); Village,(ham); Building,(botl;) or (stead); Farm (throp or thorp; or wic,); Enclosure, (worth.) ; or a Hut (shiel).

They would note the natural surroundings; Moor;(mor); Hill,(hlaw or dun); Hilltop,(copp); Dene,(denu); Valley, (dael); a Side Valley,(hop or hope); Wood, (wudu); a Small Wood or copse,(shaw); River,(ea); Stream, (burne); Sea, (sae); Headland,(naess);

and the work of men, Stones, (stan); Street, (stret) ; Fort, (ceaster or chester); Path, (paeth) ; Road,(gata); Clearing,(ryding or leah).

They would note specific properties of the land, flat land by the river, (a Haugh, originally land in an angle); an island (Eal) ; a slope or ridge, (Heugh, or Hoh); a steep rise, (stigol, or Steel); forked land, (Twisla); damp land, (Wisc); wet land, (Waet); foul (Ful); stony land, (Staener);

They noted what would grow or could be cultivated; pasture, (Lea); gorse, (Winn); rye, (Ryge); barley, (Bere); bean,(Bean); aspen, (Aespe); oak, (Ac); ash, (Aesc);, broom, (Brom);

The animals they could raise there; lamb,(Lamb);,cattle,(Kye); sheep, (Scip); (they pronounced "sc" as "sh"). There were also references to horse, colt, ox. They noted what might be seen or hunted; badger, (Broc); goat, (Gat); swan, (Elfet); wildcat,(Catt); fox, (Tod); crow,(Craw); crane, (Cran); Deer (Stag, Hart, Doe or Hind); pig or boar, (Swin).

An imagined Northumbrian landscape showing the major place name elements.

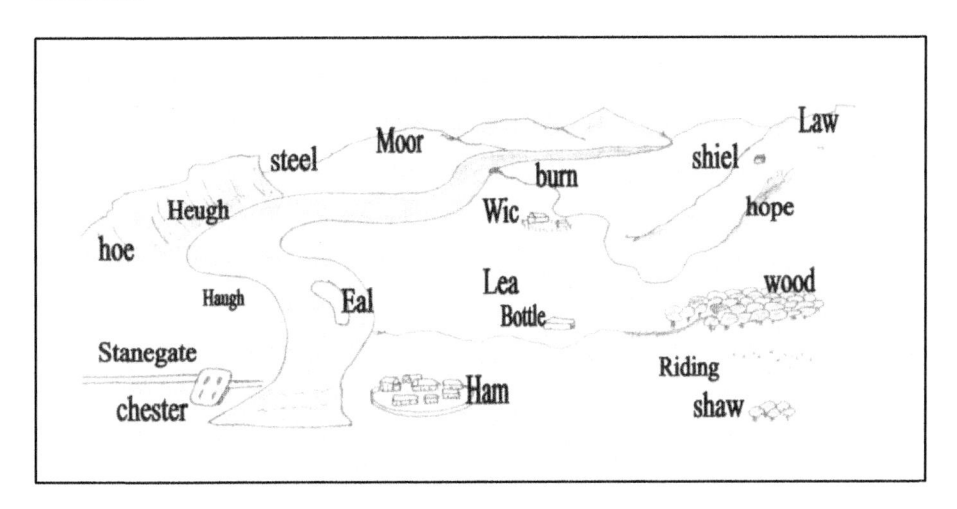

A river runs through the landscape with an island (eal), on one side there is a roman road (Stanegate) and a fort (Chester), beyond is the flat land in the bend of the river (Haugh), then the river has cut a cliff (Heugh) with steep ends (hoe and steel), beyond are the rolling moors. On the other side is a hill (Law) with a hut (shiel), a side valley (hope) feeds a stream (burn) which passes a farm (wic). Below there is a wood, part of which has been cleared (riding) leaving a small wood (shaw). Alongside the river is pasture land (lea) with a house (bottle) and a settlement (ham).

Crane, Geese and Ducks. (Cranes, common in Anglo-Saxon England, have been reintroduced at Washington Wildfowl park.)

Stag. BT
 The rivers and roman roads of Northumbria.

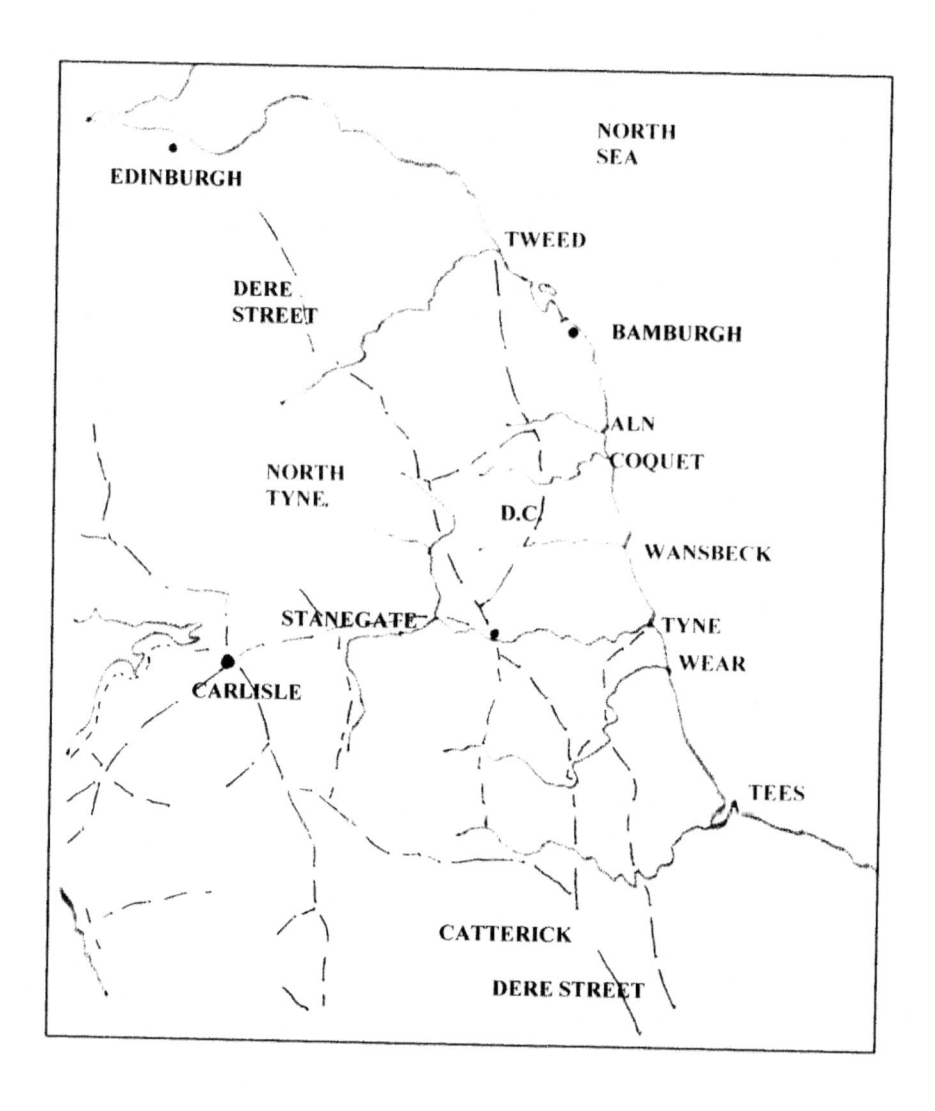

Place names; There follows a list of the place names of Northumbria. (If you wish to follow the narrative of the Kings you could skip through to Edwin). Some of the more obvious names have been left blank, (you can work them out by referring to the roots above, eg, Thornyhaugh is the thorny flat land by the river.) as have some where the origin is disputed. It begins with the coastal settlements from Berwick south. (The place names of Lothian (Berwick, northwards, feature in the chapter on Millennium Northumbria.) Then follows river settlement and settlement along the roads.

Northumbrian Coastal Settlements
Berwick   Bere, Barley farm
Spittal
Cheswick   Cheese farm

46

Goswick	Goose farm
Beal	Bee hill
Lindisfarne	
Fenwick	fen farm
Elwick	Ella's farm
Ross	promontory (celtic)
Easington	Esi's folk's place
Belford	Bela's? ford
Bradford	broad ford
Bamburgh	Bebba's town (Aethelfrith's wife.)
Sunderland	sundered(separated) land
Elford	Ella's or elders? alders ford.
Beadnell	Beada's nook
Swinhoe	swine hill
Lucker	sandpiper marsh (Norse?)
Fleetham	stream place
Tughall	
Brunton	burn(stream) place
Newton	
Preston	priest's farm
Ellingham	Ella's folk's place
Dunstan	hill stone
Embleton	Elm valley farm
Craster	crow fort
Rennington	Regna's folk's place
Howick	high farm
Longhaughton	water meadow farm
Boulmer	bullock lake
River Aln estuary	Alnmouth
Lesbury	leech (doctor's) fort
Birling	
Warkworth	Werce's enclosure
River Coquet estuary	
Amble	Anna's bill (headland)
Hauxley	Hawk's hill (or Hafoc's)
Radcliffe	
Togston	Tocga's place
Chevington	Cifa's folk's place
Chibburn	Cilla's burn
Widdrington	Wudhere's folk's place
Cresswell	cress well
Ellington	Ella's folk's place
Lynemouth	
Newbiggin	new dwelling
Seaton	sea place

Sleekburn	muddy burn
Blyth	
Seaton	
Whitley	
Shields	huts

River Tyne estuary, Tynemouth.

Marsden	marshy dene
Whitburn	Hwita`s barrow (Burial)
Cleadon	cliff hill
Monkwearmouth	

River Wear estuary, Wearmouth.

Sunderland	
Ryhope	rough hope(valley)
Seaham	
Easington	Esi`s folk`s place
Blackhall	
Mickle Hill	big hill
Crimdon	crooked dene
Nesbitt	nose bend
Middlethorpe	middle farm
Hart	stag island
Throston	Thori`s farm

River Tees estuary, Teesmouth.

The river settlements also show English names; from the North of Northumberland southwards they are;

River Aln

Hipsburn	
Lesbury	Leech (Doctor)`s fort
Denwick	Dene farm
Alnwick	Aln farm
Abberwick	Aluburg farm
Bolton	Farm cottage

(Roman Road)

Whittingham	Hwita`s folk`s place
Eslington	Esla`s place
Ryle	Rye hill
Alnham	Aln place
Prendwick	Praen`s farm.
Angerton	grazing farm
Hartburn	stag stream
Middleton	
Bolam	tree trunk place?
Wallington	the place of the welsh folk?
Cambo	crest (kame) hill spur
Kirkwhelpington	church at Puppy`s folk's place

River Coquet
Birling   once thought to be the earliest Anglian place name because of the –ing ending.
Warkworth   Werce's farm
Morwick   fen farm
Acklington   Eadlac's folks place
Acton   Acca's place
Felton   Fygla's place
Thirston   Thraesfrith's place
Swarland   heavy land
Hedley   heathery lea
Weldon   valley with stream
(Roman Road)
Thistley haugh
Thornyhaugh
Pauperhaugh   ?Papwirth's haugh
Whitton Hwita's place or white place
Rothbury   Hrotha's fort
Thropton   crossroads place
Warton   watch place
Flotterton   floating road place
Hepple   Meadow with hips
Holystone
(Roman Road.)
River Wansbeck
Seaton
Sleekburn
Ashington   (Essendun) ash dene
Stakeford
Bothal   Bota's place
Choppington   Ceabba's folk's place
Shadfen   shallow fen
Pegswood   Pecg's wood
Morpeth   murder path
Dyke neuk   bank corner
Molesden   Moll's dene
Meldon   marker hill
Tyne from the mouth
NORTH SIDE   **SOUTH SIDE**
Shields huts
Chirton church farm   Jarrow mud people's place
Howdon   Hebburn High barrow
Willington Wifel's folk's farm
                       Wardley   watch lea
Walker wall marsh

49

Byker marsh place   Felling new cleared land
Elswick Aelfsige`s farm Dunston
Lemington   Blaydon
                       Ryton rye farm
Throckley   Newburn
Wylam
Ovingham Ofa`s folk`s place Prudhoe
Ovington   Eltringham
                       Mickley big lea
Bywell bend well   Stocksfield
Styford stone path ford Ridley cleared lea
Thornborough   Shielford
Corbridge   Broomhaugh
                       Farnley fern lea
Anick Aegelwine`s farm Dilston Haugh
Oakwood
Acomb Oak place   Hexham (Hagulstad.) young warrior`s place
The Tyne divides at Watersmeet into North Tyne and South Tyne.

North Tyne
EAST   WEST
Wall   Warden watch hill
Brunton burn place
                  Chesters
Cocklaw cock hill
                  Walwick wall farm
Chollerton   Chollerford gorge ford
Barrasford wood ford
                  Humshaugh Hun`s haugh
Ellwood   Haughton
Gunnerton Gunnward`s farm
                  Coldwell
Chipchase log heap
                  Keepershiel Kepe`s hut
Blindburn   Nunwick
                  Simonburn Sigemund`s stream
                  Lyndhurst
                  Latterford
Wark defence works.

South Tyne
NORTH SIDE   SOUTH SIDE
Warden   Greenshaw
Thistle Rigg   Wharmley Quern lea
Fourstones   Woodshield
Newbrough   Keepershield
Allerwash Alder washings Elrington alder farm

50

Brokenheugh	Light Birks little birches
Plunderheath	Land Ends far off fields
Haydon hay valley	Moralee marsh lea
Rattenraw	Ridley
Chesterwood	Beltingham
White Chapel	Redburn
Whitshiel farm	Willimoteswick little Willy`s (Guillemot)
Thorngrafton thorn grove place	Haughstrother
Bardon Mill barrow hill mill	Unthank without leave
Huntercrook	
Henshaw	Sandyford Rigg
Hardriding	Broomhouse
Woodhall	Featherstone four stones
Melkridge	
Haltwhistle high forked land	
Blenkinsopp Blenkin`s valley	
Wydon Eals Wide dene pasture	

Place names on the Wear

Monkwearmouth	
Hylton	Place on a hill, or where wild tansy grows.
Washington	Waesa`s folk`s place
Penshaw	rocky top (celtic)
Chester-le-Street	
Lumley	lamb lea?
Plawsworth	games enclosure
Finchale	finch nook
Rainton	Regna`s place
Shincliffe	ghost cliff
High Houghall	
Low Grange	
Holywell	
Croxdale	
Page Bank	
Byers Green	
Willington	Wifel`s folk`s place
Todhills	
Binchester	

Several of the rivers are crossed by Roman roads. These played an important part in facilitating movement particularly of armies, most Anglian battle sites are on or near Roman roads. But roads may also have served as a line of penetration for settlement. The roads may also have been a line of demarcation, as suggested for Anglian settlement north of the Tweed, the earliest being east of Dere Street (Cramp).The same road was the western border of land granted to St Cuthbert by the Danes. The two major roman roads are the Dere Street (the road to Deira?) which is followed most of its course by the modern A 68. In Corbridge a road sign proclaims its older name of Watling Street. The other is the Devil's causeway from Berwick which joins the Dere Street at Portgate on the roman wall. A spur joins the two between Whittingham and Rochester. There were also good communications east west along the line of the Stanegate and the Roman wall. Another important road ran from York north via Crayke, and Chester-le-Street to the Tyne.

Settlements on Dere Street.
Northumbria north of the border;

Oxton
Netherhowden Addinston (?Daegestan 603AD)
Burnfoot   Cleekhimin
              Wiselawmill
              Lylestone
Midburn
Blackburn
Blackchester Lauderhaugh Newbiggin
Trabrown   Norton
Scarce law   Lauder
Woodheads
Blainslie   Whitslaid
              Galadean
Hawickshiel   Birkenside
Cocklee
Craigsford   Earlston
Sorrowless   Cowdenknowes
              Redpath
Newstead
Eildon
Monksford
Hiltonshill
Well rig
Lilliardsedge
Down law
Pennielheugh
Ancrum
Jerdonfield
Bonjedward
Walkersknowe
Ulston   Crailinghall
Overwells
Cappuck   Rennieston
Shibden Hill Whitton Edge
              Hare law
Falla knowe

      Pennymuir
Middleknowes   Hanginshaw
     Towford
       Woden Law
Hunthall   Blackhall
Gaisty Law
Greystone Brae
Brownhart law
         Border

Dere Street to Corbridge and Tyne.
         Border
Chew Green
Pepperside   Piper`s hillside
         Ridleeshope
Loanedge
Featherwood (waterfall)
Bell shiel law
       Sills Syla`s valley
       Huel crag
Rochester (junction) rook fort
Tod law Fox hill
Stobbs stumps
       Horsley horse lea
Bagraw beggar`s row
Birkhill
Rattenraw   Elishaw alder wood
Blakehope black valley
       Dargues family name?
       Garretshiels Gerard`s hut
Troughend Trequenne?
Cockridge   Dykehead

West Woodburn link west to Rochester.
Chesterhope
Ridsdale
Whitfield
       Fairlaws(waterfalls)
       Carrycoats (Caer-y-coed)fort in Woods?Celtic.
Cowden   Lousey law
       Colt crag
Swinburne pig stream
       Colwell cold well
Wheathill
       Well House
Errington   Bingfield
       Beukley

Grottington Grotta`s folk`s place
    Little Whittington Hwita`s folk`s place

Portgate on Roman Wall

Stagshaw   Halton
Corbridge   Shawell

Dere Street, Corbridge to Lanchester

    Dilston
    Riding mill
    Broomhaugh
    Broomley
    Hindley
Apperley
    Kipperlyn
    Whittonstall
Morrowfield
    (Ebchester)
    Broomhill
Shotley bridge   Medomsley
        Bradley
    (Leadgate)
    Redwell Hills
    Handwell hill
    Iveston
Newbiggin   Lanchester
    Greenwell.

Dere Street, Lanchester to Scotch corner

Bildershaw   Bilheard`s wood
Thickly   Thick wood
Houghton   hill place
Denton   dene place
Piercebridge   withy bridge
Carlbury   freeman`s fort.(Norse.)
Street House
Manfield
Aldborough
Brettonby
Barton
Waterfall beck
Middleton
Sedburgh

Junction

Devil`s Causeway place names.

Tweedmouth
East Ord   sword (shaped) place
Spital   hostel

Scremeston	the fencer's place (French)
Oxford	
Nabhill	
Ancroft	one (lonely) croft
Berryburn	Bere's burn
Berrington	Bere's folk's place
Old Dryburn	
Lickar	place between two streams
Eelwell	
Lowick	tidal pool farm
Brownridge	
Hetton	high place farm
Bill law	Billing's hill?
Redsteads	
Mealkill knowe	
East Horton	east muddy land farm
Wandon	one (lonely) hill
Fowberry	Foal's fort
Newton	
Ewe hill	
East Lilburne	east Lilla's stream
Wooperton(Wepreden)	temple hill dene
Brandon	gorse hill
Low Hedgley	Hidda's lea?
Powburn	pool burn
Glanton	look-out hill
Shawdon Hill	wooded valley hill
Low Barton	bare place

(Whittingham) (Junction).
Devil's causeway

Whittingham	Hwita's folk's place
Thrunton	Thurwine's place
High Learchield	Leofric's slope
Bisley wood	
Lumbly law	loon(diver) hill
Edlingham	Eadwulf's place
Wandysteads	Windy steads
Wellhope	
Embleton stead	the caterpillar's farm
Fram Hill	Framela's hill
Longframlington	
Healey	high lea
Todstead	fox steading
Brinkheugh	Brynca's heugh
Eldon	

Ghyllheugh	ravine hill (Scand)
North Birks	north birches
Todburn	
Whinney hill	gorse hill
Doehill	deer hill
Gallowshaw	gallows wood
Netherwitton	lower wood place
Thornton moor	thorn place moor
Hartburn	deer stream
Angerton	grazing land farm
Marlish	
Highlaws	
Huckhoe	
Shaftoe	
Ferny Chesters	ferny fort
Harnham	horn(shaped) place
Bradford	broad ford
Brandywell	St Brandon`s well?
Tongues	tongue(shaped) place
Kearsley	Cynehere`s hill?
Ingoe	Inga`s hill
Ryal	Rye hill
Grindstonelaw	
Great Whittington	Hwita`s folk`s place.
(Portgate)	gate gate

Rochester eastwards.

Rochester	
Ballyardley Hill	
Toft hill	
Branshaw	steep wood
Greenwoodlaw	
Yardhope	yard(enclosure) valley
Holystone	
Ladyswell	
Farnham(Thirnham)	Thorn place
Sharperton	Steep hill place
Burradon	fort hill
Trewhitt	fir tree clearing
Lorbottle	Leofhere`s building
Callaly	calf lea
Whittingham	

Thrunton (Devil`s causeway.)

Of course place name evidence can be treacherous. The earliest written evidence of the name is needed, and this may be different from a misleading modern spelling. The classic example is Ashington, which looks like a standard,-ington name; Ash`s folk`s place. But the earliest reference shows the spelling as Essendun meaning the ash dene. In this case as in others, local pronunciation is nearer the truth than the modern written source. Apart from the extreme north and south of the area at Chillingham and Billingham, most –ingham names in Northumbria are pronounced "-injum", as in Ovinjum. Chillingham itself may well have been pronounced with a soft "ch", Shillingham as Shilbottle.

Map (below) showing some of the people who have left their names on the map of the North East.
The places; St. Abb's Head. Berwick, Doddington, Bamburgh, Chillingham, Ellingham. Lilburn, Eglingham, Rennington, Eslington, Whittingham, Edlingham, Framlington, Ellington, Chevington, Whittington, Bedlington, Woolsington, Backworth, Killingworth, Ovingham, Willington, Elswick, Kibblesworth, Lilswood Moor, Kimblesworth, Pittington, Wolsingham, Willington, Easington, Merrington, Heighington, Stillington, Billingham, Darlington.

Aebbe

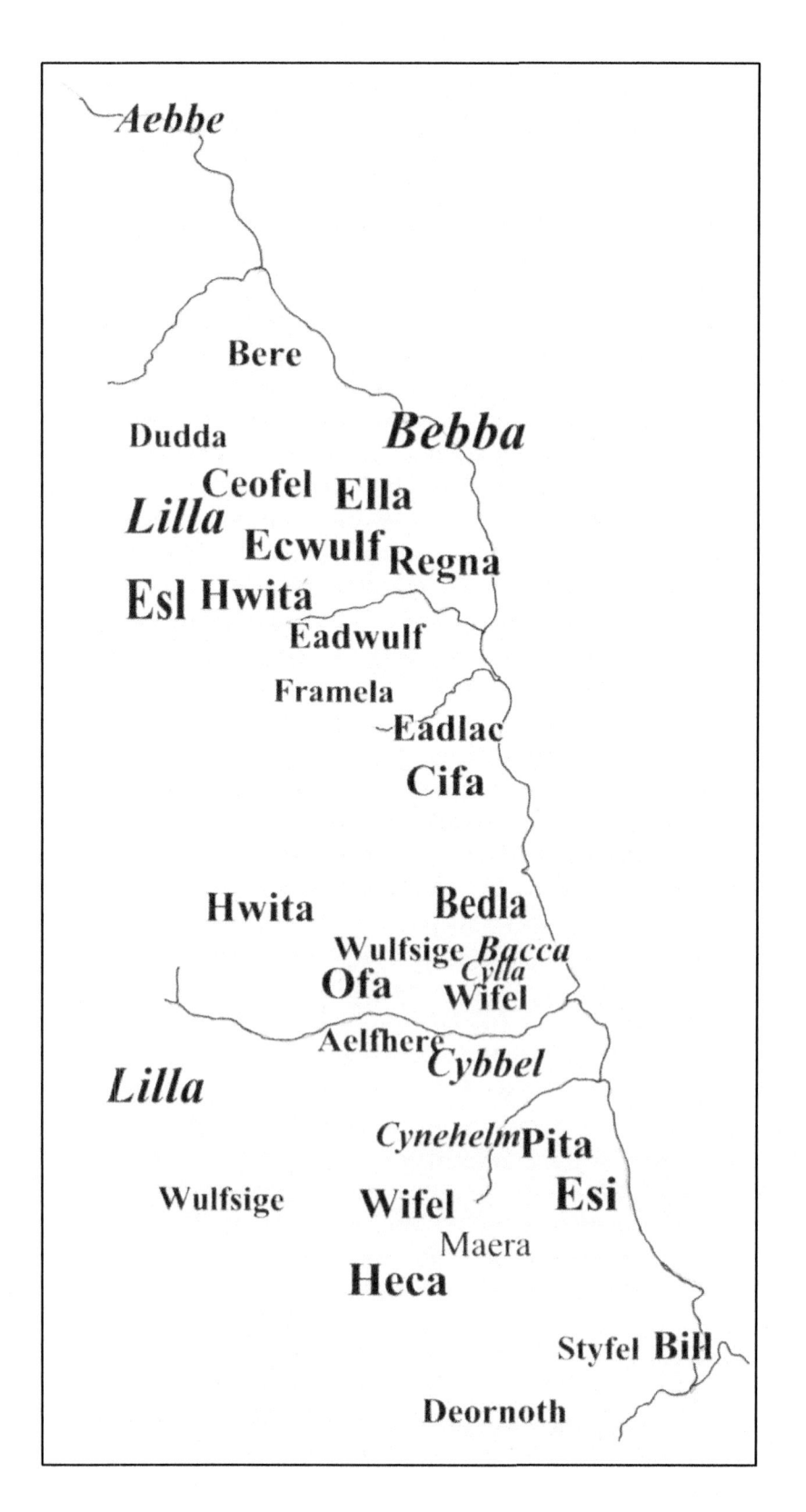

Bere

Dudda

Bebba

Ceofel Ella
Lilla Ecwulf
Esl Hwita Regna

Eadwulf

Framela

Eadlac

Cifa

Hwita Bedla
Wulfsige *Bacca*
Ofa *Cylla*
Wifel

Aelfhere *Cybbel*

Lilla

Cynehelm Pita
Wulfsige Wifel Esi
Maera
Heca

Styfel Bill

Deornoth

CHAPTER 4.

EDWIN-THE FIRST CHRISTIAN KING OF NORTHUMBRIA

> **A man is bound to take up the feuds as well as the friendships of father and kinsmen."** Tacitus
> *So I, sundered from my native land, far from noble kinsmen,*
> *often sad at heart, had to fetter my mind,*
> *when in years gone by the darkness of the earth covered my gold-friend,*
> *and I went thence in wretchedness with wintry care upon me over the frozen waves,*
> *gloomily sought the hall of a treasure-giver wherever I could find him far or near,*
> *who might know me in the mead hall or comfort me, left without friends, treat me with kindness.* The Wanderer. Gordon.

Edwin's victory over Aethelfrith forced Aethelfrith's sons, including Oswald and Oswiu, into exile. They found succor amongst the Scots. It was to be an exile that affected them profoundly, just as Edwin's had affected himself.

"Whatsoever a Man gets easily is not so precious as that which is gotten with difficulty."

Edwin (or Eadwine) had spent some of his exile in Gwynedd in North Wales, a British kingdom founded we are told by Cunedda and his 7 sons from Manau Gododdin, later North Northumbria. He was raised with king Cadfann's own son, Cadwallon. Whatever childhood rivalry there was we do not know, but Cadwallon was to pursue a bloody feud against Edwin when they both came into their respective kingdoms. Edwin was *"one of the three pests of Angelsey nurtured by itself."* Hunter Blair, Northumbria.p.42.

Edwin then married Cuenburg, daughter of Cearl of Mercia, producing two sons, Osfrith and Eadfrith. Fearing Aethelfrith, Edwin then found refuge with Raedwald of East Anglia.

"When Aethelfrith his predecessor was persecuting him, he for many years wandered in a private manner through several places and kingdoms, and at last he came to Raedwald, beseeching him to give him protection against the snares of his powerful persecutor. But when Aethelfrith understood that he had appeared in that province, he sent messengers to offer that king a great sum of money to murder him, but without effect. He sent a second and a third time, and threatening to make war on him if he refused." Bede.

Although Raedwald at last agreed, he once more changed his mind and instead raised an army against Aethelfrith. It was Raedwald's army which surprised and killed Aethelfrith in 617. Edwin then *"drove out the Ethelings ,the Sons of Ethelfrith, namely, Eanfrid, Oswald, Oswiu, Oslac, Oswood, Oslaf, and Offa"* They like Edwin before them, were driven into exile, where they sought help and nurtured plans for revenge.

Once installed as king in Northumbria Edwin in 619 AD, absorbed the little British kingdom of Elmet, which had maintained its autonomy despite its isolated position. One of his kin, Hereric, had sought refuge there from Aethelfrith and had been poisoned by King Cerdic. The only remnant of Elmet is on the modern road signs in Yorkshire.

Edwin then turned against Cadwallon, conquered Anglesey and Man, he then drove his playmate, who he had penned up in the small island of Priestholme, off Anglesey, to Ireland.

*"Cadwallawn when he went to the battle of Digoll,
and the armies of the Cymry went with him,
And Edwin on the other side,
and the armies of the Lloegr with him,
and the Severn was discoloured from its source to its mouth."* Welsh triads.

THE CONVERSION OF THE NORTHUMBRIANS

Later Edwin married Ethelburga, the Kentish princess, and fatefully came into contact with her Latin Christian adviser Paulinus. It is possible that he had met Paulinus earlier at the court of Raedwald. Raedwald himself kept a Christian altar side by side with a pagan one.

"...on a sudden in the dead of the night, (he) saw approaching a person whose face and habit were equally strange, at which unexpected sight he was not a little frightened... the stranger asked, " what reward will you give the man that shall... persuade Redwald neither to do you any harm himself, nor deliver you up to be murdered by your enemies ?...what if I further assure you that you shall overcome your enemies, and surpass in power, not only all your own progenitors, but even all that have reigned before you over the English nation?" Edwin did not hesitate to promise that he would make a suitable return to (that man)." Bede. Bede`s story suggests that Edwin`s victories were the result of divine intervention.

The Christian missionaries of Kent had been sent to England by Pope Gregory the Great. Bede tells how he first came across the English in a slave market in Rome. The event "handed down by tradition of our ancestors" as Bede records, shows that Deiran English were being enslaved before 592 AD.

"These had fair complexions, fine cut features and fair hair. Looking at them he enquired what country and race they came from." They have come from Britain he was told, *" where all the people have this appearance."* when told that they were Angles he replied *"Non Angli sed Angeli"* not Angles but Angels." Further information allowed the pope, or more likely the historian, to indulge in further puns,

> *"from Deire, was good, De Ire snatched from wrath. Their king was Aelle, Alleluia, the praise of God should be sung in those parts."*

Gregory called the English "the people at the end of the world". Later because of his role in their conversion to Christianity, it was believed that on the last day Gregory would lead the English people to the Lord.

Of course the Irish and native Britons were already Christian, but the latter had made no attempt to convert the incoming Anglo-Saxons. Christianity brought benefits other than eternal life. Paulinus could read and write, and so could make proper accounts of the tribal hidage which kept a tally on the tribute from client states. The Hidage gives an indication of the relative importance of the Anglo-Saxon tribes and Kingdoms. His skills were valuable to a King.

Not everyone was pleased with the success of the Northumbrians. Eamer a messenger from Cwichlem, king of the West Saxons, came to Edwin's Hall and in the middle of his address to the King he pulled out a poisoned dagger.

> *"And while he was artfully delivering the pretended message, he suddenly sprang up, and drawing the dagger from beneath his clothes, attacked the king. Swift to see the kings peril, Lilla, his counsellor and best friend, having no shield to protect the king, interposed his own body to receive the blow, but even so, it was delivered with such force that it wounded the king through the body of his warrior".* Bede

A second thane, Forthere, was also killed, before the assassin was brought down. Edwin survived. He saw it as an omen, and had his daughter Eanflaed, born on Easter night, baptised. She has claims to be the first Northumbrian Christian. After taking the war to the West Saxons and killing five kings, Edwin debated as to whether to become a Christian. He still took his time before making a decision,

> **"A wise man must be patient, neither too passionate, nor too hasty of speech, neither too irresolute nor too rash in battle, nor too anxious, too content, nor too grasping.**" The Wanderer.

Paulinus and Queen Ethelburga had arrived in 619 AD; it was 8 years later before Edwin took the plunge. He encouraged the introduction Christianity into his kingdom, after a discussion with his advisors.

The pagan Chief priest Coifi admitted that serving the old Gods had brought him no benefit. Another Thane said,

> *"When we compare the present life of man on earth with that time of which we have no knowledge, it seems to me like the swift flight of a single sparrow through the banqueting-hall when you are sitting at dinner on a winter's day with your thanes and counsellors. In the midst there is a comforting fire to warm the hall; outside the storms of winter rain or snow are raging. This sparrow flies swiftly through one door of the hall, and out through another. While he is inside he is safe from the winter storms, but after a few moments of comfort, he vanishes from sight into the wintry world from which he came. Even so man appears on earth for a little while, but of what went before this*

life or of what follows, we know nothing. therefore, if this new teaching has brought any more certain knowledge, it seems only right that we should follow it." Bede.

In this image Bede captures the importance of the Hall and fellowship to the English, in a harsh and hostile world, and shows an empathy with the ideas expressed by the scops.

The king with seat and drawn sword.

The priest Coifi was allowed to destroy pagan shrines at Goodmanham. Edwin himself was baptised by Paulinus in 627 AD in the wooden church of St Peter in York, on Easter Day. Since the Welsh who raised Edwin were Christians, it was likely he was christened as a child; in fact it was said that Rhun map Urien of Rheged had done it.

> *"So Edwin with all the noblemen of this race and a vast number of the common people, received the faith and regeneration by holy baptism in the eleventh year of his reign, the year of our lord 627; about 180 years from the arrival of the English in Britain."*

> *"Indeed it is said that so great was the zeal for the faith and the desire for the saving grace of baptism among the Northumbrians that on one occasion Paulinus, when visiting the royal estate at*

Adgefrin (Yeavering) with the King and Queen, spent 36 days there administering catechism and baptism. He baptised them for the remission of their sins in the River Glen which was nearby. In the kingdom of Deira, he used to baptise in the river Sualua, (Swale) which flows past the town of Cataracta. (Catterick)" Bede.

At Catterick James the Deacon, an important figure in Northumbrian Christianity, began the singing of Gregorian chant.

It was also claimed that Paulinus baptised the people at Holystone, Northumberland, close to a Roman road. Roman roads and springs were often closely linked;

Holystone, Northumberland. Paulinus's well.

"in several places where he had seen clear springs near the highways he caused stakes to be fixed, with brass dishes hanging at them, for the convenience of travelers; nor durst any man touch them for any other purpose than that for which they were designed, either through the dread they had of the king, or the affection which they bore him." Bede. One tends to feel that in Edwin's case there was more dread than affection.

Royal justice, the king, advisors and executioner

Edwin's power was such that he was named by Bede as one of the Bretwaldas of Britain.

'The fifth (Bretwalda) was Edwin, King of the nation of the Northumbrians, that is, of those who live on the north side of the river Humber, who, with great power, commanded all the nations, as well of the English as of the Britons who inhabit Britain, except only the people of Kent, and he reduced also under the dominion of the English, the Mevanian Islands of the Britons, lying between Ireland and Britain." The tribal Hidage claims to show the relative size of various Anglo-Saxon territories, for purposes of raising tribute. There is dispute as to where it was drawn up, but as Northumbrian territory is not listed it is a possibility that it shows tribute paid to Northumbria. The list has been transposed onto a map. (A hide=104 acres.)

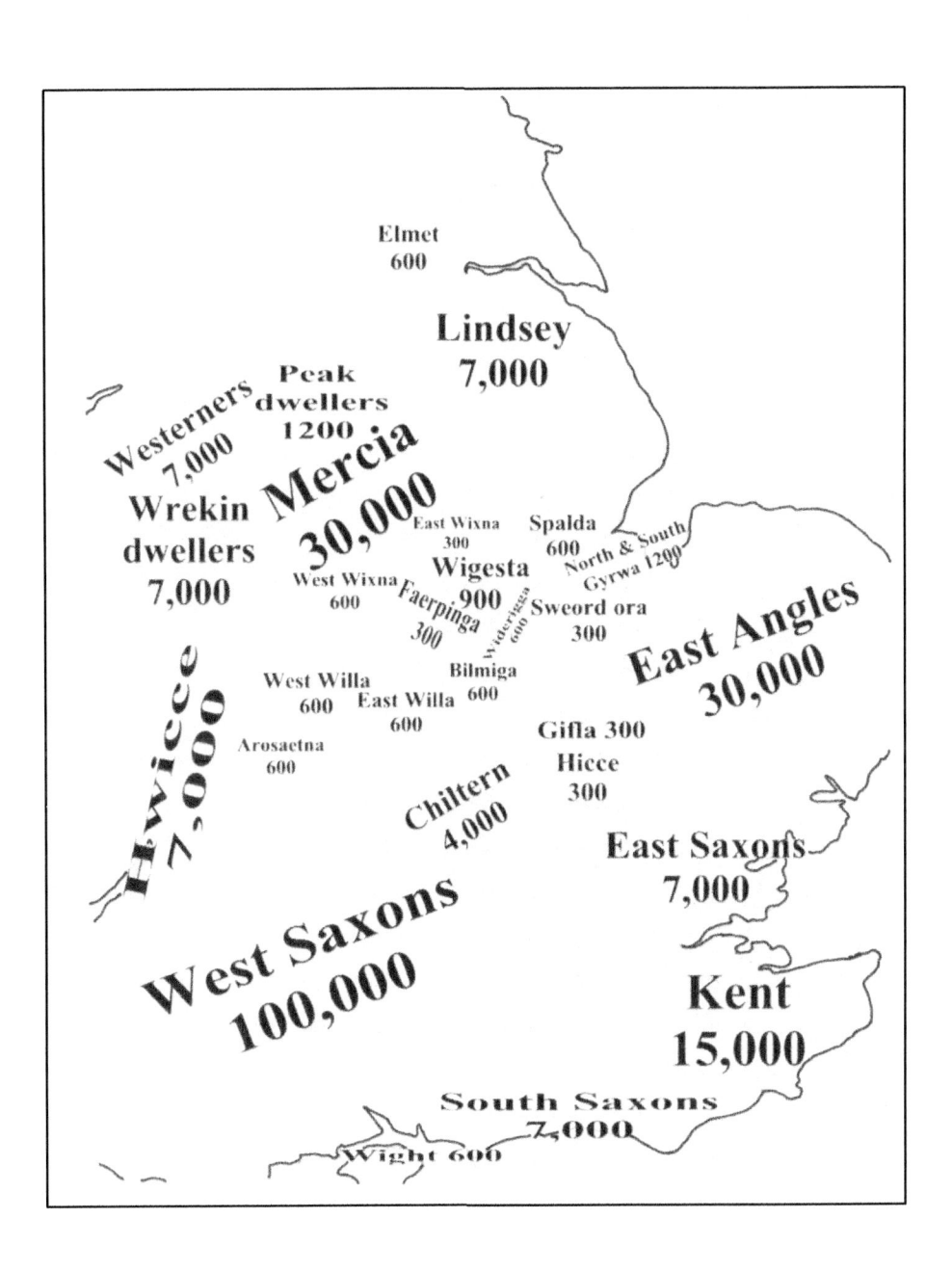

Map of Anglo-Saxon Territories

- Elmet 600
- Lindsey 7,000
- Westerners 7,000
- Peak dwellers 1200
- Wrekin dwellers 7,000
- **Mercia 30,000**
- East Wixna 300
- West Wixna 600
- Spalda 600
- North & South Gyrwa 1200
- Wigesta 900
- Faerpinga 300
- Widerigga 600
- Sweord ora 300
- **East Angles 30,000**
- West Willa 600
- East Willa 600
- Bilmiga
- Arosaetna 600
- Gifla 300
- Hicce 300
- **Hwicce 7,000**
- Chiltern 4,000
- East Saxons 7,000
- **West Saxons 100,000**
- **Kent 15,000**
- South Saxons 7,000
- Wight 600

65

A spearman from Frank's casket

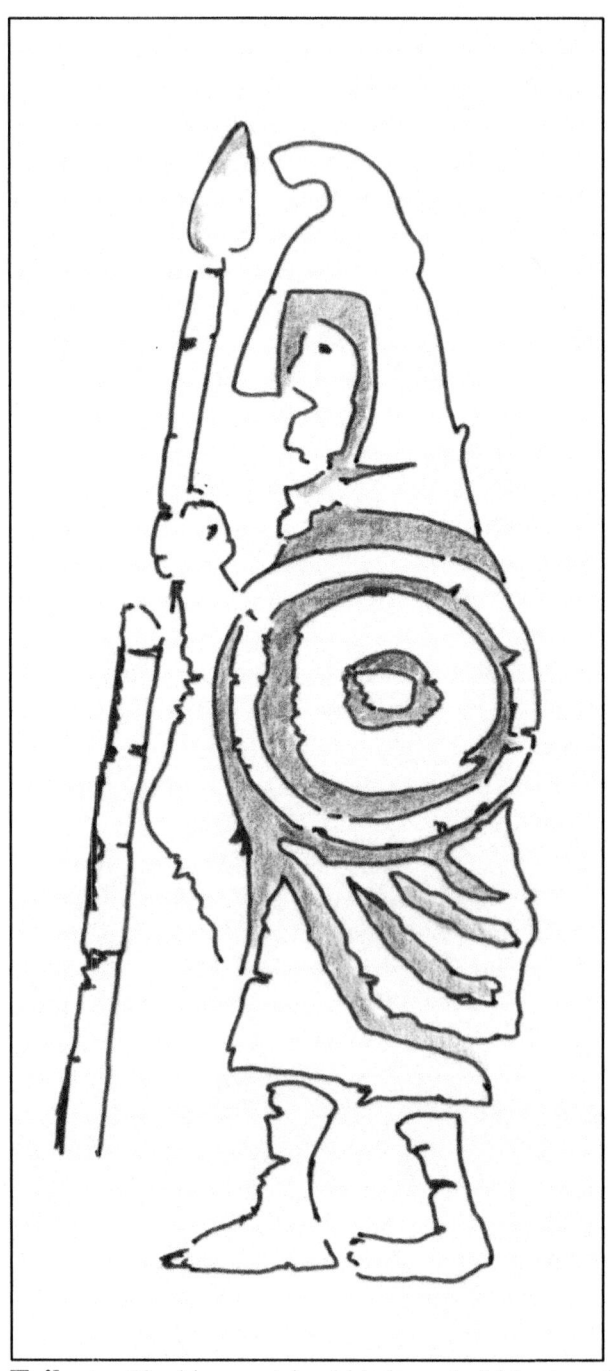

Tribute. The king sustained his household by travelling around his estates and eating their produce. Those areas furthest from his power base would have to provide tribute in something easily portable. One suitable commodity was cattle (kine).If an area refused to send tribute a cattle raid might be a way of enforcing it. "Cadwallon's cattle have not bellowed before the goads or spear points, of Edwin's men." D. Dumville in Bassett.S. ed. The Origins of the Anglo-Saxon kingdoms. P. 30. Irish history is full of references to heroic cattle raids. Northumbrians would still be indulging in cattle raiding in the 17th century. The raid was not just about taking important wealth indicators from the enemy, it was to demonstrate your superiority, to show that the enemy could not defend their own, to demonstrate their vassalage.

"Garmund servant of God,
Find those cattle and fetch those cattle,
And have those cattle and hold those cattle,
And bring home those cattle.
So that he may never have land to lead them to,
Nor ground to bear them to,
Nor houses to keep them in.
If any should do so, may he never thrive by it!
Within three nights I shall know his powers,
His strength and his skill to protect.
May he wholly wither as fire withers wood,
As bramble or thistle hurts thigh,
He who may purpose to bear off these cattle,
Or think to drive away these kine".
Charm against the theft of cattle. Gordon.p.92.

Edwin on his progresses had his Standard carried before him like a Roman Emperor. Even when he passed through the streets on foot the standard was carried before him.

> *"So peaceful was it in those parts of Britain under King Edwin's jurisdiction that the proverb still runs that a woman could carry her new-born babe across the island from sea to sea without any fear of harm."* Bede.

THE DEATH OF EDWIN.

His Christian luck was not to survive long, the Mercians gained a new king, Penda, descended from Woden via Offa, king of Angeln. He was to reign for 30 years and to fight a continuous war against his Christian kinsmen in Northumbria. He found an ally in Edwin's old playmate turned enemy, Cadwallon, the Christian British king.

In 633 AD. At Heathfield, Edwin and his son Osfrith were killed. Another son Eadfrith joined Penda but was slain by him. The battle is usually placed 7 miles NE of Doncaster at Hatfield Chase.12 October 632/33AD

> *"Then (he) began to marshall his men*
> *He rode about and advised*
> *He told men how they should stand firm, not yielding an inch .*
> *He bade them grasp their shields in their hands tightly and upright and not to be afraid."* Battle of Maldon.

> *"At intervals haughty officers from among the army ranged the highways on horseback, there before them by the banner rode the harnessed king, the ruler over men, with the ensign contingent, the warrior's overlord fastened his visored helmet, the king his cheekguard, in anticipation of fighting, the ensigns shone forth. He shook his mail coat and commanded his troop of picked men zealously to hold fast their battle array."*

> *"Birds of battle screech,*
> *The grey wolfhound howls, spears rattle,*
> *Shield answers shaft, the wandering moon gleams under the clouds."* The Finnesburgh fragment.

The head of King Edwin was carried to York, it rested in the porch dedicated to St Gregory. His body was buried at Whitby.

The victorious pagan Mercians and Christian Welsh harried Northumbria. Churches were destroyed. Cadwalla embarked on a policy of racial genocide against the Northumbrians.

"At this time a terrible slaughter took place among the Northumbrian church and nation. Cadwalla was set upon exterminating the entire English race in Britain and spared neither women nor innocent children, putting them all to horrible deaths with ruthless savagery, and continuously ravaging their whole countryside." Bede.

Paulinus and the Queen with her children, Eanfled and Wuscrea, fled south to Kent. They later fled to Gaul where the children died young. Paulinus took with him the precious gold cross and chalice of the king. Northumbria, only five years after its conversion, lapsed back into paganism. The only light recorded was James the Deacon at Catterick, who stayed on while others like Paulinus fled.

He *" continuing long after in that church, by teaching and baptizing, rescued much prey from the power of the old enemy of mankind; from whom the village, where he mostly resided, near Cataract, has its name to this day. He was extraordinarily skillful in singing, and when the province was afterwards restored to peace, and the number of the faithful increased, he began to teach many of the church to sing, according to the custom of the Romans, or of the Cantuarians. And being old and full of days, as the Scripture says, he went the way of his forefathers."* Bede on James the Deacon.

CHAPTER 5.

OSWALD AND OSWIU-the sons of Aethelfrith

*"But for a long time
sad in mind, he must dip his oars into icy waters,
the lanes of the sea,
he must follow the paths of exile,
Fate is inflexible."*

*"I heard nothing there but the sea booming the ice cold wave,
at times the song of the swan the cry of the gannet was all my gladness,
the call of the curlew, not the laughter of men, the mewing gull, not the sweetness of mead. These storms beat the rocky cliffs, the icy feathered tern answered them,
and often the eagle dewy winged screeched overhead."* The Seafarer.

"At certain places of Insular History the right men seem to have existed in the right places at the right time .Northumbria in the century from 640 is an example of this." Thomas.

OSWALD. CHRISTIANITY RESTORED.
Oswald, son of Aethelfrith, had been exiled with his brothers among the Scots. He had been baptised on Iona a centre of Irish Christianity. It was said that Iona was the oldest rock and would be the last destroyed at the end of the world. There had landed from Ulster, Columcille, of the Ui Neill dynasty, descended from Niall of the nine Hostages, who was to be called Columba. He had set up a monastery there in a place which was a 35 mile boat trip from Dunadd the rock fort which was the centre of the Scots kingdom of Dal Riata.
The island of Iona, Scotland. *"Be alone in a separate place."* Laws of Columba.

Aged about 11 years when his pagan father was killed, Oswald's exile lasted for 17 years. Not only did he learn of a Christian religion suitable for a warrior prince, he, and his companions fought for Dalriata in their wars.

Hearing of the death of Edwin, who had killed their father and driven them into exile, the sons, Oswald, and Oswiu, returned. They found their inheritance wasted. Deira devolved upon Edwin's cousin Osric, who had been converted by Paulinus but who now renounced his faith and reverted to paganism as did Oswald's eldest brother, Eanfrith who came into possession of Bernicia. Eanfrith had been exiled and married with the Picts. However the real power in the land was still Cadwalla of Gwynedd. He caught Osric by surprise and slew him and his army.

> *"after this for a year he ruled over the provinces of the Northumbrians not like a victorious king, but like a rapacious and bloody tyrant, and at length brought to the same end Eanfrith, who unadvisedly came to him with only twelve chosen soldiers, to sue for peace."* Bede.

Northumbrian Royal families.

AETHELFRITH, c.592-616. Killed at the battle of River Idle by Edwin
EDWIN, 616-633. Killed at the battle of Hatfield Chase by Penda
Osfrith (Edwin's son) 633. Killed at the battle of Hatfield Chase by Penda.
Eadfrith (Edwin's son) 634. Killed by Penda.

> OSRIC (Edwin`s cousin.) 633. Killed by Cadwalla.
> *EANFRITH* (Aethelfrith`s son.) 634. Killed by Cadwalla.
> **OSWALD,** (Aethelfrith`s son.) 634-642. Killed Cadwalla at Heavenfield. Killed at Maserfield by Penda.
> **OSWIU**, or **OSWIU**(Aethelfrith`s son.) 642-670. Killed Penda at Winwaed 655.Died.
> OSWINE .(Osric`s son.) 644-51. Killed by Oswiu at Gilling.
> OETHELWALD,(Oswald's son) 651-55?.Betrayed Penda at Winwaed.
> **ECGFRITH**,(Oswiu`s son) 670-85.Killed by Bruide at the battle of Nechtanesmere 685.
> Aelfwine, (Oswiu`s son) Killed at the battle of Trent 679.
> **ALDFRITH, (Oswiu`s son.) 685-704. Died.**
>
> Key.
>   Kings of **NORTHUMBRIA,** DEIRA, *BERNICIA,* Others.

Oswald with a small army gathered north of the Roman wall at Heavenfield, to face the conquering forces of Cadwallon. The latter's army was progressing north along the Roman road, presumably to Portgate.(a possible site of the battle.) Oswald, encouraged by a vision of Columba, before the battle raised a wooden cross in front of his troops. Like the Christian Roman Emperor Constantine, at the battle of the Milvian Bridge, it was in this sign that he would conquer.

    "Let us all kneel, and jointly beseech the true and living God Almighty, in his mercy, to defend us from the haughty and fierce enemy; for He knows we have undertaken a just war for the safety of our nation."

Marsden suggests the outnumbered Northumbrians launched a surprise night attack, tactics learned from their Scots friends. Bede says **"he advanced with an army, small indeed in number, but strengthened with the faith of Christ…advancing towards the enemy with the first dawn of the day, they obtained the victory, as their faith deserved."**

"King Oswald, as he had been directed in the vision, went forth from his camp to battle, and had a much smaller army than the numerous hosts opposed to him, yet he obtained an easy and decisive victory, for king Cadwallon was slain, and the conqueror was ever after established by God as Bretwalda of all Britain. My predecessor, our abbot Failbe, related all this to me, Adomnan, without question. He swore that he had heard the story of the vision from the lips of King Oswald himself as he was relating it to Abbot Segene." Vita Columbae by Adomnan (Abbot of Iona.)

Cadwallon himself was slain on the Denise's Burn, identified by some as Devil`s water way to the south of Heavenfield, by others as the Cor burn nearer to hand. Some place the entire battle further east around Hallington.

'From the plotting of strangers and iniquitous Monks, as the water flows from the fountain,
    Sad and heavy will be the day for Cadwallon.' Red Book of Hergest

Oswald's Cross, Heavenfield, Northumberland.

The place of victory soon became venerated, miracles occurred. People took chips from the cross. Every year the monks from Hagulstad (Hexham) held a vigil here on the eve of Oswald`s death, they later built a church,
> *"for it appears that there was no sign of the Christian faith, no church, no altar erected throughout all the nations of the Bernicians, before*

> *that new commander of the army...set up the cross as he was going to give battle to his barbarous enemy."* Bede.

Bede's statement suggests that Paulinus's mission had had only superficial success north of the Tees. (Bede also says that the place was already called Heavenfield before the battle.)

The site of Heavenfield, one of the few Anglo-Saxon battle sites to be identified, albeit approximately.

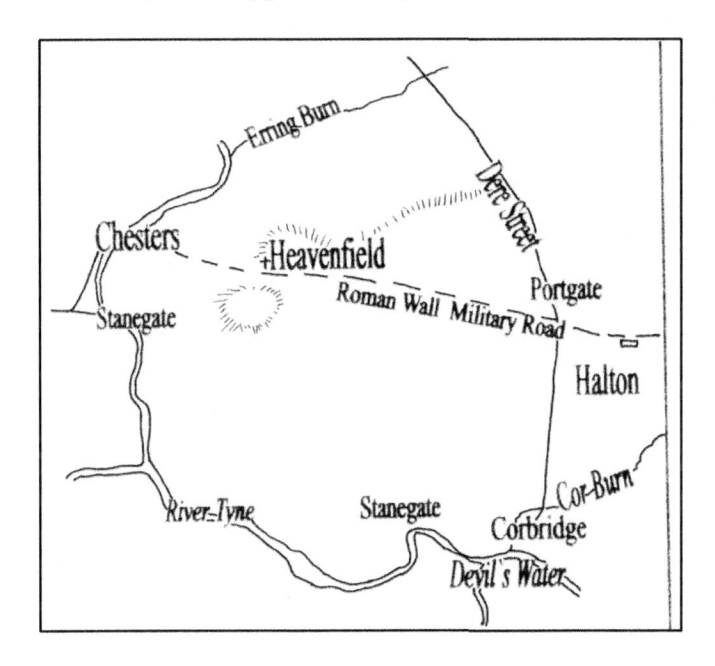

However Oswald, as son of Aethelfrith and nephew of Edwin, and with a Deiran mother was able to unite Bernicia and Deira. The victorious king was keen to support the Christianity, which had given him victory. He sent to Iona for preachers, the first returned, appalled at the barbarous ways of the Northumbrians and their stubbornness."Wild ungovernable men of harsh and barbarous disposition." but then he was sent **Aidan**, a saintly monk, who was to establish Christianity in Northumbria. He chose to settle himself on an isolated island like Iona. He chose Lindisfarne near the royal centre of Bamburgh.

"Be alone in a separate place near a chief city." Rule of St Columba.

The church at Lindisfarne was built of wood in the Irish fashion.

A model of an Irish wooden church, they could be dismantled and moved. (as Aidan's church was.)

Bamburgh seen in the distance from Lindisfarne.

Aidan's close association physically with the royal house ensured that his message reached the rich and powerful even though he himself led an austere life, much to the approval of Bede;

> *"he gave his clergy an inspiring example of self-discipline and continence, and the highest recommendation of his teaching to all was that he and his followers lived as they taught. He never*

74

sought or cared for worldly possessions, and loved to give away to the poor, who chanced to meet him, whatever he received from kings or wealthy folk. Whether in town or country, he always travelled on foot unless compelled by necessity to ride, and whatever people he met on his walks, whether high or low, he stopped and spoke to them."

"AIDAN was in the king's country-house, not far from the city of which we have spoken above, for having a church and a chamber there, he was wont often to go and stay there, and to make excursions to preach in the country round about, which he likewise did at other of the king's country-seats, having nothing of his own besides his church and a few fields about it. If wealthy people did wrong, he never kept silent out of respect or fear, but corrected them outspokenly." Bede on Aidan.

Aidan's Lindisfarne was presumably modelled on Columba's Iona. The monks fasted on Wednesday and Fridays. They ate a special meal on Sundays and feast days. The monks worked in the fields and were largely self-sufficient. Fishing and the sea no doubt played as important a part of life on Lindisfarne as on Iona. The monks of Iona built their own boats, both wooden, and skin-covered curraghs. They were well aware of the vagrancies of the seas;

"When night had passed and we rose at first light, we realized that the wind had dropped completely and we set out in the boats in still weather. Soon a south wind rose behind us, and the sailors shouted for joy and raised the sails. In this way God gave us a fast and fair voyage without the labour of rowing for St Columba's sake." Adomnan.

An image of an Irish church from the Monasterboice cross, Ireland.

Columba was credited with any beneficial change in the weather a skill which was
passed on to Aidan;

" *A certain priest, whose name was Utta,… being ordered to Kent, to bring from thence, as wife for King Oswiu, Eanfleda, the daughter of King Edwin, who had been carried thither when her father was killed; and intending to go thither by land, but to return with the virgin by sea, repaired to Bishop Aidan, entreating him to offer up his prayers to our Lord for him and his company, who were then to set out on their journey. He, blessing and recommending them to our Lord, at the same time gave them some holy oil, saying, "I know that when you go abroad, you will meet with a storm and contrary wind; but do you remember to cast this oil I give you into the sea, and the wind shall cease immediately; you will have pleasant calm weather, and return home safe.*

All which fell out as the bishop had predicted. For in the first place, the winds raging, the sailors endeavoured to ride it out at anchor, but all to no purpose; for the sea breaking in on all sides, and the ship beginning to be filled with water, they all concluded that certain death was at hand; the priest at last,

remembering the bishop's words, laid hold of the phial and cast some of the oil into the sea, which, as had been foretold, became presently calm. Thus it came to pass that the man of God, by the spirit of prophecy, foretold the storm that was to happen, and by virtue of the same spirit, though absent, appeased the same. Which miracle was not told me by a person of little credit, but by Cynemund, a most faithful priest of our church, who declared that it was related to him by Utta, the priest, on and by whom the same was wrought."
Bede. After Aidan, mastery of the weather was credited to Cuthbert.

Aidan began to teach English boys including Chedd and Chad. He ensured, vitally, that the Northumbrians would be taught in their own tongue. When Aidan preached, King Oswald would translate, the king and his brother Oswiu "having been instructed and baptized by the Scots and being very perfectly skilled in their language." Bede.

By his youth policy Aidan ensured that Christianity would survive in Northumbria. The royal family also played a prominent part. Oswald's sister Aebbe established a community at St Abbs and Coldingham. Mailros was also established, and a nunnery at Hart.

Statue of Saint Aidan on Lindisfarne by Kathleen Parbury.

Oswald himself carried the faith south sponsoring the baptism of king Cyngils of the West Saxons, whose daughter Cyneburga he married. He also established a see at Dorchester on Thames.

Under Oswald and his capable brother Oswiu Northumbrian control of Lothian was confirmed. In 628 AD Oswald attacked Edinburgh, (Dinas Eidyn.) Oswiu fought successful battles with Dalraida, Strathclyde and Manau. His welsh enemies called Oswald, "Bright blade". In English his name meant "God power". Abbot Adomnan of Iona called him Emperor of all Britain.

The death of Oswald Oswald was forced to look south where Penda of Mercia was expanding into East Anglia. Oswald`s links to Wessex threatened

Mercia's southern borders. He also tried to establish a route between Northumbria and Wessex. He detached the Hwicce from Mercia and tried to drive a wedge between the Mercians and their Welsh allies. Initially successful, he drove Penda into Wales, but gathering support from Powys, Penda struck back and Oswald was caught and killed at Maserfeld.5 August 642 AD. He was 38 years old.

The death of a king in battle.

"While St Oswald was encamped there, feeling secure and in no fear of danger. Penda unexpectedly appeared with his heathen army and endeavoured to accomplish the holy king's death in battle. But the man of God, hitherto renowned for his honour as a soldier refused to consider flight, in case he should seem a man unskilled in the conduct of battle. He considered it

dishonourable to be found vanquished and disgraced at the end, when hitherto he had appeared to all to be a vigorous and victorious warrior. And so he summoned a small force of soldiers and proceeded to commit himself to Christ." Reginald.

"When he saw he was surrounded by the enemy forces and about to be slain, he prayed for the souls of his army: and this is the origin of the proverb. "God have mercy on their souls said Oswald falling to the ground."" Bede.

His body was dismembered and his head and arms placed on stakes on the battlefield at Maserfeld, which most identity as Oswestry, Oswald's tree.

"One shall swing on the broad gallows,
hang in death, until the body, the frame,
is bloodily destroyed." Fates of Men. Gordon.

"As a rood was I raised up,
I bore aloft the mighty King
The Lord of Heaven.
I durst not stoop.
They pierced me with dark nails;
The wounds are still plain to view in me,
Gaping gashes of malice."

Dream of the Rood. Gordon.

Death of Oswald from Bamberg church.

Penda and his forces once more fell upon Northumbria. Bamburgh itself was burned and Yeavering. Oswiu was driven as far north as Stirling, amongst his troops was a young man, Cuthbert.

Within a year of becoming king Oswiu led a band of warriors south to recover the bones of his brother Oswald. He found the "remarkably spherical" head, *"and the right arm which was miraculously preserved from decomposition as prophesied by Aidan."*

"On the feast of Easter one year. Oswald sat down to dine with Bishop Aidan. A silver dish of rich food was set before him, and they were on the point of raising their hands to bless the food, when the servant who was appointed by the king to relieve the needs of the poor came in suddenly and informed the king that a great crowd were sitting in the road outside begging alms of the king. Oswald at once ordered his own food to be taken out to the poor, and the silver dish to be broken up and distributed amongst them. The Bishop, who was sitting beside him, was deeply moved to see such generosity, and taking hold of the king's right hand, exclaimed, "May this hand never wither with age." *"Later events proved that his prayer was heard; for when Oswald was killed in battle, his hand and arm were severed*

from his body, and they remain uncorrupted to this day. They are preserved and venerated as relics in the church of St Peter in Bebba's burgh." Bede.

Succouring the poor. A King and Queen dispense alms. Note the stags head on the roof.

Oswald the Christian king slaughtered by the pagan Penda was a martyr to the faith, and soon venerated. His head was taken to Lindisfarne. His arms and hands went to Bamburgh where Oswiu built a church, St Peter's on the rock, to house them. Later his head was placed in St Cuthbert's coffin when it was carried from Lindisfarne in the face of the Viking raids, ending up eventually at Durham. Later images of Cuthbert usually show him carrying Oswald's head. Queen Osthryd of Mercia, Oswiu's daughter brought his other bones to Bardney abbey in Lincolnshire,

"The monks were reluctant to admit them, for although they acknowledged Oswald's holiness, they were influenced by old prejudices against him even after his death, because originally he came from a different province and had ruled them as an alien king." Bede.

Which shows the strength of particularism among the English. Again Viking threats caused these bones to be moved, they were sent south to Gloucester by Aelfflaed, wife of Aethelred of Mercia, when Bardney came under the Danelaw. The arm was stolen from Bamburgh by monks from Peterborough. It was seen as a talisman by the English, as events in 1066 AD were to show. See below.

Many churches were named after him and a village Kirkoswald. In Northumbrian Grasmere, where it is said Oswald preached the faith, a rush bearing ceremony takes place on the Sunday nearest to his feast day of August 5th.

Grasmere church.
Saint Oswald's Heavenfield,(below).

His fame spread throughout the country and abroad. The Northumbrian missionaries encouraged the cult of their saint, Willibrord carried with him to Frisia part of the stake which had impaled the king's head. Athelstan of Wessex, when he was trying to reconquer the Danelaw, was keen to identify with an English Christian warrior king. Edith, Athelstan's half-sister, married Otto of Saxony; this reinforced the cult on the Continent. Later, Judith of Flanders, widow of Tosti, who was Earl of Northumbria in 1065, married Welf of Bavaria and carried the cult into Southern Germany. A curious ceremony in Bavaria echoes the rush bearing of Grasmere; at the end of the harvest the final sheaf is garlanded and carried through the field, it is called the Oswald. Eight villages in Austria are named St Oswald. He was often portrayed, like Woden, with a raven as a companion.

Oswald with raven. A similar image can be seen in Durham Cathedral, Oswald's banner in St.Cuthbert's shrine.

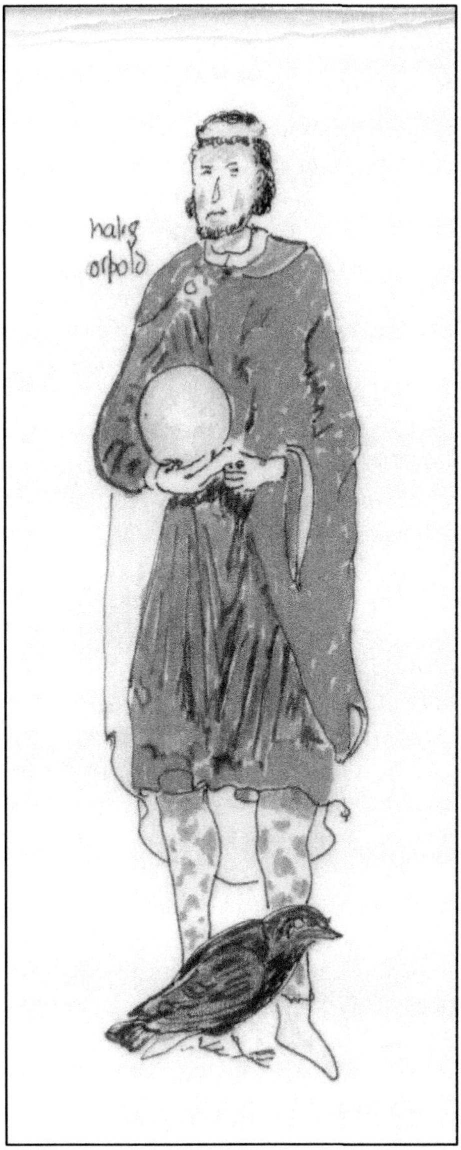
halig oſƿold

OSWIU, Emperor of All Britain.
THE MOST SUCCESSFUL NORTHUMBRIAN KING

Oswiu is also known as Oswy.

Oswald's death allowed Penda to ravage Northumbria;

"The hostile army of the Mercians, under the command of Penda, cruelly ravaged the country of the Northumbrians far and near, even to the royal city; which has its name from Bebba, formerly its queen. Not being able to enter it by force, or by a long siege, he endeavored to burn it; and having destroyed all the villages in the neighbourhood of the city, he brought to it an immense quantity of planks, beams, wattles and thatch, wherewith he encompassed the place to a great height on the land side, and when the wind set upon it, he fired the mass, designing to burn the town.

*At that time, the most reverend Bishop **Aidan** resided in the isle of Farne, which is nearly two miles from the city; for thither he was wont often to retire to pray in private, that he might be undisturbed. Indeed, this solitary residence of his is to this day shown in that island. When he saw the flames of fire and the smoke carried by the boisterous wind above the city walls, he is reported, with eyes and hands lifted up to heaven, to have said, "Behold, Lord, how great mischief Penda does!" Which words were hardly uttered, when the wind immediately turning from the city, drove back the flames upon those who had kindled them, so that some being hurt, and all frightened, they forbore any further attempts against the city, which they perceived was protected by the hand of God."* Bede. (which may account for Aidan being the patron saint of firemen, Bede supplies further evidence below.)

Even at this time of trial the Northumbrians were fighting amongst themselves for superiority. When Oswiu succeeded to Bernicia, Oswine, (or Oswin), son of Osric of Edwin's line, succeeded in Deira and reigned for 7 years. "noblemen from many a kingdom flocking to serve the bountiful Oswine of Deira" clearly Oswiu could not tolerate such a rival until. Oswiu came against him with an army. Outnumbered, Oswine disbanded his troops and sought refuge with a thane who betrayed him to Oswiu, who had Oswine murdered. Oswine was a saintly king and Oswiu did penance (after some persuasion from Queen Eanflaed,) by raising a monastery on the spot where the murder took place at Gilling. Oswine's bones were buried at Tynemouth where the church in Front Street is named after him. The murder of the saintly Oswine is supposed to have hastened the death of Aidan at Bamburgh on 31 Aug 651.AD.

"When he (Aidan) was sick they set up a tent for him close to the wall at the west end of the church, by which means it happened that he gave up the ghost, leaning against a post that was on the outside to strengthen the wall.

"It happened some years after, that Penda, king of the Mercians, coming into these parts with a hostile army, destroyed all he could with fire and sword, and burned down the village and church above mentioned, where the bishop died; but it fell out in a wonderful manner that the post, which he had leaned upon when he died, could not be consumed by the fire which

consumed all about it. This miracle being taken notice of, the church was soon rebuilt in the same place, and that very post was set up on the outside, as it had been before, to strengthen the wall. It happened again, sometime after, that the same village and church were burned down the second time, and even then the fire could not touch that post; and when in a most miraculous manner the fire broke through the very holes in it wherewith it was fixed to the building, and destroyed the church, yet it could do no hurt to the said post. The church being therefore built there the third time, they did not, as before, place that post on the outside as a support, but within, as a memorial of the miracle; and the people coming in were wont to kneel there, and implore the Divine mercy. And it is manifest that since then many have been healed in that same place, as also that chips being cut off from that post, and put into water, have healed many from their distempers." Bede

Oswine

Oswiu then appeared to make a deal with Penda, there was a double marriage agreement. Oswiu's son, Alchfrith married Penda's daughter, Kyniburga, and his daughter, Alchfled married Peada, Penda's son. Before the marriage, Peada was christened by Bishop Finan at a place called by Bede. "At the Wall", this has been taken to be Wall near Hexham, or Walbottle, but since Bede says "it is close to the wall, at the distance of 12 miles from the eastern sea" this "noted village belonging to the king" is possibly Newcastle. Despite these marriages Oswiu was still paying huge sums of tribute to Penda and Oswiu's son Ecgfrith was a hostage in Mercia.

However two years later on 15 November 655AD Oswiu, "with an insignificant force" gave battle. It was said that Penda had taken "30 legions to Bernicia" and that Oswiu had but one. He advanced south down the Roman road passed Leeds and met Penda at Winwaed. Oethelwald, Oswald's son, who had joined the pagan against his uncle withdrew as the fight began. Cadfael of Gwynedd also proved unreliable and the old pagan king went down fighting. The idea that Penda might have been 80 years old has been revised drastically to 50. Bassett. P.166.

> "King Oswiu with his son Alhfrith brought this war to a close in the 13th year of his reign to the great benefit of both populaces. For he freed his own people from the hostile pillaging of the pagans.." Liber Eliensis.

Anglo-Saxon warriors

"Then was the fight near, glory in battle; the time had come when doomed men must needs fall there.

Then clamour arose; ravens wheeled,
the eagle greedy for carrion; there was shouting on earth.
Then they let the spears, hard as a file, go from their hands;
let the darts, ground sharp, fly;
bows were busy; shield received point;
bitter was the rush of battle.
Warriors fell on either hand; young men lay low." Battle of Maldon. Gordon

Perhaps Oswiu had gained inside information on the Mercians from his daughter and her priests led by Cedd who had been sent from Lindisfarne.
The river Winwaed was swollen by rain and "many more were drowned while trying to escape as were killed by the sword."

"Not only did he (Oswiu) deliver his people from the hostile attacks of the heathen but after cutting off their infidel head he converted the Mercians and their neighbours to the Christian faith."

Oswiu dedicated another daughter, Aelfflaed, as a nun in thanks for the victory, the daughter's thoughts are not recorded. She became a nun at Hart and later Whitby, where she later died.(see below.) The degree to which the Northumbrian identity was tied up with Christianity has never been explored. Did the war against Mercia and Penda take on an element of Christian crusade? Obviously Bede makes Northumbrian success and Christianity march hand in hand, but the recently discovered Staffordshire hoard gives some support. Found in Mercia the hoard of sword trappings and other objects, plunder presumably from non-Mercian sources, includes an inscription from the Psalms, Exsurget Deus; let God arise; Let his enemies be scattered.

THE RELIGIOUS SETTLEMENT AT WHITBY.

Oswiu's latest wife Eanfled, Edwin's daughter, was raised in Kent. Her Christianity was therefore Roman, but Aidan had established Irish Christianity in Northumbria. In fact as Jocelyn Toynbee has said, *" the so-called Celtic church, surviving continuously in the West and North, was thoroughly Roman in creed and origin."* Thomas.p.75. The two brands of the same religion are often stereotyped as the aesthetic Irish monks leading lives of self-denial, in their simple island dwelling places. The Romans seeking to glorify God with large stone churches and amassing land to support the church.

If Aidan personified the first group, chief amongst the latter was **Wilfrid**, born in 614 AD. To avoid a cruel step mother he was raised in the Queen Eanfled's household. He entered the church and studied at Aidan`s Lindisfarne and Rome. Eanfled sent him to her relatives in Kent then he travelled to Gaul with Benet Biscop. Wilfrid stopped at Lyon where he so impressed the Bishop there that the latter offered to adopt him as his son, and the Count offered his daughter in marriage. Wilfrid, however, pressed on to Rome. There he prayed at the oratory of Saint Andrew, which may account for his devotion to that saint, which in turn may account t for Hexham being dedicated to Andrew along with other churches in the Tyne valley. At Rome the Pope had just been kidnapped by the Byzantines and removed from the country. The turbulent life of the higher clergy was brought home more forcibly to him when he returned to Lyons where the Bishop was murdered. Wilfrid escaped and returned to Northumbria. He was raised up as abbot of Ripon, by his new patron Alchfrith, Oswiu's son, who ruled in Deira. His reforms which included the introduction of the rule of St Benedict, caused Eata and Cuthbert, whom Alchfrith had only recently appointed, to leave Ripon.

The differences between the two traditions was symbolized by their different methods of tonsure; the Irish favoured shaving the whole of head forward from ear to ear. The Romans favoured the familiar bald circle on the crown. But the real difference was in calculating the date of Easter. The king and his wife were celebrating the main event of the Christian calendar at different times. Easter was the major Christian feast, since it celebrated the resurrection of Jesus from the dead, the central belief of Christianity. It was vital then to celebrate it on the correct day with the rest of the Churches. While the Irish and British churches held to an early method of dating Easter, the church in Rome and elsewhere had adopted a newer method. Some saw their opponents as heretics destroying the unity of the church. Bede's Ecclesiastical History discusses the dating of Easter at length. It caused him to temper his opinion of the saintly **Aidan**, though not to condemn him outright;

> *"These things I much love and admire in the aforesaid bishop; because I do not doubt that they were pleasing to God; but I do not praise or approve his not observing Easter at the proper time, either through ignorance of the canonical time appointed, or, if he knew it, being prevailed on by the authority of his nation, not to follow the same. Yet this I approve in him, that in the celebration of his Easter, the object which he had in view in all he said, did, or preached, was the same as ours, that is, the redemption of mankind, through the passion, resurrection and ascension into heaven of the man Jesus Christ, who is mediator betwixt God and man. And therefore he always celebrated the same, not, as some falsely imagine, on the fourteenth moon, like the Jews, whatsoever the day was, but on the Lord's day, from the fourteenth to the twentieth moon; and this he did from his belief of the resurrection of our Lord happening on the day after the Sabbath, and for the hope of our resurrection, which also he, with the holy Church, believed would happen on the same day after the Sabbath, now called the Lord's day."* Bede.

To solve the matter a Synod was held at Whitby, called Streaneshalch, the bay of the Beacon.

The abbess of Whitby was **Hild (or Hilda)** daughter of Edwin's nephew Herevic, who had lived in exile in Elmet during Edwin's exile. She had wished to join her sister Hereswith who was nun at Chelles in Gaul but Aidan gave her land at Wearmouth where she became abbess. Then she succeeded Heiu as abbess of Hartlepool. She was sympathetic to the Irish. Hild was well respected and kings and ecclesiastics often sought her advice. Hilda then became abbess at Whitby, a double monastery of Monks and Nuns. Whitby was the first monastery to emphasize education. Five scholars from Whitby were to become Bishops. Whitby also witnessed the birth of English poetry, for it was here that the monk Caedmon discovered his talent for turning his Christian lessons into poems in the English language.(see above).Under Aelfflaed, Oswiu`s daughter, it was to become the burial place of the Northumbrian kings and Queens.

Whitby the burial place of Northumbrian royalty. The medieval ruins.

At the Synod Cedd acted as translator for the Irish. Agilbert, the Gaulish Bishop of the West Saxons chose Wilfrid, whom he had consecrated, to speak for him, and the Romans. The Synod of 664AD was portrayed by Bede as the intransigent Irish rejecting the true tradition of St Peter. Wilfrid launched into an insulting diatribe against the stupid Scots and obstinate Picts and Britons. The king sided with the Roman position, declaring he would side with St Peter, as he held the keys of the kingdom of Heaven. Wilfrid was exultant. Many Celts, led by Colman returned to Scotland taking with them some English monks from Lindisfarne, and some of the bones of Aidan and others. They eventually set up a monastery on Innisboffin in the west of Ireland. However the Irish and English monks fell out as the Irish went on walkabout during the year, and returned to share in the food harvested by the English after all the work was done. The English moved away and set up their own monastery in Mayo.

How far Oswiu's sympathies lay with the Romans is hard to judge. **Wilfrid** was an insufferable man, Oswiu`s son had appointed Wilfrid as

Bishop of York, but Oswiu appointed Chad who had been educated on Lindisfarne and in Ireland. When Wilfrid went to Gaul for his consecration, Oswiu appointed Eata to Lindisfarne The arrival of the aged and prestigious Theodore of Tarsus,(a refugee from the expansion of Islam in the Middle East) as Archbishop of Cantebury saw Wilfrid restored. Wilfrid had been consecrated by Agilbert in Gaul, when he returned to this country he had survived a shipwreck in Sussex. His followers stoned and killed the local pagan priest who was cursing them, and had to fight their way to safety from attacks by the pagan South Saxons. He moved back to Ripon where he began building a new church, the crypt can still be viewed there. He also restored Edwin`s church in York. His church acquired land from the defeated Britons around the Ribble, at Yeadon, Dent and elsewhere. But his career under Oswiu's children was to be chequered.

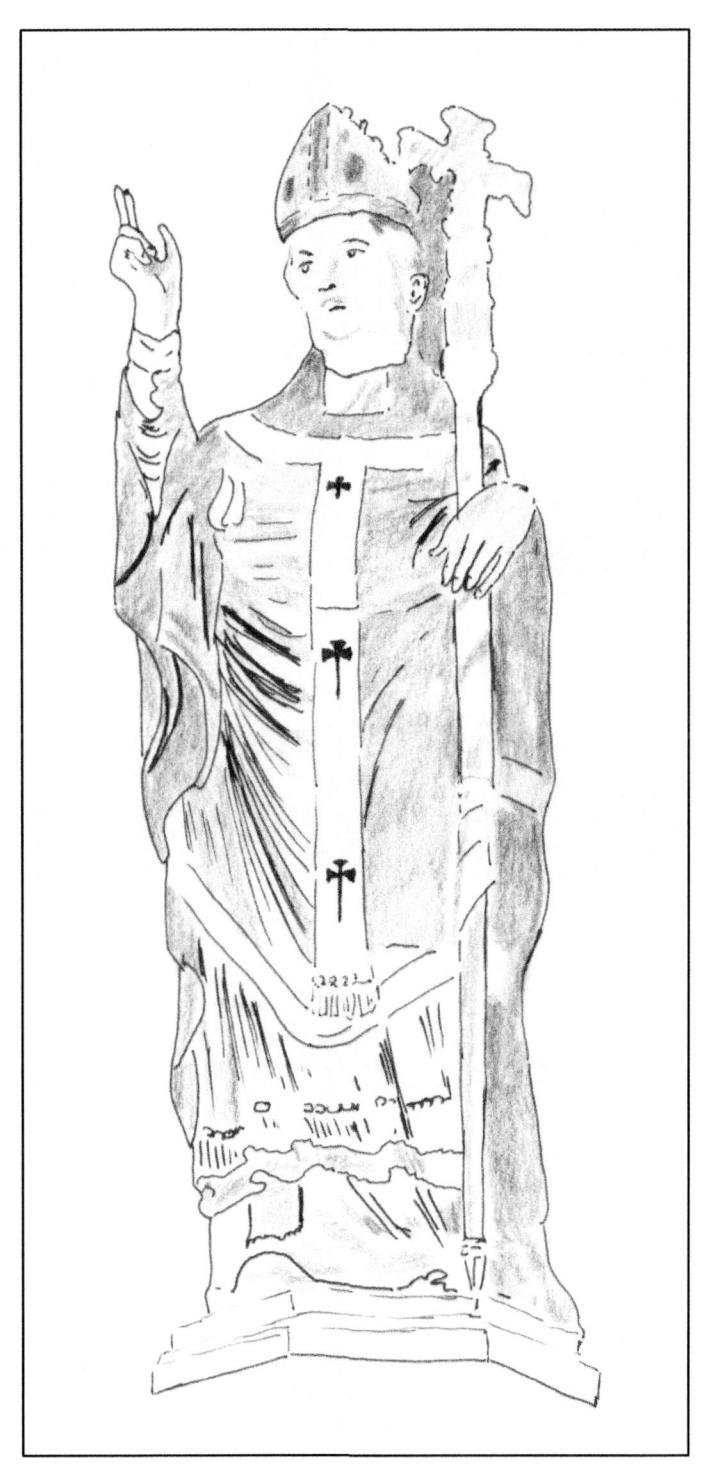

Wilfrid from a Statue in Ripon Cathedral.

Theodore was already 67 years old when he arrived in England in 669AD. It was a time of plague which had carried off the previous archbishop-elect. Theodore after a series of visits reorganized the English church along Gregorian lines. He created more and smaller bishoprics. Northumbria being divided initially into 3, then in 681AD into 5. The other kingdoms were similarly divided. The original scheme lasted until the Reformation. The aim was to allow bishops to carry out a more pastoral role in their smaller dioceses. Rich bishops of large territories like Wilfrid objected. Theodore died in 690AD aged 88 years.

But under Oswiu Northumbrians had played a large part in the conversion of Mercia. After the Council at Chelsea had barred Irish ecclesiastics from jurisdiction in England **Chad** was removed from York, he declared, *If you know I have not duly received episcopal ordination, I willingly resign the office, For I never thought myself worthy of it; but, though unworthy, in obedience submitted to undertake it."* Bede

Consecrating a Bishop. (below)

Theodore was impressed by Chad's humility. He re-consecrated Chad and made him bishop of the Mercians. He had to force him to ride a horse as Chad, like Aidan, travelled everywhere on foot, so he could preach to those he met along the way. Chad set up the see of Lichfield. He also established a monastery at Barrow in Lindsey. He was a friend of Sigebert king of the East Saxons, who had been driven into exile by Raedwald of East Anglia, Sigebert was also baptised by Finan at "At the wall". Chad helped in his conversion and that of the people of Essex sending his brother Cedd to preach to them. **Cedd** was a terrifying character who on one occasion berated Sigebert for visiting a thane who had been excommunicated. While the trembling king prostrated himself, Cedd prodded him with his rod and prophesied that the king would die in that very same Thane's house, which came to pass. Cedd built a church at Bradwell-on-Sea in the gateway of the roman fort. Northumbrian bishops held sway throughout the country.

Cedd was later given land at Lastingham to build a monastery by Aethelwald of Deira, whose priest Celin was Cedd's own brother. The monastery was completed by Cedd and another brother Cynebil. It was at Lastingham that Cedd died of plague. Hearing of this 30 of his followers came from Essex to be near the body, they all in turn caught the plague and died, with the exception of one boy.

Chad died and was buried at Lichfield where "as a testimony to his virtue, frequent miraculous cures are wont to be wrought." Bede. Much later an abbot from Lindsay visiting Egbert in Ireland was told,

St Chad

"I know a man in this island, still in the flesh, who, when that prelate passed out of this world, saw the soul of his brother Cedd, with a company of angels, descending from heaven ,who, having taken his soul along with them, returned thither again." Bede.

The continuity of personnel was maintained when one of Chad`s monks Trumberht taught Bede. Bishop Wilfrid later took a mission to the South Saxons, baptising many and setting up a monastery at Selsey.

Northumbria was therefore responsible for the conversion of the better part of England

Oswiu, Bretwalda of Britain, had extended Northumbrian dominance to its greatest extent, and unlike most of his ancestors and successors died in his bed. Just before his death the Mercians murdered his son-in-law Peada, who was betrayed by his wife, Alchfled, Oswiu's daughter.

Peada held the kingdom of the South Angles until foully murdered through the treachery on the part of his wife at the very time of the Easter festival." Fairweather. Liber Eliensis.

Cedd

Despite his many achievements; the destruction of the pagan Penda, the conversion of other nations, and most important the decision in favour of Rome at Whitby, Oswiu does not get a very sympathetic report from Bede, particularly when compared to Oswine (God's friend) who is promoted to sainthood. Yet Oswine was the son of the apostate Osric and on his father's death fled to the pagan west Saxons. Oswiu was obviously blamed for Oswine's death and the latter's holiness was suggested by the death of Aidan only 12 days later. Perhaps Oswiu's marriage to Eanfled counted against him, as they were first cousins, both grandchildren of Aelle of Deira. Oswine was buried at Tynemouth, Oswiu at Whitby, perhaps Bede who was a Bernician Northumbrian looked upon Oswiu as too much of a Deiran.

His daughter Aelfflaed was buried at Whitby "together with her father Oswiu, her mother Eanfled, her grandfather Edwin and many other nobles, all in the church of the holy apostle Peter." And her Aunt, Acha.

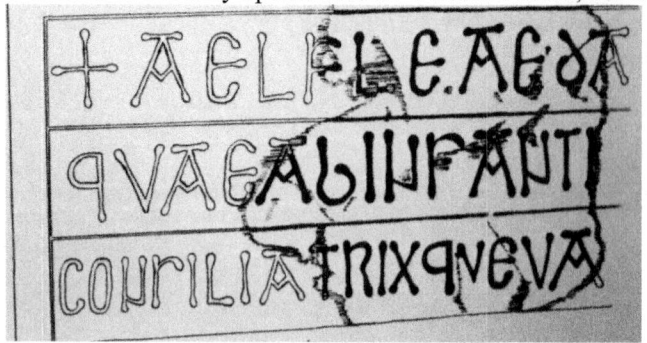

Aelfflaed's tomb inscription, Whitby.

CHAPTER 6.

ECGFRITH and ALDFRITH. THE SONS OF OSWIU.

The throne now fell to Ecgfrith, "the Sword's edge", an aptly martial epithet, who at the very start of his reign with Earl Beornheth defeated the Picts.

When Ecgfrith was about 15 years old he was married to Aetheldreda of East Anglia, the lady's second marriage. Also known as Aethelthryth she was the daughter of Anna of East Anglia who had been killed by Penda. Her mother was Hereswith, sister of Abbess Hild and a relative of Edwin. Aethelthryth was unfortunately in favour of perpetual virginity, being encouraged in this by Wilfrid. It is not recorded as to whether Ecgfrith was given this information about his Queen before the wedding.

"Although she lived with him for twelve years, she preserved intact the glory of perpetual virginity. I enquired about this myself, when some had cast doubt on it, and was assured of its truth by Bishop Wilfrid of blessed memory, who said he had indisputable evidence of her virginity in that Ecgfrith had promised to give him lands and great wealth if he could persuade the Queen to consummate the marriage; for Ecgfrith knew that she loved no man more than Wilfrid." Bede.

After a trying 12 years, they were divorced and the lady joyfully retired to a nunnery. Aetheldreda entered the double monastery at Coldingham under abbess Ebba who was Ecgfrith's aunt. Ebba (Aebbe) is remembered by the name of an earlier monastery she set up at St Abb's head. Ebchester is also said to be named after her, her brother King Oswiu had given her the fort there for her to build a monastery. Craster AA NSxvi.1894. Aetheldreda, then moved to Ely. After her death at Ely, ignoring her pleas for a plain coffin, the monks went to the roman remains at Grantchester near Cambridge to search for a suitable stone coffin for her. Her tomb and uncorrupt body attracted pilgrimages. She is remembered as St Audrey, and cheap mementoes sold at the fair on her day gave us the word Tawdry. She was succeeded by her sister Sexburg.

It was under her sponsorship that **Wilfrid** built extensively at York, Ripon and also Hexham where his crypt using the roman stone of Corstopitum can be seen.

"It's crypts of wonderfully dressed stone, and the manifold building above ground, supported by various columns and many side aisles and adorned with walls of notable length and height surrounded by various winding passages with spiral stairs winding up and down" Eddius,

Wilfrid's follower and biographer claimed that there was none north of the Alps built on such a scale.

The Frith stool, Hexham. Statue of Aethelthryth, (Etheldreda) at Ely.(below.)

To impress people he had had the gospels written in letters of gold on purple parchment. But on another occasion, according to Eddius, after he had saved a child's life, he demanded that the child at 7 years old be handed over to the church, and when the family fled to live with a "gang of Britons", he had the king's reeve bring them back and the boy "lived in the service of God", until he died in the Great plague.

Ecgfrith's new wife Iurminburga was less infatuated with Wilfrid and began seeking to reclaim royal land which had been alienated by her predecessor, in particular Hexham. The King called in Theodore of Tarsus the Archbishop, to restrain his troublesome cleric. Theodore appointed Bishops to Lindisfarne, York, the newly annexed Lindsey, and later to Hexham and Abercorn. At a meeting between king and Archbishop at Twyford on the Aln, (possibly Whittingham) they picked out Cuthbert as bishop of Lindisfarne. Wilfrid, who remained truculent, was expelled from the kingdom, he went prophesying doom. He intended to seek redress from the Pope so once more headed off to Rome. His ship was however blown off course to Frisia. Never one to miss an opportunity Wilfrid began preaching the Gospel and converted numbers to Christianity, so starting the Frisian Mission. When he returned with papal backing, he found that letters from the pope did not count for much at the court of Ecgfrith, who had the bishop imprisoned at Dunbar. He was only released on the death of the Queen. He was however expelled once more. He sought refuge in Mercia but the Queen was Ecgfrith's sister, when he moved to Wessex he found that the Queen was Iurminburga's sister. It was while in the south that he converted the south Saxons and founded the monastery at Selsey. In 686AD he helped the exiled Caedwalla regain the throne of Wessex. He was given one quarter of the Isle of Wight and a large amount of booty which he passed on to his nephew. Wilfrid and his followers were a political, as well as religious force, in the country. Apart from sponsoring Cuthbert, Ecgfrith "the most devout and Christian king" Eddius. gave land to Biscop Baducing, a young nobleman who had served Oswiu, then had been drawn to the church and journeyed to Rome six times. He had observed many monasteries (about 17) abroad including that at Lerins, off the Mediterranean coast of France. He escorted Theodore of Tarsus to England and had been made abbot of St Peter and Paul at Cantebury. He only returned to Northumbria on Oswiu's death. He was given 50 hides of land at Wearmouth by Ecgfrith to set up a Monastery in 673AD. **Benedict** (Benet) **Biscop** (as he is better known.) reintroduced the making of glass and crucially, cement. Skilled workers from Gaul were able to build churches at Wearmouth and 7 years, later in 681AD, at Jarrow when Ecgfrith gave a further 40 hides of land. The two sites were run as one monastery. By 716AD there were 600 monks and lay brothers, which was greater than any Medieval English monastery.

Dedication of the Church at Jarrow Dedication of the Church (Basilica)
Of Saint Paul, on 9th Kalends of May
Year 15 of Ecfrith, king,
Ceolfrith, abbot, with God's help,
Church's founder,
His year 4

(Dedication Jarrow St Pauls, South Tyneside. below)

It was the latter place built alongside the Slake (an area of land which fills up with the tide.) known as Ecgfrith's harbour that a young boy called Bede was taken into the monastery. Benet Biscop was helped at Wearmouth by Ceolfrith who accompanied him to Rome.
They brought back John the archchantor to teach chant to the monks.

(he taught) *"singing and reading aloud, and committing to writing all that was requisite throughout the whole course of the year for the celebration of festivals; all which are still observed in that monastery, and have been copied by many others elsewhere. The said John not only taught the brothers of that monastery; (Wearmouth) but such as had skill in singing resorted from almost all the monasteries of the same province to hear him; and many invited him to teach in other places."* Bede on John the Archchanter. Benet Biscop and Ceolfrith also bought large numbers of books and paintings creating one of the finest libraries in Europe.

"He journeyed so many times to places across the sea that we are abounding in all the resources of spiritual knowledge and can as a result be at peace within the cloister." Bede.

He observed that there was no learning without books. Although his own influence had been exclusively for the good he opposed the growing trend of royal and aristocratic influence on the monasteries. When Biscop's kinsman Eosterwine, also an ex-soldier, became abbot of Wearmouth, he happily shared in the hardest physical work done in the monastery. The latter died of the plague which also wiped out all but two of the community in Jarrow. Eosterwine is buried in the porch at Wearmouth. The two who survived at Jarrow were Ceolfrith and a small boy.

Anglo-Saxon doorway at Jarrow (below)

Anglo-Saxon window at Jarrow (below)

Not all religious were so dedicated as Benedict. Adomnan criticised the monastery of Coldingham;

"where the cells, which were built for prayer and study, are now converted into places for eating drinking, gossip and other amusements. When they have leisure, even the nuns vowed to God abandon the propriety of their calling and spend their time weaving fine clothes which they employ to the peril of their calling, either to adorn themselves like brides or to attract attention from strange men." Coldingham was destroyed by fire.

The Sword's edge

Despite his close involvement in religion Ecgfrith lived up to his martial name. In 672 AD. He with "Beornhaeth, his trusty sub-king," Eddius defeated the Picts, two rivers were filled with corpses, a not uncommon occurrence according to Chroniclers.

"so that, marvellous to relate, the Northumbrians passing over the river dry shod, pursued and slew the crowd of fugitives." Eddius.

Then, assisted by Cuthbert's prayers, he defeated Wulfere of Mercia, Peada's son, in 674. Wulfere had already conquered Essex, Sussex, and the Isle of Wight, and had led "all the southern nations against Ecgfrith" an indication of the growing power of Mercia but also the continuing power of Northumbria. Five years later Ecgfrith's brother Aelfwin was killed in battle by Aethelred of Mercia. Despite the fact that the death of a brother demanded revenge, Archbishop Theodore was able to make peace between the two kings. After this battle a young Northumbrian thane Imma who was wounded was captured by the Mercians. He pretended to be a peasant but when it was found out "from his appearance, clothing, and speech that he was of noble birth." his captor said , "You deserve to die, because all my brothers and kinsmen were killed in that battle:" He was not killed however but taken to the slave market in London and sold to a Frisian. However, his brother was a priest and prayed for him, and at the very same time his fetters fell off. He was able to ransom himself from his master. The tale indicates a thriving slave trade and continued links to Frisia. Also that nobles were recognizable by speech and dress. It also shows that the Anglo-Saxon ideal of the feud in revenge for the deaths of kin was strongly held. and survived in Northumbria for a thousand years, it was commented on by 16th century observers of the reiving families.

Ecgfrith's wide ranging capabilities were shown by a raid into Ireland in 684AD which brought condemnation from Bede and Egbert.

"In the year of our Lord's incarnation 684, Ecgfrith, king of the Northumbrians, sending Beort, his general, with an army, into Ireland, miserably wasted that harmless nation, which had always been most friendly to the English; insomuch that in their hostile rage they spared not even the churches or monasteries. Those islanders, to the utmost of their power, repelled force with force, and imploring the assistance of the Divine mercy, prayed long and fervently for vengeance; and though such as curse cannot possess the kingdom of God, it is believed, that those who were justly cursed on account of their impiety, did soon suffer the penalty of their guilt from the avenging hand of God" Bede

This suggests the existence of a Northumbrian fleet and naval base on the west coast.

The death of Ecgfrith The next year he turned his mind once more to the Picts who were being reorganised by Bruide son of Beli, a grandson curiously of Eanfrith, son of Aethelfrith. (Eanfrith was Ecgfrith's uncle.) The sword's Edge was to meet his fate at the hands of the kin of the Twister, his grandfather. **Cuthbert** warned the king against the expedition. While the king set off north regardless, Cuthbert accompanied the Queen to Carlisle where they, like tourists, were being shown the Roman remains including the roman fountain, when Cuthbert had a vision of the disaster that had taken place.

> *"The day after, a man who had escaped from the war explained, by the lamentable news which he brought, the hidden prophecies of the man of God. It appeared that the guards had been slain, and the king cut off by the sword of the enemy, on the very day and hour in which it was revealed to the man of God as he was standing by the well."*
> Bede Life.

Miles to the south Wilfrid also saw the doom. Ecgfrith's army had advanced towards Forfar and there 3 mile SE at Dunnichen, (Dun Nechtain, or Nechtan's fort), on Saturday 20th May, 685AD he and his army were surprised and massacred by the Picts. His companions fell with him. The battle is sometimes called, the Heron's pool, or **Nechtanesmere.** The mere has now been drained. The site does not fit well with Bede's description of a more mountainous place,

> *"The enemy made show as if they fled, and the king was drawn into the straits of inaccessible mountains, and slain, with the greatest part of his forces, in the fortieth year of his age, and the fifteenth of his reign."* Bede.

Nearby was erected an amazing stone, the Aberlemno stone, in fact there are three Aberlemno stones, but the main one has been removed to the Museum of Scotland in Edinburgh. It does in stone for the battle of Nechtanesmere, what the Bayeux tapestry does in cloth for the battle of Hastings.

The Aberlemno stone

The top (not shown) has some Pictish symbols, a "z rod", and a triple circle. Below shows a battle. In it helmeted Northumbrians on crop tailed horses are opposed by bareheaded Picts. The first image sees a Northumbrian horseman, having lost or thrown away his weapons and shield, fleeing from a Pictish horseman who is about to cast a spear. The middle image shows a Northumbrian horseman with round shield attacking Pictish infantry, who stand in formation, the front soldier with raised shield and sword, is covered by the man behind who grips a long spear, while a third man stands in reserve. The bottom line shows two horsemen each about to cast spears at each other, then in the bottom right hand corner we see a fallen Northumbrian

108

figure being pecked at by a carrion bird. From the exaggerated size of this figure, we may presume that it is a representation of Ecgfrith himself. The carrion bird on the battlefield is a constant theme in Anglo-Saxon poetry, it also appears in the Goddodin, and also in later Northumbrian Border ballads. (see **Singin' Hinnies, by Chris Kilkenny.(Amazon books)**)

"685 The same year Ecgfrith was slain by the North sea." ASC
"This day the son of Oswiu was killed with green swords,
Although he did penance, he shall lie in Iona after his death.
This day the son of Oswiu was killed, who had the black drink."

"Thought shall be harder, heart the keener
courage the greater, as our might lessens.
here lies our leader all hew down,
the valiant man in the dust, I am old in age;
I will not hence but I purpose to lie by the side of my lord". Battle of Maldon. Gordon.

'Then the proud thanes went forth there
The brave men hastened eagerly
They all wished, then, for one of two things
To avenge their lord or to leave this world."

The Northumbrians were driven south of the Forth, the monastery at Abercorn was abandoned. The body of Ecgfrith was buried, according to Simeon, on Iona in 685 AD. It may well be that his successor and half-brother, Aldfrith, was living there or had contacts there.

Grave mound associated with Ecgfrith on Iona.

> *"From that time the hopes and strength of the English crown "began to waver and slip backwards" for the Picts recovered their own lands, which had been held by the English and the Scots that were in Britain, and some of the Britons their liberty, which they have now enjoyed for about forty-six years. Among the many English that then either fell by the sword, or were made slaves, or escaped by flight out of the country of the Picts, Trumwine, who had been made bishop over them, withdrew with his people that were in the monastery of Abercurnig, seated in the land of the English, but close by the arm of the sea which parts the lands of the English and the Scots."* Bede.

Cuthbert it seems had served in the army of Oswiu as a young man. But he was working as a shepherd or at least guarding sheep on the hills near Northumbrian Melrose when he saw a bright light to the south-east, it was the night that Aidan died at Bamburgh. He decided to join the monastery at Melrose and was taken in by Boisil.

> *"He knew that the church of Lindisfarne contained many holy men, by whose teaching and example he might be instructed, but he was moved by the great reputation of Boisil, a monk and a priest of surpassing merit, to choose for himself an abode in the abbey of Melrose. And it happened by chance, that when he was arrived there, and had leaped from his horse, that he might enter the church to pray, he gave his horse and his travelling spear to a servant, for he had not yet resigned the dress and habits of a layman. Boisil was*

standing by the doors of the monastery and saw him first. Forseeing in spirit what an illustrious man the stranger would become, he made this single remark to the bystanders: " Behold a servant of the Lord" I was told this by that veteran priest and servant of God, the pious Sigfrid, for he was standing by when Boisil said these words." Bede Life.

From Melrose he went with Eata to Ripon where he was in charge of receiving guests, but was turned out when Alchfrid gave the monastery to Wilfrid.

"Meanwhile, as everything in this world is frail and fluctuating, like the sea when a storm comes on, Eata with Cuthbert and the other brethren were expelled from their residence, and the monastery given to others." Bede. Life.

He returned to Melrose where he was been made Prior when Boisil died of plague. From there he would travel out usually on foot to preach the truth "to those who had gone astray", for as Bede says in times of disaster or plague many returned to the old gods and used spells and amulets.

"In those days whenever a priest visited a town, English folk always used to gather to his call to hear his message. But Cuthbert was so skillful a speaker, and had such a light in his angelic face all openly confessed their wrong doings. He used mainly to visit and preach in the villages that lay far distant among high and impenetrable mountains, which others feared to visit and whose barbarity and squalor daunted other teachers. Many villages and hamlets of our people are situated in inaccessible mountains and dense woodlands, here is not even a teacher to teach the difference between good and evil conduct. Often he was away for a month at a time". Bede Life.

The Anonymous "Cuthbert" written on Lindisfarne is more precise; Penna recounts, "making his way from Hexham to the city which is called Carlisle. A halt was called in the middle of the journey in a district called Ahse" the people gathered from the mountains to hear him. Colgrave Anon.p117. Tydi recalled "he was going along the river Teviot and making his way southward, teaching the country people among the mountains and baptizing them." Ibid.p.85

Cuthbert also visited the Pictish church for Epiphany, January 6th.Once while visiting Aebbe, abbess of Coldingham, as night fell he left,

"the monastery, went down to the sea, which flows beneath, and going into it, until the water reached his neck and arms, spent the night in praising the Lord. When the dawn of day approached, he came out of the water, and, falling on his knees, began to pray again. Whilst he was doing this, two quadrupeds, called otters, came up from the sea, and lying down before him on the sand, breathed upon his feet and wiped them with their hair: after which having received his blessing, they returned to their native element." A monk who witnessed this, *"concealed this miracle during St Cuthbert's life; but, after his death, took care to tell it to as many persons as he was able."* Bede. Life.

Aebbe was King Oswiu's sister.
Cuthbert at Coldingham.

From Melrose Eata transferred him to Lindisfarne. There he won over the monks to a stricter observance of discipline,
"there were some brethren in the monastery who preferred their ancient customs to the new regular discipline. But he got the better of these by his patience and modest virtues." Bede life.

But while at Lindisfarne he tried to get away from the other monks by living on a tiny island next to the monastery which can still be seen, called St Cuthbert's Island.

Saint Cuthbert's island, Lindisfarne.

Later he moved to the isolation of the Farnes "lying off several miles to the east, and, consequently, surrounded on all sides by the deep and boundless ocean. No one before God`s servant Cuthbert, had ever dared to inhabit this island alone, on account of the evil spirits which reside there."
Bede Life.

Inner Farne, Northumberland, an important bird sanctuary today. The small building is a later medieval chapel the larger a "Pele tower".

There he built an oratory with walls so high only the sky could be seen. He tried to grow wheat but it failed .Barley however did grow. He was also lucky enough to find a large piece of wood to enable him to build a toilet in a place where the sea flushed it out twice a day .Although he had little contact with humans Cuthbert had always had a strong affinity to animals and birds. The Eider ducks are still called Cuddy's ducks in Northumbria. They still nest by Cuthbert's chapel to this day.

An Eider duck nesting by the wall of Cuthbert's chapel, Farne Island.

Cuthbert consecrated Bishop from a wall painting at Pittington church, County Durham. King Ecgfrith looks over Bishop Theodore's shoulder.

The meeting at Twyford arranging the Northumbrian bishoprics had chosen Cuthbert as Bishop of Hexham originally. King Ecgfrith himself went to Cuthbert`s Hermitage on the Farne and knelt down and begged him to become bishop. He reluctantly accepted but swapped Hexham for Lindisfarne.

While Bishop he travelled quite widely and he talked at least once a year with a hermit, Herebert, who lived on an island in Derwentwater in the Northumbrian Lake District, near Keswick, (the cheese farm.)It was to Herebert that he foretold his death. Herebert prayed that they might not be separated, and they died on the same day.

When Cuthbert fell sick on the Farne a monk was sent from Lindisfarne to look after him. When he died on the 20th of March torches were lit to inform the brothers. He had wished to be buried on Farne, but consented to return to Lindisfarne.

Ecgfrith meets Cuthbert on Farne from the painting by William Bell Scott in Wallington Hall. The painter pictured Theodore as the third figure but it was in fact Trumwine.

Prophetically, he had said that in the event of an incursion of unbelievers at the monastery his body should be taken up and move with the brothers ***"When 11 years had passed since the period of this death, the brethren opened his tomb and found his corpse quite as fresh as if he had been recently buried. The limbs were flexible and his whole appearance was***

more like that of a man who was asleep than of one dead, the vestment also in which he was clothed not only were entire, but they exhibited as marvellous a freshness and sheen as they had done when they were new.'

The life of Cuthbert and the miracles accredited to him were to be well publicized by the monks of Lindisfarne and later Durham, their wealth and standing in the Community was dependent on the belief in the sanctity of Cuthbert and his efficacy as an intermediary. He was credited with finding food fortuitously; a loaf in an abandoned shiel, a dolphin on the beach, a salmon, *"I have been young and now I am old, yet I have not seen the righteous forsaken".* Anon. Cuthbert. He changed the weather, winds changed to stop fire, he cured a variety of people, he foresaw the future. The miracle of the uncorrupted body was to attract pilgrims and Cuthbert as the patron saint of Northumbria was to become the centre of a cult which lasted until the Reformation, and beyond.

The body is discovered uncorrupted.

ALDFRITH, THE MOST CIVILISED NORTHUMBRIAN KING.

> I found in Innisfail the fair,
> In Ireland while in exile there,
> Women of worth, both grave and gay men,
> Many clerics, many laymen. **Attributed to Flann fina, Aldfrith.**

John Mitchel Poems

Aelfflaed, Oswiu's daughter, dedicated as a nun in thanks for the victory of Winwaed, had been joined in the cloister by her widowed mother Eanflaed. Together they had succeeded Hilda as joint abbess of Whitby. Aelfflaed was a powerful supporter of Cuthbert. She claimed that she had been restored to health by his help. She was also a prime supporter of the royal house of Northumbria to which she belonged. Worried about the succession if the childless Ecgfrith should be killed, she had arranged to meet Cuthbert in the monastery on Coquet Island. There "with feminine boldness" she confronted Cuthbert, who prophesied of Ecgfrith's death, and that he would be succeeded by his half-brother Aldfrith.

"Aldfrith, who was said to be the son of her father, and who was then exiled to the Scottish islands, on account of his love of Literature." Bede. Life. Oswiu had had a number of wives. He had married Rhiainfelt of Rheged, and he had married Fin daughter of Colman of the Ui Neill. Aldfrith was the child of the latter union, and nephew to Finan, Bishop of Lindisfarne. Bede was not totally enthusiastic,"Aldfrith, *said to be* brother to the other, and son to king Oswiu." Bede. (my italics).Both scholar and warrior, Aldfrith had trained in Ireland and was recognised for his learning. His exile in Ireland might have been more for the good of his health than his love of literature, since Northumbrian kings had a track record of having rival claimants killed. Consider the actions of Ecgfrith's grandfather Aethelfrith attempting to have Edwin killed, and his own father Oswiu's, removal of Oswine. The failure of Aldfrith's Irish hosts to oblige may give us a reason for Ecgfrith's expedition to Ireland.

Aldfrith does however seem to have been;

"A scholar of great powers of eloquence, of piercing intellect, a king and a teacher at the same time."

"He stands beside Alfred of Wessex among the few Old English kings who combined skill in warfare with desire for knowledge." Stenton.

In Ireland Aldfrith was known as Flann Fina and was recognized as a famous poet. Many sayings are attributed to him; Some suggest a different approach to problems than his half-brother Ecgfrith.

"Better old debts than old grudges"
"Better to flee than to stand still".
"Better a conference than a contention."

Others suggest a love of learning;
> " Docility is the beginning of wisdom."
> "Enquiry is the beginning of knowledge."
> " A teacher should be honoured." T.F. O'Rahilly, A Miscellany of Irish

proverbs.

Some claim that he is the author of Beowulf and Widsith, which would place him amongst the most important of Northumbrian kings. He once paid 8 hides for a book. (a hide being enough land to keep a family.) He was interested in all things;

> Drycthelm who lived at Cunningham in Northumbria died after a fever, but the next morning sat up startling those around him. He would regale people with visions of what he had seen while he was dead. "on the left it appeared full of dreadful flames, the other side was no less horrid for violent hail and cold snow flying in all directions." He entered a monastery from where in all weathers he would stand in the river, sometimes up to his loins sometimes up to his neck, and pray even in winter "the half broken cakes of ice were swirling around him which he had broken to make a place where he could stand in the water." When the other monks said, "Brother Drycthelm it is wonderful how you can manage to bear such bitter cold," he replied "I have known it colder' King Aldfrith himself would always speak with him when he was in the area." Bede.

> Bede said of Aldfrith, "he nobly retrieved the ruined state of the kingdom, though within narrower bounds."

Although there were still problems on the borders,

> "697 This year the Southumbrians slew Ostritha, the queen of Aethelred (the sister of Ecgfrith)
>
> 699 This year the Picts slew Alderman Burt." ASC

Aldfrith set about restoring the fortunes of Northumbria. He tried to restore goodwill with the Irish by returning the prisoners Ecgfrith had taken. He sent them to Adomnan Abbot of Iona, a friend he had made while visiting the monastery there. Adomnan made visits to Northumbria. He gave Aldfrith a book on the Holy Places, he was given gifts in return. It was not an auspicious time for a visit,

> *"I visited my friend King Aldfrith while the plague was at its worst and many whole villages on all sides were stricken. But both on my visit after Ecgfrith's battle and on my second two years later, though I walked in the midst of this danger of plague, the Lord delivered me."* Adamnan.

(Later in 716AD Iona was to adopt the Roman Easter. Also the former enemies, the Picts, asked Jarrow for masons, and advice about the dating of Easter. The Northumbrians, unlike the Britons, continued to be capable of converting their enemies. Ruling over both Jarrow and Wearmouth with their 600 inhabitants was Ceolfrith, who decided at the age of 74 to travel to Rome, taking with him Northumbrian Bibles as presents.)

Under Aldfrith, Wilfrid temporarily returned to Hexham and York only to be expelled again in 691 an event, which led to the king being excommunicated.

His late call to the throne, and late marriage meant that Aldfrith's death in 704 left a disputed succession. His son, the 8-year-old Osred, was protected by Berhtfrith, a thane of Dunbar, who slaughtered the Picts in 711 AD. (He seems to be one of a family with names including "Berht", who may have held vice regal status in Lothian.) Osred was under the influence of **Wilfrid** and Aelfflaed of Whitby, the boy's aunt. For a couple of months Eadwulf, son of Aethelwold of Deira, seized the throne, driving Wilfrid and Berhtfrith to hide at Bamburgh. They found "refuge in a narrow place in the stony rock at Bamburgh." Eddius. Such a cleft can still be identified at Bamburgh. But Osred was eventually slain by Coenred and Osric. Coenred reigned for two years 716-718AD. He was then succeeded by Osric, another son of Aldfrith, according to Simeon.

Amidst all this turmoil the restless Wilfrid was restored, partly because Aelfflaed confirmed that a reconciliation had been the dying wish of her half-brother Aldfrith. Wilfrid died soon after on 12th October 709AD at Oundle. He was buried at Ripon. He left a store of treasure to his supporters and urged them to use it to buy the friendship of Kings, something he was singularly unsuccessful in acquiring himself.

Acca succeeded to Hexham where his cross can be seen. Acca also had a very fine library and encouraged singing.

"710.AD. Acca succeeded to the bishopric, and Alderman Bertfrith fought with the Picts between Heugh and Carau." ASC.

After Osric, warring factions replaced the dynasty of Aethelfrith. Led by Coenred and his brother Ceolwulf they also claimed descent from Ida, the first king of Bernicia, but through his son Ocga rather than through Ida's son Aethelric, the ancestor of Oswiu and Aldfrith's line. This change of dynasty may have caused Bede to insert Ida into his history.

Osric was succeeded by Ceolwulf, who was so persecuted that he decided to retire to Lindisfarne. There the austere rule of Aidan, which had allowed only water and milk, had been replaced and the monks were now allowed wine and beer. ***"To drink wine with reason was better than to drink water with pride."*** Palladius. In Craster AA 1894. The arrival of a rich patron boosted the monastery's finances;

"when he entered the monastery of Lindisfarne, he gave to St Cuthbert his royal treasures and lands, that is to say, Bregesne, and Werceworde, with their appurtenances, together with the church which he had built there, and four other vills also Wudecestre, Hwitingham, Eadulfingham and Eagwulfingham." (Brainshaugh, Warkworth, Woodchester, Whittingham, Edlingham, Eglingham.). Symeon.

His body was buried on Lindisfarne, but later moved to Norham. Later his head was taken to Durham.

It was to Ceolwulf that Bede dedicated his great History. In that book Bede perceptively wondered what was to become of the kingdom if more nobles and warriors entered the church. It seemed to be an increasing trend for the nobility to copy the actions of royalty by setting up monasteries run by their own families. This seemed to mean that thereby they not only avoided personal service to the king, but that the land became the hereditary possession of the church. The "land bank" available to the king to use in rewarding his followers was thereby diminished and consequently fewer would rally to his banner. Certainly the nobility seem to play an increasingly influential role in the politics of the kingdom. Unfortunately Bede died in on 25th of May 735AD, so the details of Northumbria's fortunes in the later 8th century are missing from his work.

"As such peace and prosperity prevail in these days, many of the Northumbrians, both noble and simple, together with their children, have laid aside their weapons, preferring to receive the tonsure and take monastic vows rather than study the arts of war. What the result of this will be the future will show." Bede.

CHAPTER 7.

8TH CENTURY NORTHUMBRIA. THE GOLDEN AGE.

POLITICAL UPHEAVAL AND CULTURAL ACHIEVEMENT
"**Northumbria achieved a position that without exaggeration may be described as supreme in western civilisation.**" Kendrick 1938.
*"Days of great glory
in the kingdom of earth are gone forever,
Kings, Emperors and gold-giving lords are no longer as they were."*

"Weaklings thrive and hold sway in the world."

8TH CENTURY KINGS OF NORTHUMBRIA. PART 1.
Aldfrith 685-704. Descended from Aethelric, son of Ida.
Eadwulf, 704.
Osred, son of Aldfrith, 705-716.
Coenred. 716-718. Descended from Ocga, son of Ida.
Osric, son of Aldfrith.718-729
Ceolwulf, brother of Coenred. He was forcibly tonsured in 731,but regained the throne.Abdicated.729-737.
Eadbert, cousin of Coenred. 737-758.Abdicated and entered monastery at York.
Oswulf, son of Eadbert. 758-759.Murdered.
Aethelwald Moll. 759-765.Removed.

The years after the death of Bede saw a decline in the political fortunes of Northumbria, but it was not all downhill. Although Ceowulf had in 731AD been captured and forcibly tonsured, and retired permanently in 737AD.His successor, was his cousin, **Eadbert** who brought stability for 20 years. **"wearing the crown of his ancestors upon his head". "He extended the bounds of his kingdom, often subduing the enemy ranks with terror."**

In 740AD Eadbert fought the Picts, but the Mercians invaded. The next year York itself was burnt. Undaunted Eadbert attacked Argyll, and annexed Kyle. In 750 AD he conquered Ayrshire and established Northumbrian bishops on the Isle of Whithorn. In 756AD, allied to the Picts he attacked Dumbarton, the capital of the Strathclyde Britons, but 9 days later he was defeated and his army lost. Nonetheless he continued to rule until 758AD.

Since Eadbert's brother, Egbert, was Archbishop of York the king had control of both royal and church lands. He imprisoned Cynewulf, Bishop of Lindisfarne, for allowing his kinsman Offa to be dragged from the tomb of St Cuthbert and murdered.Egbert wrote the Penitentials which showed aspects of Anglo-Saxon life and pointed to drunkenness as the especial English sin. He established the school at York that was to be famous throughout Europe. Egbert succeeded in persuading the Pope to implement Gregory the Great`s plan and make York an Archbishopric, so lessening the power of Cantebury and extending the prestige of Northumbria. The coinage showed both king and Archbishop, this was the first large scale issue of coinage in Northumbria. **"These were happy times for the people of Northumbria."** Alcuin. (Like Bede he extols the virtues of a previous generation.)

"When at length he had either reduced to subjection or overcome in battle all who opposed him, not only did all the neighbouring kings of the Angles, Picts and Britons and Scots keep peace with him, but were happy in showing him marks of deference."

Eadbert`s contacts extended to the continent and he received gifts from the Frankish king Pepin. However like his predecessor he abdicated, and went to become a monk in York with his brother. They were eventually both buried beneath the one porch in that city.

Sceattas (silver pennies) of Eadberht and Bishop Ecgberht.

Later kings did not always have a relative as Archbishop. For some the Archbishop had often been appointed by the rival they had replaced, like an incoming soccer manager faced with a team chosen by his predecessor. The kings became more dependent on the aristocracy.

Nonetheless for the time being Eadbert left Northumbria at its greatest extent since Nectansmere. However his son Osulf was killed by his own family at Market Weighton within a year.

A thane, Aethelwald Moll, from outside the royal line, (possibly a descendant of Oswine of Deira) then seized the throne. He killed Eadbert's son Oswine at Edwin's cliff .

There were other problems; in 764AD the winter was so cold that the monks could not hold a pen to transcribe their books.

"But the conditions of the past winter oppressed the island of our race very horribly with cold and ice and long and widespread storms of wind and rain so that the hand of the scribe was hindered from producing a great number of books.' Abbot Cuthbert to Lull.

Despite hardship the monks of Northumbria produced the works of **THE GOLDEN AGE**

Christianity continued to prosper in Northumbria itself. But as always they were also prepared to convert their enemies.

THE NORTHUMBRIAN MISSIONARIES.

The indomitable Wilfrid had in 678 preached to the Frisians with some success on his way to Rome but there was no follow up. However the Northumbrian monk Egbert survived an attack of the plague and vowed he would abandon his home and go on a mission to the Saxon homelands of Germany. However a vision told him to remain on Iona. He did so and it was Egbert the Englishman who persuaded the community of Iona to adopt the Roman tonsure and Roman Easter in 716AD. (In the same year Abbot Ceolfrith persuaded former enemy Nechtan and the Picts to do likewise.) However Egbert did send Wictbert, then Willibrod and 12 others to the continent, who began to convert the Heathen. Willibrod was a Northumbrian from Deira. He preached to the Frisians with the support of the Frankish king Pippin. He was made Bishop of Utrecht and performed miracles with relics of St Oswald which he had taken with him. He also went on mission to the Danes. He died in 739AD and was buried at Echternach.

Other missionaries were the two Hewalds, known as the Fair and the Dark, who were killed by the Saxons and buried at Cologne.

King Alhred, (765-774AD) sent missionaries abroad, Aluberht to the north Germans, and Willehad to Frisia. Willehad was sent to the Saxons by Charlemagne who looked upon missionary work as a way of extending Frankish influence. The Emperor's attempt to force laws against eating meat in Lent and cremation led to Willehad being expelled by the Saxons. After a visit to Rome and being sent to Echternach, he returned to Saxony. He eventually became Bishop of Bremen in 787 AD. Alhred was in contact with the Bishop of Mainz, and sent ambassadors to the court of Charlemagne. In 767AD Aluberht was consecrated Bishop of the continental Saxons at York.

The relative success of the Northumbrians was in part due to the lack of a language problem in Frisia and Saxony. So Northumbria was not so isolated or decrepit as the bare events of the chronicles suggest.

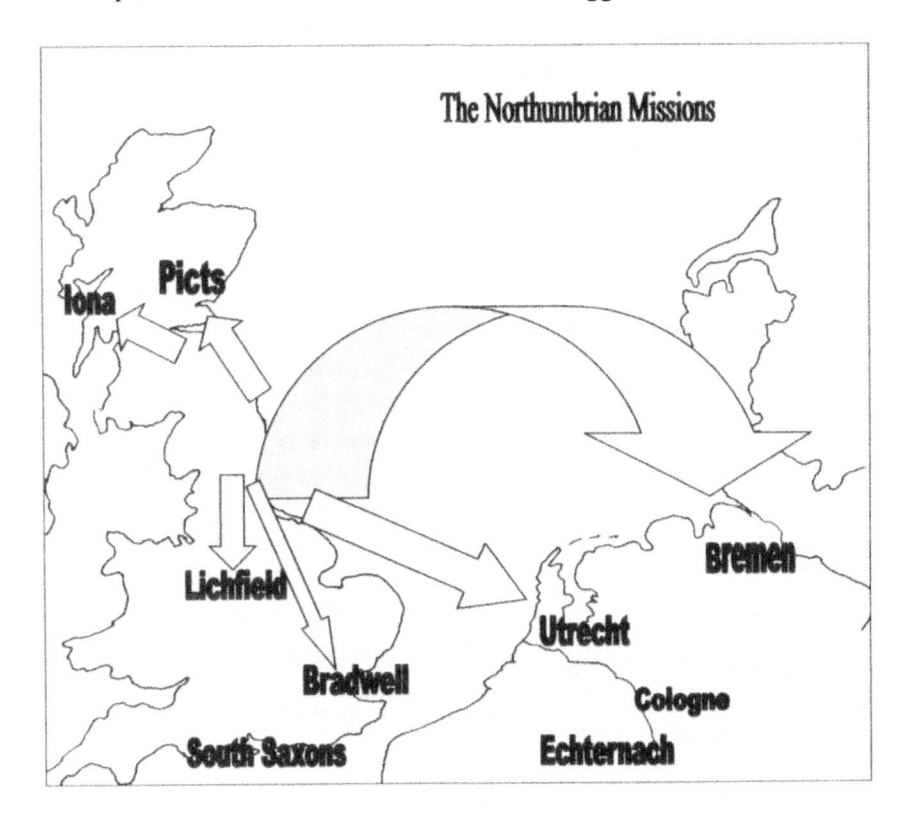

The Northumbrian Missions

Map showing Iona, Picts, Lichfield, Bradwell, South Saxons, Utrecht, Bremen, Cologne, Echternach

There were also still famous servants of God working in Northumbria. John of Hexham who had founded Beverley, had set up a chapel at St John Lee (although Warden also claims the site),

"There is a certain building in a retired situation, and enclosed by a narrow wood and a trench, about a mile and a half from the church of Hagulstad (Hexham), and separated from it by the river Tyne." Bede. The description sounds more like St John Lee on its wooded hill, than Warden on the flat Haugh at the juncture of the North and South Tyne. Warden however does have some visible Anglo-Saxon work.

He was renowned for healing the sick and teaching a dumb child to speak. He ordained Bede. He was buried at Beverley in the woods of Deira when he died in 721.AD. His banner was used as a talisman in war.

The political strength of Northumbria and the riches that attended it, followed the success of Oswiu at Winwaed in 655 AD. Oswiu and Ecgfrith after him, and their Queens had encouraged the growth of the monasteries. It was in the monasteries, which were peopled by English men and women who possessed a knowledge of and often a skill in traditional Germanic art forms that the cultural renaissance of 7th and 8th century Northumbria took place with an outpouring of literature and art. At the centre of this achievement is the **Lindisfarne Gospels,** by Bishop Eadfrith, the illustrated text showing the skills of the Northumbrian monks with their mixture of English, Irish and Byzantine art forms. It was bound by Aethelwald and ornamented by Billfrith. Aldred of Chester-le-Street later glossed the Latin text in the Northumbrian dialect. As such the Gospels are the oldest surviving English Gospels.

The Lindisfarne Gospels were dedicated to "God and St Cuthbert". The Gospels were made from sheep or calves skin. The skin was scraped and prepared as vellum. The writing area was then pricked and ruled out. They were written in an insular majuscule script using ink made from soot or lamp black using pens of quill or reed. But the glory of the work is the illumination of the capitals and the illustrated pages. The elaborate patterns were prepared by use of feint grids, and compass arcs, but also by eye. The colours came from minerals, chemicals, plants and insects. The decoration often includes birds which resemble Mergansers, Goosanders or Cormorants so common on the Northumbrian coast. Amidst all this perfection, Eadfrith in his humility left small parts unfinished or uncoloured, lest his work be considered perfect. Although the illustrations show various potential influences, they remain a Northumbrian work, and as such are much more than a piece of art or an historical document they are an icon to the people of this land.

A Goosander by the Northumbrian artist Thomas Bewick, shows similarities to the Gospel illustrations.

Initials from the Lindisfarne gospels, (below).

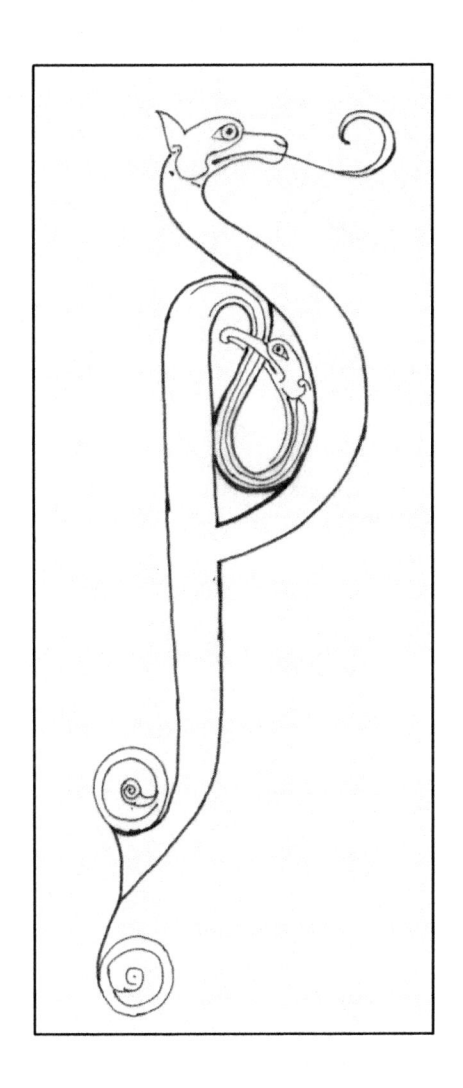

"this particular book has never been regarded merely as a museum curiosity, of interest only to scholars and connoisseurs, but has kept something of the mystique of a holy relic, even into the twentieth century."
Backhouse. Curator British Museum.

The book was stolen by Henry VIII's Commissioners at the time of the Dissolution of the Monasteries, the precious cover ripped off. By luck the Gospels book survived a fire that destroyed many priceless early works, including another Northumbrian bible, and it now lies in the British Library, although it is due to return to Durham in 2013 AD for six months, a situation which hopefully may become permanent. **(for more on this see "The Lindisfarne Gospels and Cuthbert, the body, book and banner" by Chris Kilkenny.Amazon.)**

A monk writing
The British Library holds other scraps of Northumbrian bibles which had been used as wrappers for estate papers. Another bible lies in the library of Corpus Christi, Cambridge. Leningrad State Library has a copy of Bede`s Ecclesiastical history. This work includes the first example of an initial incorporating an image of the subject of the text, in this case Pope Gregory. The Rushworth Gospels were glossed, in part, in a south Northumbrian dialect.

Bishop Ceolfrith at a great age set out on a Pilgrimage to Rome (1,419 miles) taking with him a vulgate Bible as a present for the Pope. He died just about half way at Langres (692 miles). Situated on a long crest with the endless plain stretching away to the south the future might have seemed daunting, nonetheless some of his companions continued, but the Bible never reached Rome. It now lies in Florence it is known as the Codex Amiatinus, it is the earliest surviving complete Latin bible. It takes its name from the abbey of Amiata whose abbot Peter the Lombard rubbed out the dedication to abbot Ceolfrith and inserted his own name. *Petrus Langobardorum* replacing *Ceolfridus Anglorum.* Claims that the work was Northumbrian were dismissed with scorn, it was too fine a work to be made anywhere other than Italy. Later scholars discovered the forgery. The huge number of calf hides needed to make the book is an indication of the wealth of the Monkwearmouth-Jarrow monastery.

The Echternach gospels now in the Bibliotheque Nationale de Paris, are Northumbrian work probably taken abroad by Willibrod to help with his mission. The same could be said of the St Chad Gospels at Lichfield. The Durrow bible at Trinity College Dublin is possibly Northumbrian.

The stages in making a book with vellum. Cleaning the animal skin, folding the skin.(below)

Pens are made from quills, the skin is scraped of its hairs.(below)

It is bound with boards, the text is copied from another book. (below)

The book is bound and used to instruct youths. (below)

131

A riddle tells the same tale;

*A foe deprived me of life,
took away my bodily strength;
afterwards wet me, dipped me in water, took me out again,
set me in the sun where I quickly lost the hairs I had.
Afterwards the hard edge of the knife cut me, with all impurities ground off;
fingers folded me, and the bird's delight sprinkled me over with useful drops;
it made frequent tracks across the dark brim, swallowed the tree-dye, part of the stream,
again moved on me, journeyed on leaving a dark track.
Afterwards a man covered me with binding, stretched skin over me, adorned me with gold;
and so the splendid work of smiths, circled with wire, decked me.
Now the ornaments and the red dye and the glorious possessions
make renowned far and wide the Protector of multitudes,
in no wise the torments of hell.
If the sons of men will use me they will be the safer and the more victorious,
the bolder in heart and blither in thought, the wiser in mind;
they will have the more friends, dear ones and kinsfolk, true and good, worthy and trusty,
who will gladly increase their honour and happiness, and lay upon them benefits and mercies
and hold them firm in embraces of love.
Ask what is my name, useful to men; my name is famous, of service to men, sacred in myself.
myself.*   Riddles. A Book. Gordon.

In 1104 when St Cuthbert's coffin was opened a St John's gospel, was found, it ended up with the Jesuits at Stonyhurst. (It was on loan to the British library, but has recently been sold by them, and will hopefully be displayed at Durham, whence it came.) It is the only known bible with its binding in situ. There are other works of art; the wooden coffin of Saint Cuthbert itself survives in Durham cathedral it is incised with figures of the apostles. St Cuthbert's vestments remain the only proven example of Early English embroidery. (With the possible exception of the Bayeux Tapestry.)

Figures of Andrew and Peter on Cuthbert's coffin, Durham Cathedral.

A whalebone casket, named after its collector, Franks, is Northumbrian workmanship. It shows the legend of Weland Smith as well as Christian religious figures. It has a theme of good and bad rulers, it also shows brothers in exile, illustrated by carvings of Romulus and Remus. Exile was a theme also shown by the flight of the Jews from Jerusalem. It was a theme readily recognized by Northumbrian rulers and their thanes, especially Edwin, Oswald, Oswiu and Aldfrith. The links implied were from Jerusalem, to Rome to Northumbria. The journey taken by Christianity. The Northumbrian rulers saw themselves as successors to Jews and Romans as the chosen people. But there is also the more pagan element of revenge present shown by Titus's destruction of Jerusalem and the themes of the Weland saga.(see above for illustrations. The original is in BM. There is a copy in MA and Bede's World.)

The Frank's casket, the gifts of the Magi are contrasted to Weland's "gifts" to Nithad.

(That some Northumbrians saw themselves as inheritors of Rome may be inferred; Edwin was preceded by a standard bearer. Oswald had a banner of purple and gold, adopted now as the red and gold flag of Northumberland. Oswiu was called Emperor of Britain. Many Northumbrians journeyed to Rome. Roman techniques in building, singing and religious observance were all quickly adopted.) An important part of Northumbrian Christian culture was the cross.

"On the estates of nobles and good men of the Saxon race it is a custom to have a cross, which is dedicated to our Lord and held in great reverence, erected on some prominent spot for the convenience of those who wish to pray daily before it" Huneberc "Life of Willibald.

This image was central to Christian life particularly after St Helena, the Emperor Constantine's mother, discovered the remains of the true cross. The story is engraved on a cross in St Helen's Kelloe, County Durham. Constantine had won a battle at Milvain Bridge and the Empire after seeing a vision of the cross. Similarly Oswald raised a cross before the battle at Heavenfield. Stone crosses were raised in Northumbria, before the construction of churches, as a centre where preaching may take place. Only a

134

handful survived the ages and the iconoclasm of the Puritans. But collections such as that in the Monk`s dormitory at Durham Cathedral and Newcastle University`s Museum of Antiquities, (now in the Museum of the North) show that the free standing cross was once a common sight in Northumbria. Most remote, and still in its original open air position is that at Bewcastle lying on the roman road, The Maiden's Way. It shows Christian scenes and many scrolls of foliage decoration. It has the name of Cuniburga Penda`s daughter and Oswiu's daughter-in- law on it. The broken cross of Ruthwell has been reassembled and can be clearly seen in the church in Dumfries. Hexham has Acca`s cross. Many other parts of crosses survive such as at Rothbury and Auckland. The illustrations could clearly have been used as a preaching aid to an illiterate audience, as they show scenes from the old and New Testament. The decoration shows that the masons were not merely dependent on outside influences, such as Celtic or Roman, but brought their own Teutonic traditions into play. Crosses are found in many parts of Europe.

The Bewcastle Cross

The Bewcastle cross showing the "inhabited vine" decoration.

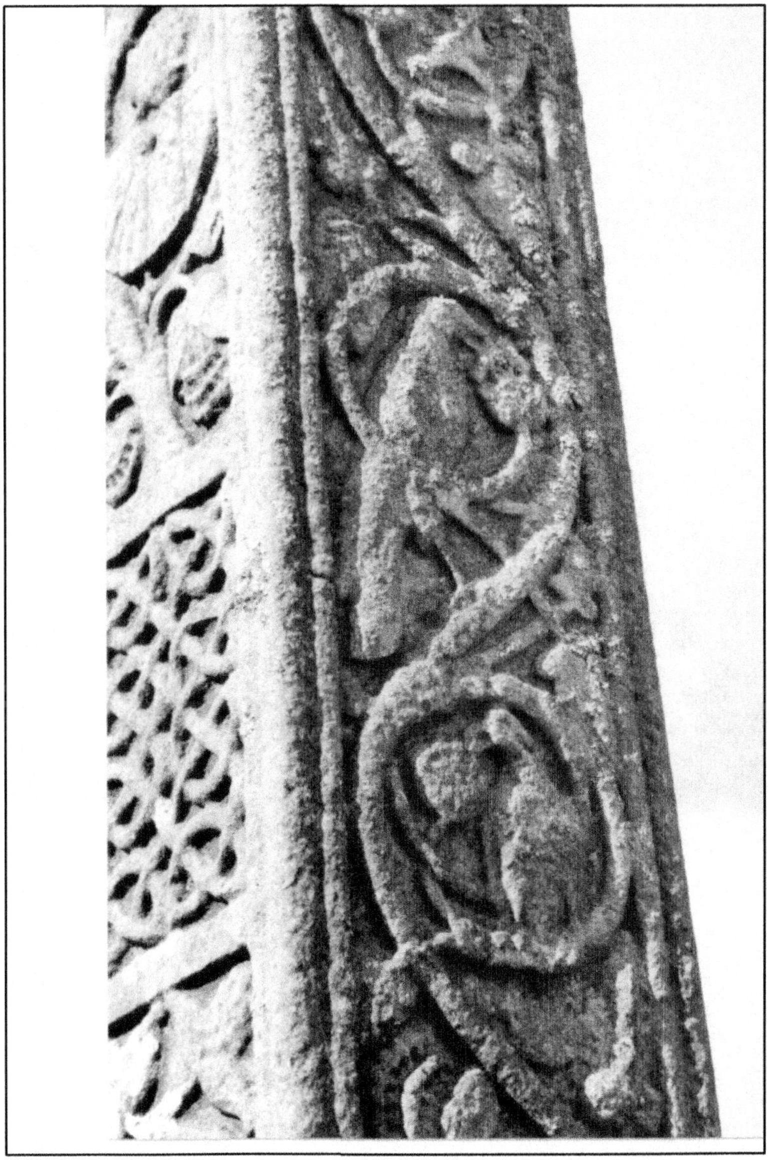

The Ruthwell cross, showing Christ.

The Rothbury cross, part is incorporated in the Church font, part is now in the Museum of the North, Newcastle.

Sundial from St. Gregory's Kirkdale, North Yorks.

Sundial from Bewcastle, Cumbria

139

Apart from the crosses many churches were built, though not all were of the dimensions of Wilfrid's churches at Ripon and Hexham. Many, however, like those two, used roman remains as a convenient Quarry. Corbridge also has a Roman arch. The stone church at Chester-le-Street stands in a Roman fort, as does Bewcastle. The Church at Escomb took stones from nearby Binchester. This church is the finest surviving complete Northumbrian church of the Anglian era, and one of "only 3 complete Saxon churches surviving in Britain". Pevsner.

Many other Northumbrian Anglian churches have been incorporated into later buildings and suffered from restorations.

Escomb church, near Bishop Auckland, County Durham.

140

Benet Biscop's church at Monkwearmouth-The Anglo-Saxon tower.

The Anglian tower at Warden on Tyne, Northumberland.

Some original Anglo-Saxon sites in Northumberland and Durham. There are collections of material in Durham cathedral and the Museum of the North, Newcastle.

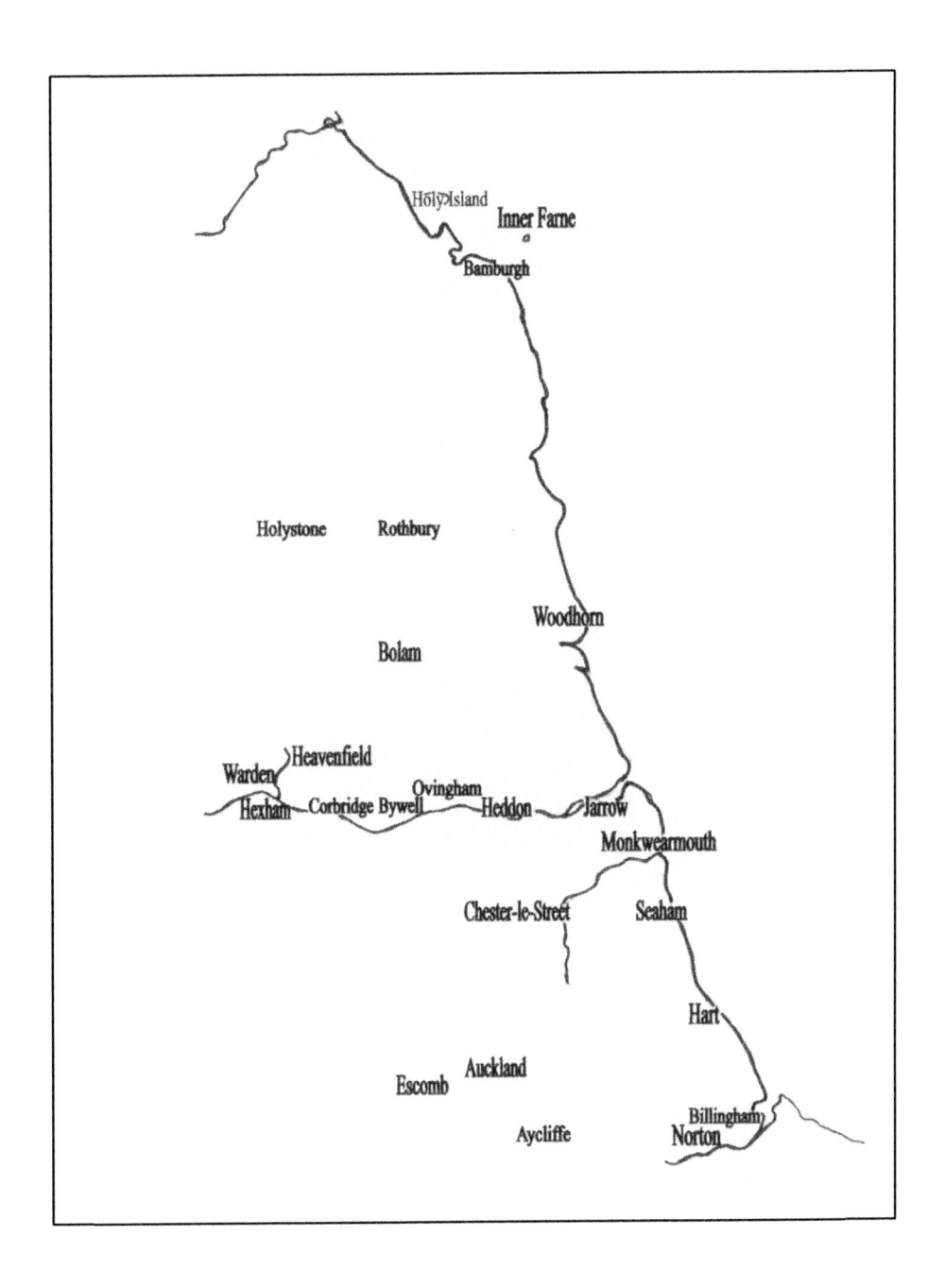

The Venerable Bede. The first English Historian. (artist's impression.)

143

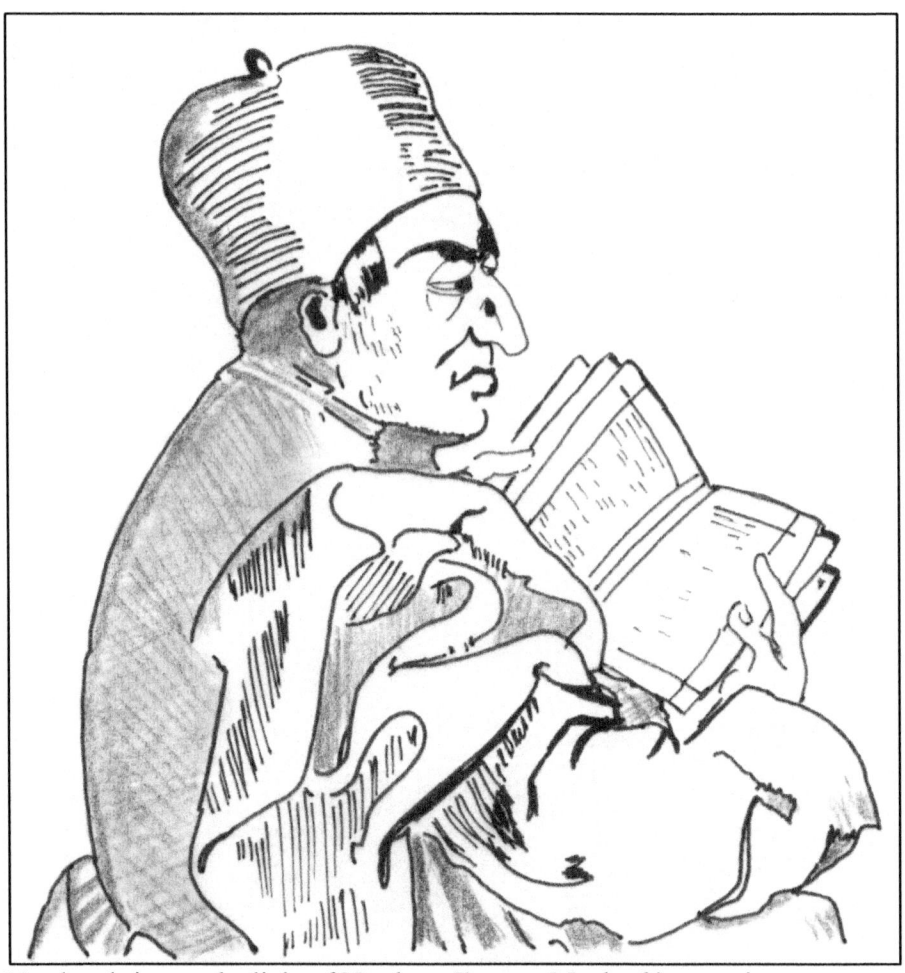

Northumbria was the light of Northern Europe. Much of its prestige came from the works of Bede, as the Abbot of Jarrow-Wearmouth said;

"Indeed it seems right to me, that the whole race of English in all provinces wherever they are found, should give thanks to God, that he has granted to them so wonderful a man in their nation, endowed with diverse gifts, and so assiduous in the exercise of those gifts, and likewise living a good life." Abbot Cuthbert of Wearmouth to Bishop Lul.

Others agreed;

"the monk Bede, who, we have heard, has lately shone in the house of God among you, with knowledge of the Scriptures like a candle of the church." Boniface.

Later historians echoed Bede's praises;

"During his lifetime this Beda lay hidden within a remote corner of the world but after his death his writings gave him a living reputation over every portion of the globe." Symeon

"the greatest jewel in the Northumbrian crown was the Venerable Bede." K Crossley-Holland The Anglo-Saxon world.
Bede, humbly, said little about himself,

> *"I was born in the lands of this monastery and at the age of seven was entrusted by the care of my family to the reverend abbot Benedict and then to Ceolfrith, to be educated. Since then I have lived my whole life in this monastery, devoting myself entirely to the study of the scriptures."*

He may, in fact, have visited York and Lindisfarne. He certainly sent monks to all centres of learning for information. It was also by chance that the young Bede survived. Plague struck the monastery and only the abbot and one small boy survived, that boy was Bede. Plague death was a fact of life in early Northumbria. Tuda Bishop of Lindisfarne died of it as had Cedd.

Bede's achievements were many; he popularized the use of AD, that is dating events from the birth of Christ. Without Bede there would be no Millennium. He also popularized the term Northumbrians to describe his people. He knew the world was round and of "the frozen sea, one day's sail north of Thyle". He observed the movements of the tides, how could he not from a monastery lying alongside Jarrow slake, and was aware they were caused by the moon. His abbot, Hwaetberht caught the moment between land and sea of the high tide turning;

> **"We do not want to be peaceful, nor do we wish to be parted.**
> **War is ever between us, yet with arms that are yielding;**
> **Peace established below, and therefore the battle quiescent:**
> **Each from the other one guiltless always plucking the harvest."**

Hwaetberht.in Hunter Blair .Northumbria.p.80.

In his History he was concerned to check his sources, but his aim was to describe the history of Christianity amongst the English and particularly the role of the Northumbrians in its preservation and expansion. He was also commissioned by Bishop Acca for a commentary on Luke's gospel for those needing a simple commentary. Bede's St John's Gospel, the book he was working on when he died, was the first known English translation of the Gospel. Although much of his work was in Latin which he spoke fluently, he was also knowledgeable of English poems and was in favour of the use of English for the Creed and Lord's prayer. Since his pupil Egbert was a member of the Northumbrian royal family he was ideally placed to have a knowledge of the history and poetry of his people. Unfortunately he recorded none of the pagan heroic verse. In this he was like Alcuin who disapproved of those Lindisfarne monks who like Bede enjoyed the old poems, "What has Ingeld to do with Christ?" Alcuin asked. Ingeld being a Teutonic hero who features in *Beowulf* and other poems.

> **"Let the word of God be read at the priestly repast. There should the reader be heard, not the harpist; the sermons of the fathers, not the songs of pagans. What has Ingeld to do with Christ? The house is narrow, it cannot hold both."** In Girvan p 41.

Prophetically, Bede warned about the way nobles were using monasteries as a means of avoiding tax and military service. The increasing amount of land being given to the church meant that noblemen's sons were moving abroad as there was no land left for them. These were the people who should have been forming the backbone of the army.

Aware that he was dying he shared out his possessions amongst his brethren, unlike Wilfrid, Bede had only some pepper, some napkins and some incense. He struggled to finish the English St John's Gospel before he died;

"Then the boy said once again "There is still one sentence, dear master, that is not written down." And he said "Write it." After a little the boy said; "There! Now it is written. "And he replied, "Good it is finished; you have spoken the truth. Hold my head in your hands, for it is a great delight to me to sit over against my holy place in which I used to pray, that as I sit there I may call upon my Father." And so upon the floor of his cell, singing "Glory be to the Father and to the Son and to the Holy Spirit" and the rest, he breathed his last."

Bede died on 25th of May, 735AD

"I know that angels visit the canonical hours and the assemblies of the brethren. Will they not say "where is Bede? Why does he not come to the devotions of the brethren?"

> *" before he leaves on his fated journey*
> *No man will be so wise that he need not*
> *Reflect while time still remains*
> *Whether his soul will win delight*
> *Or darkness after his death-day."* Bede's Death Song.

Bede's pupil Egbert set up a school at York. Together with Aelberht he established one of the foremost schools in Europe. Thanks to Aelberht's efforts many books were bought from the continent. It was eventually taken over by their scholar **Alcuin,** "The first Englishman to be fully conscious of the call of teaching as the avenue to satisfaction in life." Alcuin favoured specialist teachers of reading, writing and singing. He said that salvation was not possible without teachers. Scholars came from the continent to learn at York like Liudger who came from Frisia, he returned to become Bishop of Munster.

The monastery schools of Northumbria were the centres of civilisation, with robust methods of teaching;

*"***Teacher;** *Do you wish to be flogged in your studying?*
Pupils*; We would rather be flogged for the sake of learning than be ignorant, but we know that you are gentle and will not inflict blows upon us unless we force you to do so."* Bede.

Alcuin after Bamberg State Lib

Aelberht's curriculum was recollected by Alcuin,

There he dispensed the streams of learning drawn
From many sources, slaking thirsty souls:
To some he diligently taught the arts
Of Grammar and the principles of style;
Others he sharpened on the stone of law;
Others he taught to write in Latin verse
And run with lyric feet on helicon,
Or make their music on the shepherd's pipe;
And others still the master brought to know
The harmony of heaven, the sun and moon,
The five zones and the seven wandering stars..

He showed the fixed return of Easter time,
Expounding holy scripture mysteries,
And plumbed the depths of law, both new and old.
Whatever youths he saw of special gifts,
He took and tended, taught and made his friends;

Alcuin was an early example of the Northumbrian brain drain. He travelled abroad and was called upon by the Emperor Charlemagne, the most powerful man in Europe, to run his school at Aachen.
"For all other subjects he was taught by Alcuin, surnamed Albinus, a man of

the Saxon race who came from Britain and was the most learned man anywhere to be found. Under him the Emperor spent much time and effort in studying rhetoric, dialectic and especially astronomy...the Emperor went so far as to have himself called Alcuin's pupil, and to call Alcuin his master."
Einhardt. YME.

He was the foremost scholar in Europe becoming eventually the abbot of Troyes, Ferrieres and St Martins at Tours. From there he sent back to York for books;

"send some of our boys to get everything we need from there and bring the flowers of Britain back to France, that as well as the walled garden in York there may be off-shoots of paradise bearing fruit in Tours." YME
Northumbria was educating the Continent.

"He is a very foolish man, who will not increase his understanding while he is still in this world, and long to reach that endless life where all shall be made clear."

All of this culture and education was to be swept away by invaders.

CHAPTER 8.

POLITICAL UNREST

"Traitors, murderers of their lords and worse than Heathen,"
Emperor Charlemagne on Northumbrians.

Alchred who had seized the throne in 765 AD, from Aethelwald Moll held it for nine years. He had married into Eadberht`s line, so strengthening his claim, but he was betrayed by his nobility and he was replaced by Aethelred, Moll's son in 774AD. Aethelred murdered a number of prominent Ealdormen. Simeon calls him "that most wicked King." He was expelled in 777AD to be replaced by Aelfwold, a grandson of Eadbert, the murders continued,

"780AD. The high sheriffs of Northumbria committed to the flames Alderman Bern at Silton, on the ninth day before the calends of January.(Christmas Day.)"

The murder of victims while feasting was to be a feature of Northumbrian history. As was the Anglo-Saxon predilection for feud. All members of a family were duty bound to revenge an injury to one of their members. These clannish score settlings could last for generations. A spectacular example was to occur in the 11th Century but the feud would continue to feature amongst the border clans until the 17th century.

Aelfwold received legates from the English Pope Hadrian, the first for 200 years. He was "A man of exceeding devotion and justice." He was however murdered, and a church erected on the site near the Roman Wall at Halton Chesters, it was later dedicated to the Northumbrian Saints Cuthbert and Oswald.

"Aelfwold was murdered at Scytlechester i.e. Chesters and buried at Hexham. His murderer Sicga committed suicide and was carried to Lindisfarne for burial. He had been a supporter of Osred, son of Aldred of Ida's line."

Halton Chesters

Northumbrian Kings 765-867 AD
Alchred, descended from Ethric son of Ida. Married Oswulf's daughter. 765-774.Expelled.
Aethelred, son of Aethelwald Moll. 774-779.Expelled.
Aelfwold, son of Oswulf. 779-788.Murdered.
Osred II, son of Alchred. 788-9.Expelled.
Aethelred, son of Aethelwald Moll, returned. 789-796.Murdered.
Osbald. Reigned for 27 days.796
Eardwulf. 796-806.Expelled.
Aelfwald II. 806-808.Died.
Eardwulf. returned. 808-811.Replaced .
Eanred, son of Eardwulf. 811-840.Died.
Aethelred, son of Eanred. 840-844.Expelled.Returned 844-48.Killed.
Raedwulf.844. Killed by Vikings.
Osbert. 848-866.Expelled.
Aelle. Killed with Osbert by Vikings at York.866-7.

"AD 789 This year Aelfwold king of the Northumbrians was slain by Siga, and a heavenly light was often seen on the spot where he was slain. He was buried in the church of Hexham, and Osred the son of Aldred, who was his nephew succeeded him." ASC

Osred lasted barely a year before he was driven into exile in the Isle of Man.

As the power and prestige of the monarchy declined, aristocratic families began to build up their own power bases to rival that of the king.

Often it seems that the churches at Lindisfarne and Hexham (and Ripon) supported different families, as is indicated by the treatment of Aelfwold and his murderer, they were buried at different centres.

Aethelred returned. He drowned Aelfwold`s sons Oelf and Oelfwine. He also killed Osred Aethelwold`s nephew. "Osred`s body is deposited at Tinemouth" Aethelred hoped to maintain his position by marrying the daughter of Offa of Mercia, the rising power.

Offa had restored **Mercian power**. "How much blood Offa shed to secure the kingdom for his son." Alcuin. Aethelred's marriage into the Mercian family may have been a sign of dependency as was the marriage of Beorhtric of Wessex to another of Offa`s daughters. Like Eadbert of Northumbria, Offa had succeeded in getting an Archbishopric for his kingdom, at Lichfield, although it did not survive his death. Also like Eadbert he produced an extensive coinage after he had taken over the Kentish mint. The Northumbrians were also minting. The coins provide some evidence of the rulers of the period.

A bronze bucket found at Hexham contained 8,000 Northumbrian century coins (stycas-brass coins) more than all of the south of England coinage pre 900 AD. In January 1999 AD.223 English coins were found on Francis Armstrong's farm near Bamburgh by the Ashington and Bedlington Metal detectors club. The coins included those of Eanred (810-840), Aethelred II (840-844) and Redwulf (844) (Newcastle Journal) .They were later displayed in the Museum of Antiquities, Newcastle University. The low percentage of precious metal in the Northumbrian coins was blamed on Offa of Mercia who had drained Northumbria of gold. His coinage was renowned despite his minter being called Dud.(A Northumbrian minter was called Monne.) His power was indicated by the construction of the 150 mile dyke that bears his name, although some believe it to be an earlier work. But Mercian power, like its prestigious archbishopric did not survive his death, and significantly although Northumbria did not conquer at this time, it was not conquered.

The link to Mercia did Aethelred no good he was assassinated in 796 AD. Osbald a nobleman, his successor, was expelled. He had only reigned for 27 days. He went to live among the Picts. Eardwulf, whose dynasty was to dominate the next 50 years and longer, succeeded him.

"795.AD Erdulf succeeded to the throne and was consecrated at York.

798 AD This year a severe battle was fought in the Northumbrian territory during Lent, wherein Alric son of Herbert was slain, and many others with him.

806 AD Erdulf was banished." ASC

CHAPTER 9.

THE COMING OF THE VIKINGS

But in the midst of this internecine bickering and murder, monumental events intruded; in
787AD Danes had landed in the south of England and killed the Reeve.

"In King Bertic's days came first three ships of the Northmen from the land of robbers. The reeve then rode thereto, and would drive them to the king's town; for he knew not what they were; and there he was slain. These were the first ships of the Danish men that sought the land of the English nation." ASC

The Northumbrians ignored the warning,

"793AD This year came dreadful fore-warnings over the land of the people most woefully, these were immense sheets of light rushing through the air, and whirlwinds and fiery dragons flying across the firmament. These tremendous tokens were soon followed by a great famine; and not long after, on the sixth day before the ides of January in the same year, the harrowing inroads of heathen men made lamentable havoc in the church of God in Holy Island, by rapine and slaughter."

This was the first attack on Northumbria and the news of the attack would echo around Europe.

THE VIKING ATTACK ON NORTHUMBRIA.

"The said army of pagans, spread themselves over the whole country, and filled all with blood and grief; they destroyed the churches and the monasteries far and wide with fire and sword, leaving nothing remaining save the unroofed walls; and so thoroughly did they do their work, that even our own present generation can seldom discover in those places any conclusive memorial of their ancient dignity, sometimes none." Simeon.

"So general was the decay in England that there were very few on this side of the Humber who could understand their rituals in English, or translate a letter from Latin into English; and I believe that there were not many beyond the Humber. There were so very few of them that I cannot remember a single one south of the Thames when I came to the throne." Alfred the Great

"To argue that the skills shown by Scandinavians in trading, manufacturing and colonization in any respect compensated for their aggression, terrorism and looting is little short of offensive, irrespective of the scale on which that occurred." Higham.

"But with the best will in the world, the idea of the early Vikings as speedy Baltic commercial travellers, singing their sagas as they rowed to a new market opening, doesn't quite ring true." Schama.

The Viking attacks were a disaster for Anglo-Saxon England in general and Northumbria in particular. The kingdom was destroyed and with it a centre of civilisation. The Viking remains at Jorvik are scant recompense for the glories of the schools of Lindisfarne, Jarrow and York, for Alcuin's walled garden with its off-shoots of paradise. The libraries disappeared. Northumbria has no surviving charters which would have told us so much about land holding. Northumbrian book mounts are found as loot or jewelry in Scandinavian graves. (such as Bjorke ,Norway a pendant now in Historik museum , Bergen, Norway. Campbell.p.147.)

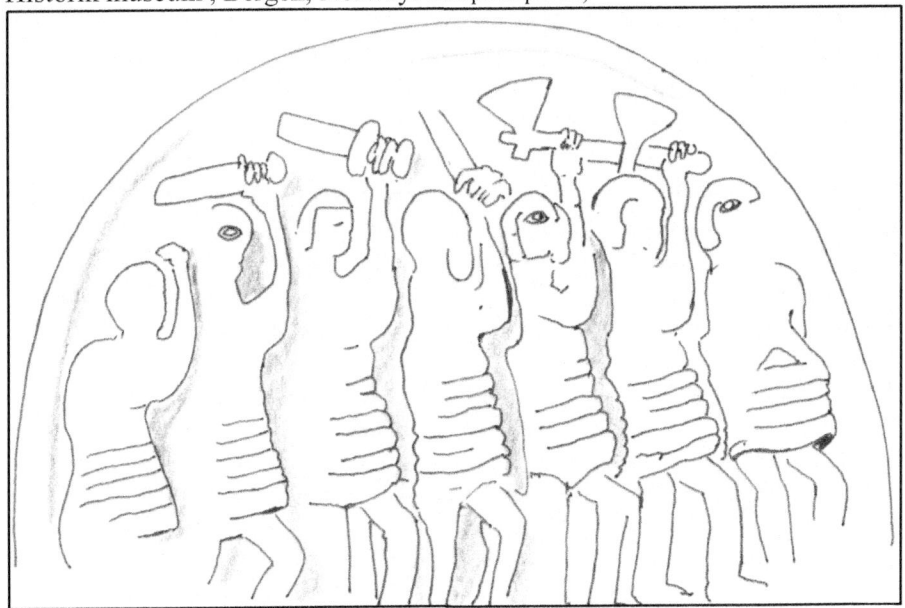

Stone from Lindisfarne thought to show Vikings.
There had been portents of disaster, an eclipse, floods and gales;

"Lo it is nearly 350 years that we and our fathers have inhabited this most lovely land, and never before has such terror appeared in Britain as we now have suffered from a pagan race, nor was it thought that such an in road from the sea would be made. Behold the church of St Cuthbert spattered with the blood of the priests of god, despoiled of all its ornaments, a place more venerable than all in Britain is given as a prey to pagan peoples, and where first after the departure of St Paulinus from York, the Christian religion in our race took its rise, Here misery and calamity have begun." Alcuin on the Viking attack on Lindisfarne 793AD.

"(the church of Lindisfarne)…miserably filled with devastation blood and rapine and all but entirely thoroughly ruined."

"they miserably ravaged and pillaged everything. they trod the holy things under their polluted feet, they dug down the altars and plundered all the treasures of the church. Some of the brethren they slew, some they carried off with them in chains. The greater number they stripped naked, insulted and cast out of doors, and some they drowned in the sea."

As usual, Anglo-Saxon priests deduced that the calamities were sent by God as a punishment for the sins of the people;

"from the days of King Aelfwold fornications, adulteries and incest have poured over the land."

"Consider the dress, the way of wearing the hair, the luxurious habits of the princes and the people. Look at your trimming of beard and hair, in which you have wished to resemble the pagans. Are you not menaced by terror of those whose fashion you wished to follow? What also of the immoderate use of clothing beyond the needs of human nature, beyond the customs of our predecessors."

"The prince's superfluity is poverty for the people. The saiety of the rich is the hunger of the poor."

Alcuin did however warn Jarrow of its exposed position, the next year it was attacked, not without loss to the attackers;

"while plundering the port of King Ecgfrith, that is Jarrow and the monastery which is situated at the mouth of the Don, their leader was put to a cruel death and shortly afterwards their ships were shattered and destroyed by a furious tempest, some of themselves were drowned in the sea, while such of them as succeeded in reaching land alive speedily perished by the swords of the inhabitants."

The depredations, however, continued particularly of the rich monasteries near the coasts;

'the most impious army of the pagans cruelly despoiled the churches of Hertenes and of Tinemutha and retired with its plunder to the ships." AD 800 Roger of Wendover.

Viking raiders also struck at the coast of Scotland and Ireland after similar easy pickings. There at Innisboffin, where the Lindisfarne monks had gone after the Synod of Whitby, they destroyed the shrines of Aidan and Colman, the Bishops of Lindisfarne.

Ivarr the Dane also sacked and enslaved the monastery at Ely which had been established by Ecgfrith's wife Aethelreda.

At Coldingham the nuns avoided ravishment by the Danes by the extreme measure of mutilating themselves;(according to the over imaginative Roger of Wendover.)

"There have come lately into these parts wicked pagans, destitute of all humanity, Who roam through every place, sparing neither the female sex or infant nor aged, destroying churches and ecclesiastics, ravishing holy women, and wasting and consuming everything in their way. If therefore you will follow my counsels, I have hope that through divine mercy we shall escape the rage of the barbarians and preserve our chastity'

She then took a razor and with it cut off her nose, together with her upper lip as far as the teeth, presenting herself an horrific spectacle to those who stood by. Filled with admiration for this admirable deed the whole assembly followed her maternal example." Ivar's attack on Coldingham.
The horrified Vikings retired in haste but gave orders for the monastery and nuns to be burned
Soon many were saying,

> *"Bitter is the wind tonight*
> *It tosses the white locks of the ocean,*
> *I fear not the coursing of a clear sea*
> *By the fierce warriors of the lochlann."*

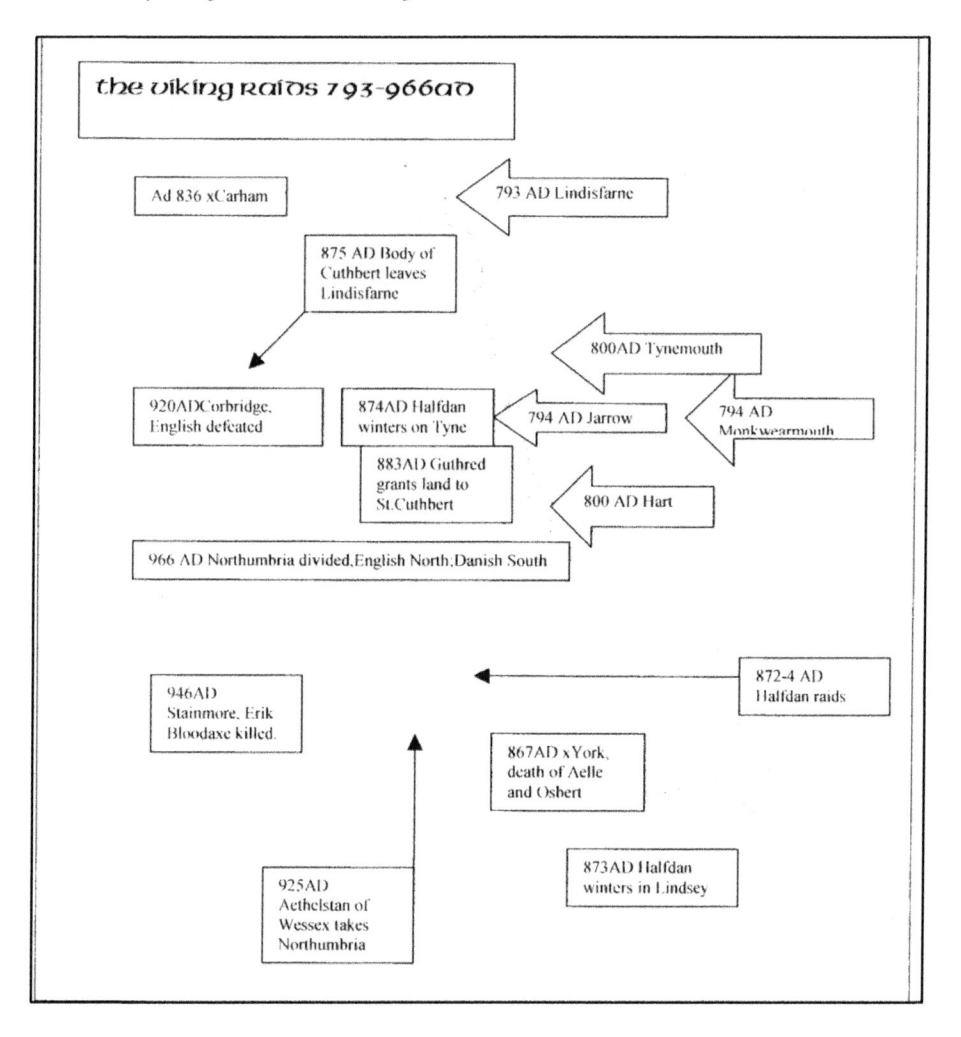

the viking raids 793-966ad

- AD 836 xCarham
- 793 AD Lindisfarne
- 875 AD Body of Cuthbert leaves Lindisfarne
- 800AD Tynemouth
- 920AD Corbridge, English defeated
- 874AD Halfdan winters on Tyne
- 794 AD Jarrow
- 794 AD Monkwearmouth
- 883AD Guthred grants land to St.Cuthbert
- 800 AD Hart
- 966 AD Northumbria divided, English North, Danish South
- 946AD Stainmore, Erik Bloodaxe killed
- 872-4 AD Halfdan raids
- 867AD xYork, death of Aelle and Osbert
- 925AD Aethelstan of Wessex takes Northumbria
- 873AD Halfdan winters in Lindsey

THE THREATS TO NORTHUMBRIAN INDEPENDENCE

Eardwulf was banished and replaced by Aelfwald II for two years. Eadwulf however had married into the most powerful European family, the

155

Carolingians. He travelled to Rome and Aachen visiting the Pope and the new Holy Roman Emperor, Charlemagne. He returned with envoys from both Pope and Emperor and was accepted again as king. His son Eanred ruled for 30 years and died in bed an achievement for a Northumbrian king and he was succeeded by his son Aethelred II. This succession from grandfather to grandson shows signs of stability.

But by the ninth century Northumbria was also beginning to feel the power of the **West Saxon threat** which had replaced the Mercian. King Egbert of Wessex was the first Bretwalda since Oswiu (according to Wessex Chroniclers). Egbert became king in 802AD and was quick to exploit Mercia's problems on their king Offa's death. He also turned his attention to Eanred's Northumbria.

"In 827 AD Egbert of Wessex led an army against the Northumbrians as far as Dore, where they met him ,and offered terms of obedience and subjection, on the acceptance of which they returned home.
Egbert was the eighth king who was sovereign of all the British dominions." ASC

But more pressing for Northumbria with its long vulnerable coastline, on both east and west, was the **Viking threat**. The Danish raids became more persistent, in 836AD the Danes won a victory at Carham. In 844 AD Aethelred II was expelled by Raedwulf who died fighting the Vikings in the same year. Aethelred returned only to be killed in 848 AD. In the face of these attacks Bishop Egred transferred the relics of Cuthbert and Ceolwulf and others from Lindisfarne to Norham. Along with these he took St Aidan's wooden church. The relics had been returned, prematurely as it turned out, to Lindisfarne by 875AD

But now a **Scots threat** emerged. In 849AD Kenneth MacAlpin ,King of Scots who had absorbed the kingdom of the Picts, burned St Cuthbert's monastery at Melrose.

In 849AD Osberht became king he was expelled in 866AD by Aelle. In that year the Vikings captured York, the destruction of the kingdom of English Northumbria was at hand.

Again significant events were occurring in the south,
"854 AD this year the heathen men for the first time remained over winter in the Isle of Sheppey."
"866AD the same year came a large heathen army into England, and fixed their winter quarters in East Anglia, where they were soon horsed; and the inhabitants made peace with them." ASC
The Danes were coming to stay

The next year that Danish army moved North, upon an already weakened and divided Northumbria. Osberht (848/9-867AD) a Bernician was contending with a Deiran Northumbrian, Aelle. Both were accused of plundering the lands of St Cuthbert to finance their armies.

"In 867 it (the Danish Army) went over the Humber as far as York. And there was much dissension in that Nation among themselves, they had deposed their king Osbert, and had admitted Aella, who had no natural claim. Late in the year, however, they returned to their allegiance, and they were now fighting against the common enemy, having collected a vast force, with which they fought the army at York; and breaking open the town, some of them entered in. Then there was there an immense slaughter of the Northumbrians, some within and some without, and both kings were slain on the spot. The survivors made peace with the army."

"Then they took horses
And the best of their men
And most of them went in ships
As far as the Humber. Sails set
More than 20,000 went on foot
At Grimsby they passed the Humber
And those on foot likewise.
Great plenty they had of men
And those who were with the ships
All went to York,
Both by water and by land.
They waged great war at York.
Those who came by water
sailed as far as the Ouse.
But directly the sun was hidden,
The tide turned
And they then quartered themselves there,
Some on the water, some in tents.
But the chief men, the lords
Went into houses in the town."   Geoffrey Gaimar. L'Estoire des Engles

The Northumbrian king suffered a grisly fate:
"And Ivarr, Who ruled at Jorvik
Cut an Eagle On the back of Aella"   Knutsdrapa

"They caused the blood-eagle to be carved on the back of Aella, and they cut away all the ribs from the spine, and they ripped out his lungs"   Thattr of Ragnar's sons.

The blood eagle barbarity appears to be a speciality of Ivaar the Boneless. Later the descendants of these Danish raiders who had settled in Deira, (later Yorkshire) encouraged the myth that Aelle had thrown Ivar's father Ragnar Lothbrok into a snake pit, in order to justify, in part the son's action. Since Ragnar had died 10 years previously fighting in Ireland, the snake pit was pure fiction, which did not stop Hollywood from adapting the tale in the Kirk Douglas film, "The Vikings".

Vikings attacking a town.

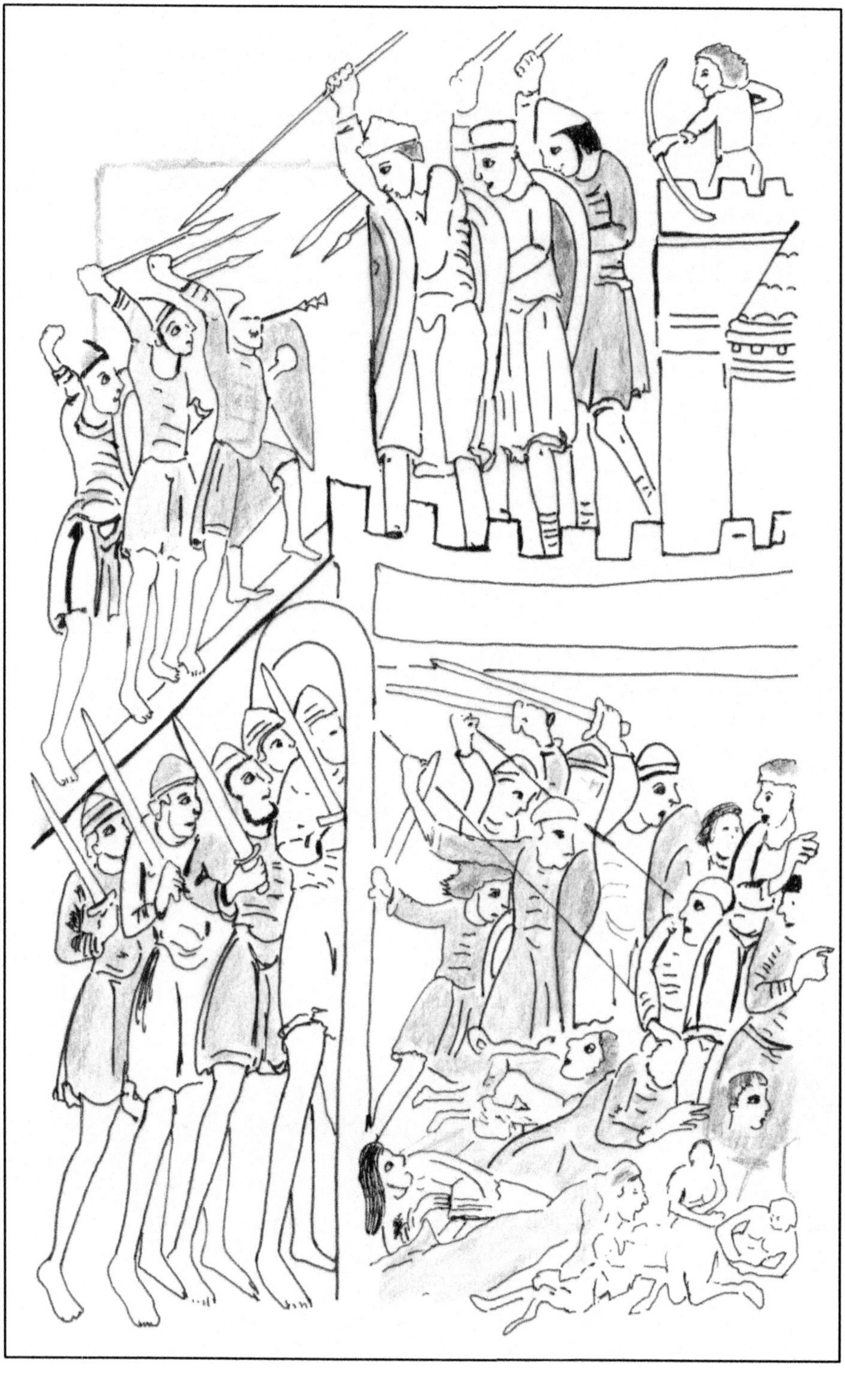

On 867 AD the barbarians advanced no further north than the mouth of the Tyne, but returned from thence to York. Here at Jorvik they established a Danish Kingdom and exacted tribute from the Northumbrians of Bernicia. The prosperity of York increased, by trade and because the Viking leaders remained in one place unlike the peripatetic Northumbrian rulers. The English Northumbrians were tolerated for the time being;

"The Danes appointed Egbert as king over such of the Northumbrians as survived, limiting his jurisdiction to those only who resided upon the north of the Tyne." Symeon.

The Northern English however drove him out along with Wulfhere, Bishop of York, for accommodating the Danes. The Northumbrians chose Ricsige instead. Halfdan returned to impose his will,

"In 872AD Halfdan attacked the north.

In 873AD the army went against the Northumbrians and wintered in Lindsey.

In 874AD he wintered on the Tyne, subdued the land and harried the Picts and Britons."

"Halfdene, king of the Danes, entered the Tyne and sailed as far as Wyrcesforde, ravaging everything and sinning cruelly against St Cuthbert." Historia Sancto St Cuthberto.

Wyrcesforde is believed to be on the tributary the Don where the Roman Road, the Wrekendike, crosses it. He occupied Tynemouth for a time.

"Everywhere did he burn down the monasteries and the churches. He slew the servants and handmaidens of God after having exposed them to many indignities, and in one word, fire and sword, were carried from the eastern sea to the western."

Significantly the same year the chronicle recorded,

"Rolla penetrated Normandy with his army and he reigned fifty winters". ASC

190 years later Rollo's descendants, who had ceased to be called Vikings and had become French speaking Normans would fall on England and Northumbria, and seize the land.

But in 875AD the Danes also had not come only to raid in Northumbria,

"Halfdene apportioned the lands of the Northumbrians and from that time they (the Danes) continued ploughing and tilling them."

Whether the Danes controlled the areas they settled as landowners or peasants is open to debate, it has been suggested that "ploughing" should be translated as "harrying". (Woolf.p.87.)

Precisely which areas were settled by the Danes the chronicle does not state. Egbert II replaced his father Ricsige as ruler in English Northumbria from 876AD. Place name evidence shows that Yorkshire as far as the south bank of the Tees was heavily settled. The characteristic Danish place name suffix is " –by". The English –ham, -ton, -burn.

Place names on the Tees

North Side	South Side
Hartlepool	Warrenby
Greatham	Thornaby
Billingham	Stainsby
Haverton	Ingleby
Norton	
Stockton	Barwick
Preston	Leven Bridge
Eaglescliffe	Yarm
Aislaby	Worsall
Newsham	Girsby
Middleton	Staindale
Dinsdale	Eryholme
Sockburn	Dalton
Neasham	Croft
Hurworth	Monkend
	Stapleton
Darlington	Cleasby
Coniscliffe	Manfield
Carlbury	Cliffe
Piercebridge.	

The list of place names on the Tees indicates the Danish presence, as does *Danby*, *Raby* and the Danish *Wapentake of Sadberge*. However "There is little evidence of heavy Scandinavian settlement in Northern Durham or North of the Tyne."

There was to be a growing rift between those areas under direct Danish control and the English Northumbrians. In some measure this division was a reflection of the old borders between Deira and Bernicia.

"from approximately this time the North East assumed the air of a region distinct from the rest of England which remains with it until the present day."

Halfdan took his army across Strathclyde to Ireland and later returned. By then he was suffering from disease and unpopular with the troops. Halfdan had a suitably gruesome death for a despoiler of the church,

" he was attacked at the same time by mental instability and the severest bodily suffering; the intolerable stench exhaling from which made him an object of abomination to the whole army. He left the Tyne with three ships and perished."

After Halfdan's death. Northumbrian kings re-emerged at Bamburgh, Ecgberht II and Eadwulf. Meanwhile the monks of Lindisfarne had once more taken up the body of their saint:

THE JOURNEYS OF ST CUTHBERT'S BODY

"Raising then the holy and uncorrupt body of the Father, they placed beside it in the same shrine the relics of the saints, that is to say, the head of

Oswald the king and Martyr, part of the bones of Aidan, the bones of Eadbert, Eadfrid, and Aethelwold, this occurred in 875AD, 241 years since King Oswald and Bishop Aidan founded that church and 189 years after the death of father Cuthbert, and 83 years since this church had been devastated under bishop Higbald." The enclosed bones therefore contain the men responsible for the creation of the Lindisfarne Gospels.

In doing this they were following the wishes of the saint who had said,

"If it should happen that you must decide one of these two things, it would be much more pleasing to me that you should take my bones up from the tomb, and remove them from this spot, and should continue to reside wherever God shall provide an abode for you, rather than that you should tamely submit to evil and bow your necks to schismatic". Simeon.

The body of St Cuthbert was carried by his followers the length and breadth of Northumbria. The original community were held in high esteem in Northumbria.

"when the monks left, they had followed the venerable body of the holy confessor from the island of Lindisfarne, vowing never to part with it as long as they lived. Four of these, who are remembered as being more important than the other three, Hunred, Stitheard, Edmund and Franco. Many of their descendants in the kingdom of the Northumbrians-clergy and laity-take pride that their ancestors are said to have served St Cuthbert so faithfully." Simeon

Cuddy's Corse. The travels of Cuthbert's Coffin based on Prior Wessington's list.

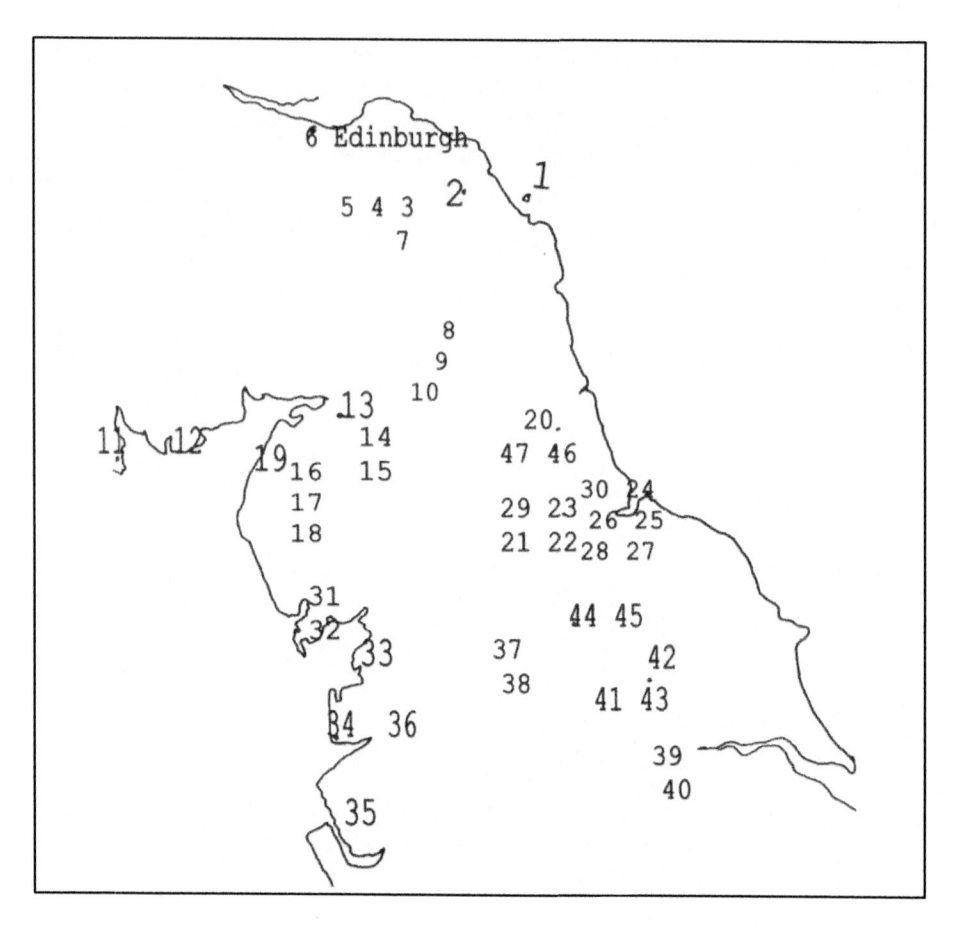

1,Holy Island, 2,Norham, 3,Carham, 4,Kelso,5,Melrose, 6,Edinburgh, 7,Cavers,
8,Elsdon,9,Bellingham,10,Haydon Bridge,11,Whithorn, 12,Kirkcudbright,13,Carlisle,
14,Salkeld, 15,Edenhall, 16,Plumbland,17,Embleton (Cu.), 18,Lorton, 19,Cockermouth,
20,Chester-le-Street,.21,Marske, 22,Cowton, 23,Darlington, 24,Kirkleatham,25,Wilton,
26,Ormesby, 27,Marton, 28,Middleton-under-Leaven,29,Forcet, 30,Billingham, 31,Ireleth,
32,Aldingham,33,Over Kellet, 34,Lytham, 35,Halsall,36, Mellor,37,Burnsall, 38,Bolton,
39,Ackworth, 40,Fishlake,41,Overton, 42,Barton, 43,Peaseholme Green (York),
44,Ripon,45,Crayke, 46,Warden Law, 47,Durham.

The coffin was taken to the mouth of the Derwent in Cumbria; they nearly transported it to Ireland but were miraculously driven back. The gospels were washed into the sea and lost, but restored to one of the community, Hunred near Whithorn; Adomnan told similar stories, about Books written by St Columba.

> "A young man fell off his horse into the river Boyne and was drowned. Lying for 20 days under water. At the time of the fall he was carrying a leather satchel of books,…the pages of all the books were found to be ruined and rotten except one page, which St Columba had written out with his own hand."

In 882 AD they were in Crake in North Yorkshire. To move nearer the Scandinavian centre of York has suggested to Aird that the progress of the community was less a flight than a procession with their saint to confirm their landholdings in the North. Certainly relationships with the Danes were (temporarily) transformed after the death of the murderous Halfdan, and in 883AD a vision of St Cuthbert approved the appointment of the Dane Guthfrith as king. He was the son of Hardacnut, whom the Danes had sold to a certain widow of Whittingham after a fight with the English at Edlingham burn. Bishop Eardwulf and abbot Eadred were instructed that;

> "the whole army pay the widow for him... lead him before the whole gathering so that they might elect him king...take him and the whole army up the hill which is called Oswigesdune, and there place on his arm a gold bracelet,"

Guthred in return gave to the Community of St Cuthbert all the land from the Tyne to the Wear, East of Dere Street, as well as making the church a refuge for fugitives for 37 days. The community settled at Chester-le-Street. Eadred further extended the Community's land by buying Sedgefield from the Danes. He also bought Bedlington.

Having helped the community, Guthred now came under the protection of the Saint, so when the Dane was attacked by a Scots army, it was no surprise that the enemy were swallowed up by a miraculous earthquake.

> "After a lapse of sometime the nation of the Scots collected a numerous army and among their other deeds of cruelty, they invaded and plundered the monastery of Lindisfarne. Whilst king Guthred, supported by St. Cuthbert, was about to engage in battle with them, immediately the earth opened her mouth and swallowed them all up alive."

Rather biblical and incredible, but an army fleeing north from Lindisfarne would probably use Cheswick sands, notorious quicksands.

Although it is not clear whether Guthred was a Christian at the time of his accession, many Danes did convert, Bede would have been pleased to see that the Northumbrians had achieved what the Britons did not. "The conversion of the Danes to Christianity was the most remarkable memorial of the 9th century Northumbrian church." And the conversion, indeed the survival, of Christianity in Northumbria owed a great deal to the efforts of the Community. The lands of St Cuthbert in Durham were to prove a buffer between the English of Bamburgh and those of Yorkshire, the latter increasingly controlled by Danes.

While the Danes ruled at York, Eadwulf of Bamburgh was still able to rule from the Tees to the Forth having succeeded Ecgbert. From their Bamburgh base, his descendants, the Eadwulfings would maintain an autonomous English Northumbria for two hundred years. "Northumbria was nothing more than a geographical expression," claimed DJV Fisher in "The Anglo-Saxon age" much as Metternich had said of early nineteenth century Italy. But those who wrote off the separateness of Northumbria were somewhat premature.

Meanwhile the Danes were triumphant nearly everywhere else in England,

"878AD they rode over the land of the West Saxons; where they settled, and drove many people over the sea; and the rest the greatest part they rode down, and subdued to their will;-ALL BUT;
ALFRED THE KING."

Alfred knew little of what was happening in Northumbria. Although it was said he was friendly with Eadwulf. Nonetheless, (according to the Chronicler`s) in Alfred's darkest hour he received a vision. While hiding from the Danes he gave all his food to a mysterious pilgrim.

"But when he returned again he found that the pilgrim had disappeared but the wine and food had not been touched. Nor could they discover how he had found his way through the marshes, as there was no sign of a boat. When the rest of the household returned they had three boats filled with fish and declared they had caught more in that one day than in the 3 months they had lived in the marshes.

That night when he retired with his wife as she lay sleeping Alfred was awake pondering on the events of the day when a bright light shone out like the sun, and there appeared an old priest with black hair, wearing episcopal regalia and holding in his right hand a text of the gospel decked with gold and jewels, and as Alfred lay awake he blest him with these words:

"Do not be alarmed at my appearance and let not fear of the heathen's fury trouble you any longer, For God, who does not despise the tears of his poor people, will presently put an end to your troubles. And henceforth I shall be a most ready ally to you.

And when asked by Alfred who he was and what was his name, he said, "I am he to whom you generously offered food today, and my name is Cuthbert, a soldier of Christ. Be strong, and attend carefully and with a glad heart to what I tell you, for henceforth I shall be your shield, and your friend, and the defender of your sons. And now I shall tell you what you must do thereafter."

He was told to rise at dawn and sound the horn three times "and by the ninth hour you will have 500 men in arms and after 7 days by God's gift you will have the whole army of this land ready to support you, at the hill of Ethandune. And thus you will fight against your enemies and without doubt will overcome them." Historia Sancto Cuthberto Miracles and Translations of St Cuthbert

Alfred, according to the story, was to have the blessing of the Northern English Saint, as Oswald had had the blessing of the Scot Columba. Alfred and his family were to begin the reconquest of the country from the Danes, in this he would appeal "to the shared sense of Englishness conveyed by the language."

"It seems better to me that we should also translate certain books which are most necessary for all men to know, into the language we can all understand, and also arrange it…so that the youth of free men now among the English people are able to read English writing as well." Alfred.

164

Alfred The Great. Winchester. (below.)

In 911AD Alfred's son, Edward, caught a Danish Northumbrian army raiding ,and slew many thousands of them.

"There fell King Eowils and King Healfden, Earls Ohter and Scurf, Governors Agmund, Othulf and Benesing, Anlaf the swarthy, and Governor Thunferth, Osferth, the collector, and Governor Guthferth."

Irish success against the **Norwegian Vikings** caused problems for Northumbria. In 902AD the Norwegians were driven from Dublin and crossed over to the North West. This led to an exodus of English to avoid them. The abbot of Heversham moved to Norham, and a fugitive called Alfred arrived.

"Alfred fleeing from the pirates came from beyond the mountains towards the west, and sought the pity of St. Cuthbert and of Bishop Cutheard, that they might grant him some lands. The Bishop Cutheard, for the love of God and for the sake of St. Cuthbert, granted him these estates: Easington Heseldon, Thorpe, Horden, Castle Eden, the two Shottons, (South) Eden, Fulam, Hutton, Willington, Billingham with its appurtenances, and Sheraton. All these estates . . . the bishop gave to Alfred that he might be loyal to himself and the Community, and should render full service from them. This also he faithfully did, until King Raegnald came with a great multiple of ships, and occupied the land of Ealdred the Earl."

In 913AD Raegnald, grandson of Ivarr the Boneless, leading a force of displaced Irish and Breton Vikings attacked the English Northumbrians. As in earlier Viking attacks the event seems to have been precipitated by Northumbrian infighting.

" Eadred, son of Ricsige rode to the west beyond the mountains and killed prince Eardwulf and seized his wife against the peace and the wishes of the people, and he fled to the patrimony of St Cuthbert." Not only was he received there, but he was leased a substantial parcel of land by Bishop Cutheard.

The Vikings defeated Ealdred of Bamburgh, Eardwulf's son, and Constantine II, king of Scots at Corbridge. A few years later another battle appears to have been fought near the same place, when in 918 or 920AD an anti-Danish coalition was built up against Raegnald by the English of Bamburgh with the Scots and Strathclyde Britons, again Raegnald was victorious. In this battle Alfred the refugee was killed as was Eadred, but the leaders of the Bamburgh English escaped;

" the pagan king triumphed, put Constantine to flight, scattered the Scots, killed Alfred and all the English nobles except Ealdred and his brother Uhtred." HSC

Raegnald did however allow Eadred's sons to succeed to his lands, which raises a question over Eadred's part in the battle. Raegnald then divided the land of St Cuthbert south of the Tyne, part of which he granted to one of his followers, Olaf Ball. The latter was however paralysed by the saint,

"What can this dead man Cuthbert do against me...I swear by my mighty gods, Thor and Odin, that from this hour I will be a great enemy to all of you...But when he had put one foot outside the threshold, he felt as if iron was deeply fixed in the other foot. With this pain piercing in his diabolical heart he fell and the devil thrust his sinful soul into Hell. And St Cuthbert, as was right, received his land." HSC.

CHAPTER 10

THE RISE OF WESSEX

Raegnald's death in 921AD allowed the West Saxon influence to increase in the North.
In 920AD Edward of Wessex who had gained the resources of Mercia following the death of his formidable sister Aethelflaed, was recognized by all Northumbrians.

"In 924AD the son of Eadulf, and all that dwell in Northumbria, both English and Danish, chose Edward as their father and lord."

WEST SAXON KINGS

EGBERT recognised as Bretwalda 827Ad. Died 839.AD. succeeded y his son,
ETHELWULF Died 855 AD. Succeeded by four sons,
ETHELBALD. Died 860 AD
ETHELBERT Died 866 AD
ETHELRED. Killed 871 AD
ALFRED. Died 899 AD. Succeeded by his son;
EDWARD THE ELDER. Succeeded by three sons (by two women.)
ATHELSTAN. (mother Egwina) died 939AD. No issue.
EDMUND (mother Eadgifu) murdered 946AD. Sons Edwy and Edgar succeeded below.
EDRED (Died 955AD)
EDWY (son of Edmund) died 959AD
EDGAR (son of Edmund) Died 975AD succeeded by two sons (by two women).
EDWARD II, THE MARTYR. (son of Ethelfreda) murdered 979AD.
ETHELRED II, THE REDELESS. Murdered 1016 AD.

Edward of Wessex was succeeded by the equally powerful Athelstan;

"In 925AD Sihtric, King of the Northumbrians married the sister of Athelstan of Wessex. The next year Sihtric died and Aethelstan took the kingdom of Northumbria, and governed all the kings that were in this island including Aldred, son of Eadulf of Bamburgh. This was done at Eamont on the 12th of July"(927AD).

This was a major turning point in the fortunes of Northumbria. The West Saxon king whose only claim was as an in-law, seized York and the old Northumbrian lands west of the Pennines.

Aethelstan's real claim was the power of his army, but he still took care to appease Cuthbert:

167

In 934AD Aethelstan took a combined land and sea force into Scotland and laid it waste. He left gifts at St Cuthbert's tomb at Chester-le-Street.

"a Gospel Book, two chasubles and one alb, one stole with a maniple, and one belt, and three altar cloths, and a silver chalice, and two patens, another worked in gold and another worked in Greek style, and a silver thurible, and a cross skillfully worked in gold and ebony, and a royal cap woven in gold, and two altar tables worked in gold and silver, and two silver candelabra worked with gold, and a missal, and two texts of the Gospels, decorated in gold and silver, and one life of St Cuthbert written in verse and prose, and seven pallia, and three hangings, and three tapestries, and two silver bowls with lids, and four great bells, and three horns, worked in gold and silver, and two banners and a lance, and two gold bracelets."

Some of those gifts can still be seen today with St Cuthbert's coffin in the cathedral at Durham. The lavish copy of Bede's life of St Cuthbert is at Cambridge university having been pillaged during the Reformation. A precious copy of the bible was reduced to fragments in the great fire at Ashburnham house in the 18th century.

Aethelstan makes a gift to Cuthbert.

The Jonas silk The stole was ordered by Queen Aelfflaed for Frithestan , Bishop of Winchester.

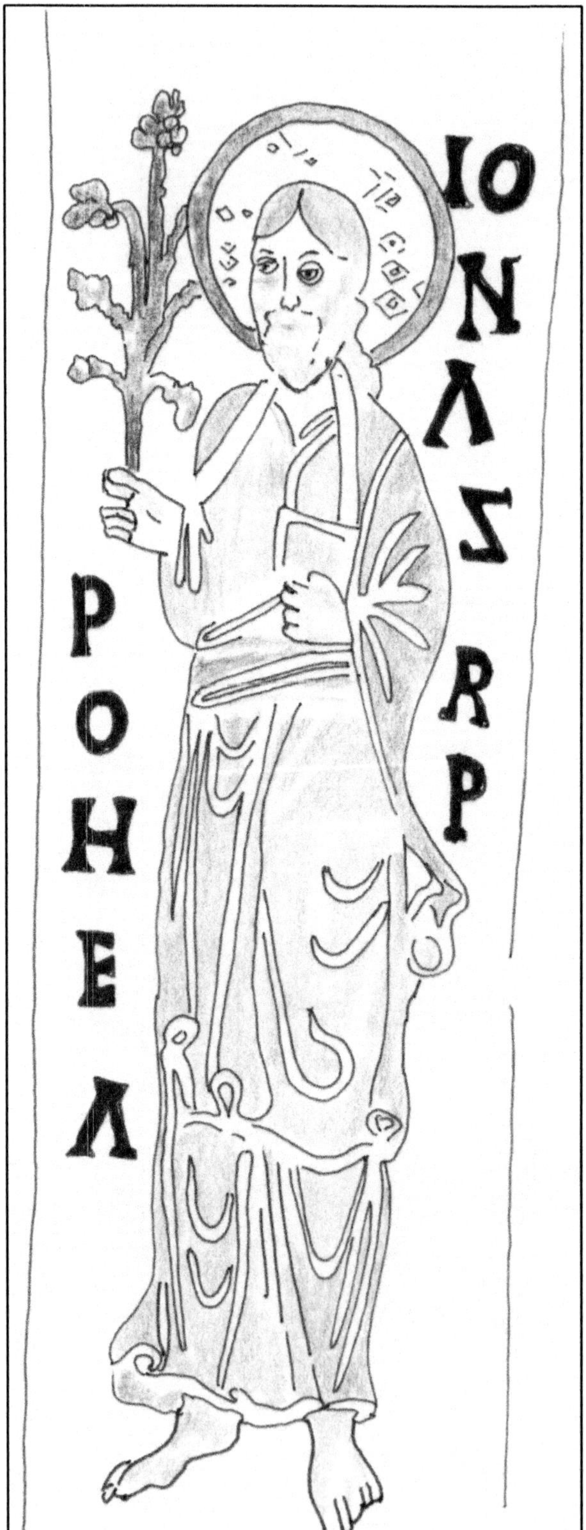
IO
N
A
S
RP
P
P
O
H
E
A

Some Northumbrian like to trace their lineage back to the reign of Aethelstan, in particular the Roddams who claim to be the oldest family,

" I King Aethalstan give unto thee Pole Roddam For fee and fine, to thee and thine Before my wife Maude, my daughter Maudlin and eldest son Henry for a certain troth I bite this wax with My gang tooth. So long as muir bears moss and cnout grows hare, A Roddam of Roddam for ever mare."
Tomlinson.

In 938AD Olaf Guthfrithson claimed the kingdom of York and gained allies in Owain of Strathclyde and Constantine, King of the Scots. They were defeated by Athelstan at Brunaburgh.

"Here Athelstan king
Of earls the lord,
Rewarder of heroes,
And his brother eke,
Edmund atheling
Elder of ancient race
Slew in the fight
With the edge of their swords
The foe at Brumby
The sons of Edward
Their board-walls clove
And hewed their banners."   ASC

Aethelstan credited St John of Hexham and Beverley with the victory. The Northumbrian bishops at Chester-le-Street, (who still called themselves Bishops of Lindisfarne.) were present at councils of Aethelstan in Dorset and Colchester.

However when the king died in 939AD Olaf returned to York and even gained part of Mercia east of Watling Street. He then invaded English Northumbria north of the Tees, reaching as far as Tyningham near Dunbar. Fortunately for the English he died in 941 AD and was succeeded by his less martial cousin Olaf Sihtricson. Edmund, Athelstan`s successor and brother quickly recovered these lands;

171

The Fryd.

"Here, Edmund king,
Of Angles lord,
Protector of friends,
Author and framer
Of direful deeds,
O`erran with speed
The Mercian land.

In thralldom long
To Northmen Danes
They bowed through need
And dragged the chains
Of heathen men;
Till, to his glory,
Great Edward`s heir,
Edmund the king,
Refuge of warriors,
Their fetters broke." ASC

The Chronicler sees the West Saxon king freeing the Mercians from the heathen yoke. English Northumbrians however were facing a choice between Scandinavian or West Saxon domination.

A civil war now broke out between Olaf and his cousin Raegnald Guthfrithson which allowed Edmund to subdue Northumbria the following year. He also prayed and left gifts at Cuthbert's shrine at Chester-le-Street.

The next year he overran Cumbria which had fallen to the Strathclyde Britons and gave it to Malcolm King of Scots on condition he became an ally. This buying off of the Scots by the southern king was a disaster for the Northumbrians, as it meant that a potential enemy outflanked their territory.

Edmund was just 25 years old when he was stabbed to death at a feast as he tried to restrain a banished warrior. His brother Eadred succeeded and subdued the Northumbrians and had Archbishop Wulfstan swear allegiance at Tadden's cliff. The Archbishop preferred the Danes to the Wessex kings. The southern chronicles do not differentiate between Danish controlled Northumbria, (Yorkshire) and English controlled Northumbria,(North of the Tees)

"In 946AD Northumbria swore fealty to Eadred but then chose Eric Bloodaxe, son of Harold Fairhair of Norway as king." Eric had been evicted from Norway by Haakon the Good after a short but bloody reign.

Eadred once more attacked Northumbria, Wilfrid's minster at Ripon was burned. Although Eadred lost men at York while his main army was at Chesterford, the Northumbrians fearing further reprisals abandoned Eric. But within 2 years they had had chosen Olaf Sihtricson again from Dublin. However, in 952AD Eric returned to York. His style of government is hinted at by the saga;

" where the king kept his people cowed
under the helmet of his terror
from his seat in York he ruled unflinchingly
over a dank land." Egil skalla-grimson

Two years later Eric was betrayed to his death at Stainmore by Osulf of Bamburgh, who became Earl of Northumbria. Eric was killed by Maccus, son of Olaf. Eadred had the rebellious bishop Wulfstan imprisoned at Jedburgh.

" He was treacherously killed by Earl Maccus in a certain lonely place which is called Stainmore, with his son, Haeric and his brother Ragnald, betrayed by Earl Oswulf; and then afterwards King Eadred ruled in these districts" Roger of Wendover.

"Here the kings of Northumbria came to an end, and henceforth the province was administered by earls". Simeon.

Some like to see Eric as the last king of an independent Northumbria and a romantic figure, in fact he was a bloodthirsty tyrant driven out of his homeland and his removal was at the hands of the English Northumbrians.

They were struggling to maintain their identity against Scandinavians, West Saxons and Scots.

Eadred's early death left his two nephews fighting for the throne. Edgar with the backing of Northumbria and Mercia eventually supplanted Eadwig in 959AD at the age of 16 years. In 966AD Northumbria was split between Eadwulf, son of Osulf, who gained the North, old Bernicia; and the Dane Oslac who took Deira. This recognized the division between Danish Yorkshire, and Northumbria. The latter included Durham, Northumberland and Lothian. Some would say that Deira and Bernicia had been recreated.

Edgar then ruled Northumbria. Thereafter the Earls of York were under the Wessex kings. The king's power was shown by the annual circumnavigation of Britain by his Fleet and by six kings rowing him on the River Dee in 973AD.

KING EDGAR ROWED UP THE DEE TO ST JOHNS CHESTER 973

It was claimed later that one of those kings, Kenneth, king of the Scots ,was brought to Edgar by Aelfsige, Bishop of Chester-le-Street, and Eadwulf, Ealdorman of Bernicia; and that Edgar gave Kenneth Lothian and other estates in England to facilitate his visits to Edgar's court. (Roger of Wendover in Stenton p365) If the king did cede Lothian to the Scots the reaction of the Northumbrians who lived there, or the effect on them of this diplomatic move, are not recorded. Barrow believes that the Scots were already in possession of Lothian by this date. Whatever the situation, it marked increasing pressure from the north on the English of Bamburgh. It also showed that the solutions proffered by southern rulers to the problem of the northern frontier were not always to the benefit of the English who lived there.

Edgar also established Oswald as Bishop of York. Archbishop Wulfstan I, who had died in 955 AD was to be the last Archbishop from the North. The Wessex kings began a process of centralization that aimed to ensure that the North would lose its religious and political separateness. Oswald was the nephew of Oda, the Danish Archbishop of Cantebury, he was also Bishop of Worcester, so linking Northumbria with English Mercia. Oswald with the support of Dunstan, Archbishop of Cantebury, reintroduced monasticism. He had visited Fleury the resting place of St Benedict, the founder of the Benedictine order. Worcester was turned into a monastic establishment. He also founded Evesham, Pershore and Winchcombe. Monks from the last place were to re-found Jarrow after the Norman Conquest This monastic reformation alienated many important families who were linked to the older monastic establishments.

"One misdeed he did too much however that foreign tastes he loved too much; and heathen modes into this land he brought too fast." ASC on Edgar.

THE NEW DANISH ATTACK.

But once more events in the south were to have a devastating effect on the North.

Edgar's early death in 975AD, aged just 32 years, again left a problem of succession between two half brothers, Edward and Aethelred. There were ominous portents; a great famine in 976AD, Oslac the ruler of Deira was expelled, then in 978 AD.

"This year all the oldest counsellors of England fell at Calne from an upper floor; but the holy Archbishop Dunstan who stood alone upon a beam. Some were dreadfully bruised; and some did not escape with their lives. This year was King Edward slain, at eventide, at Corfe gate."

Aethelred II succeeded his murdered half-brother Edward. Aethelred's mother, Edward's stepmother, Aelfthryth, is usually blamed for the murder. Archbishop Dunstan of Canterbury was unimpressed with both mother and son. At his baptism the infant Aethelred defecated into the font, causing the Archbishop to predict "he will be a wastrel when he is a man". O'Brien p.53. and later that England would suffer for the death of Edward. After the Queen Mother's death Edward's remains were taken to Cantebury and a cult of Edward the Martyr developed.

Aethelred was to be known as the "unready" or rather the "unraed" or lacking in counsel. But this was a critical time when England needed a strong ruler. Unfortunately after a series of strong rulers with brief reigns, the incompetent Aethelred was to rule for 38 years, and to preside over the rapid decline of Anglo-Saxon England.

Pub sign at Corfe, Dorset. Much history is to be gleaned in public houses. (see "The Inn sign story". By Chris Kilkenny.Amazon books.For the story behind the pub signs of North East England.)

EDWARD THE MARTYR KING OF WESSEX TREACHEROUSLY STABBED AT CORVES GATE IN A.D. 978 BY HIS STEPMOTHER ELFRIDA

In 993AD the battle of Maldon in Essex marked a new Danish offensive. Made famous by the poem of the same name, the battle came about when the English leader Byrhtnoth allowed a Danish force to cross over a causeway onto dry land to give battle. His gallant, or stupid, gesture led to his death and his men's defeat. He was curiously called "Northanumbrorum Dux", leader of the Northumbrians, by the Liber Eliensis, but no link with Northumbria has been traced. There was a Northumbrian present however, he was a hostage and fought alongside his host;

"the hostage helped them with all his might-
his name was Aescferth, the son of Ecglaf;
he came of a brave family in Northumbria.
He did not flinch in the battle-play
But fired arrows as fast as he could."

The English were defeated. Byrhtnoth's body was taken to Ely for burial. His widow presented the abbey with a tapestry recording his deeds. The first Danegeld was paid to buy the Danes off. But Danish attacks were now organized, backed by royalty, and based on armed camps at Trelleborg, Fyrkat and elsewhere. Olav Tryggvason a major player in the wars, led the Danes at Maldon.

It was not long before disaster struck Northumbria.

Brythnoth's memorial at Ely.

BRITHNOTHUS
NORTHUMBRIŌR.
DUX, PRÆLIO
CÆSUS A DANIS
A.D.DCCCCXCI.

CHAPTER 10.
Millennium Northumbria-the fight for survival.

"By its very geographical position it lay open to the Picts, the Scots, the Danes, the Norwegians and anyone else who came ashore to ravage the island", 1135 Geoffrey of Monmouth.

"**Northumbrians had a native ardour of their minds which brooked no master'** William of Malmesbury.

"The revolt (of Guttred) was caused by a suggestion made to him by the Northumbrians, that their county had always been want to have a king of their own and to tributary to none of the south Angles. From that time to the present, Northumbria has been subjected to the south Angles and has been grieving through want of a king of their own, and of the liberty they once enjoyed." John of Wallingford.

The strong feeling of self-reliance and independence in the face of hostile neighbours was well attested by writers, and was to be tested by events. As the new Millennium approached, Northumbria was not a tranquil place. For those who believed that the Millennium would herald the end of the world, the events of the nine hundred and nineties seemed appropriate, starting with the unimaginable fall of Bamburgh;

"AD 993 This year was Bamburgh destroyed, and much spoil taken. Afterwards came the army to the mouth of the Humber; and there did much evil both in Lindsey and in Northumbria. Then was collected a great force; but when the armies were to engage, then the generals first commenced a flight. In this same year the king ordered Elfgar, son of Aelderman Elfric, to be punished with blindness.

AD994 Next (the Danish army) took horse, and rode as wide as they would, and committed unspeakable evil. Then resolved the king and his council to send to them, and offer them tribute and provision on condition that they desisted from plunder. And they gave them 16,000 pounds in money.

AD995 This year appeared the comet star.

AD 999 This year came the army about again in the Thames...where the Kentish army came against them, but alas! They too soon yielded and fled; because they had not the aid that they should have had." ASC

The inability of the English to coordinate their efforts against the Danes led to a feeling of despair. The payment of Danegeld did show the remarkably sophisticated tax raising capabilities of the Anglo-Saxon monarchy, but did nothing to stop the Danish raids. The casual violence of the king towards his enemies did not necessarily increase respect for the monarchy.

Apart from the Viking threat, in 986 AD there had been a great pestilence amongst cattle and 1005 AD was to see the worst plague in living memory. For some the times were apocalyptical. Wulfstan, Archbishop of York, saw a warning in events of the past;

"There was an historian in the days of the Britons called Gildas, who wrote about their misdeeds, how they by their sins so overly much angered God that in the end he permitted the army of the English to conquer their land and to destroy the Briton's power. And true it is that I say: we know of worse deeds among the English than we heard of anywhere among the Britons."

Within sixty one years his warning would be fulfilled. He detailed the failings of society;

" the public laws have deteriorated all too extremely and holy places are widely devoid of immunity…widows are unduly forced into marriage and too many of them impoverished and grievously humiliated, poor people are cruelly ensnared and widely sold from out of this land into the power of foreigners."

Women were particularly vulnerable,

"they club together and jointly buy one woman, and with that one they commit filth, one after one and each after the other, and afterwards for profit they sell out of the country into the control of enemies God's creature."

The new Millennium then began as a crucial time for Northumbria. It was a time of raid and warfare, treachery and murder with racial hatred of Balkan dimensions. The protagonists were the Northumbrian English based on Bamburgh, the Community of St Cuthbert based at Durham. The Danes based on York. The Danish army. The rising power of the Scots, who under Kenneth MacAlpin had taken over Pictland and under Indulf had captured Edinburgh in 962 AD; and the English Kings based on Wessex who had been recognized by the Lords of Bamburgh.

The Danes of York had stood aside when the Vikings had sacked Bamburgh in 993AD. Southern monarchs looked upon them as unreliable. They seemed to sympathise with Danish invaders. Yorkshire, suspiciously, escaped the raids on other parts of the North. When Danish leaders sailed up the Humber the locals tended to readily submit, as they were to do in 1013 and 1066 AD. It was said of Yorkshiremen, "They are all Danes on their father's side." Wulfstan complained of the different treatment given to Christian and heathen,

"the servants of idols one does not dare mistreat in any wise among the heathen peoples in the way that God's ministers are too widely mistreated now."

"If a thrall runs away from his master, a thane, and turns from Christianity as a Viking…and if later he kills the Thane, the thane lies without right of compensation for his kin; but if the Thane kills the thrall, whom he formally owned, he must pay compensation as if he was a Thane."

The Community of St Cuthbert.

The Community remained at Chester-le-Street for 113 years, while there during the time when Aelfsige was Bishop (968-990) Aldred the provost inserted a translation between the Latin lines of the Lindisfarne gospels. This translation in Northumbrian Old English is the oldest surviving translation of the gospels. Another Viking threat caused them to temporarily move south to Ripon.

ST CUTHBERT ARRIVES AT DURHAM 995 AD.

"After three or four months, peace being restored, as they were returning with the venerable body to its former resting place, and had now reached a place near Durham named Wurdelau, on the eastern side of the city, the vehicle, on which the shrine containing the holy body was deposited, could not be induced to move any farther. They, who attempted to move it were assisted by others, but their efforts though vigorous, were equally ineffective; nor did the additional attempts of the crowd which came up produce any result in moving it. This circumstance clearly intimated to all that he refused to be conducted to his former resting place; but at the same time they did not know where to deposit him, for the place on which they were at that time standing, in the middle of a plain, was then uninhabitable. Hereupon the Bishop ordered a three-day fast to find the explanation from heaven. At the end, a revelation came to a certain religious person called Eadmer, who said that they were to remove the body to Durham and there prepare a resting place for it." Symeon of Durham.

The tradition is that they found the site by following a woman and her Dun Cow. The plateau itself may have been uninhabited but Elvet just across the river is usually taken to be the place where Peohtwine was consecrated Bishop of Whithorn in 762AD. It seems unlikely that the community which had lived at Chester-le-Street for 113 years, had not heard of Durham, 7 miles away.

"Where the corpse had rested at first, miracles began to be performed, and sick people restored to health. Some considerable time afterwards a certain Scottish woman, who had continued in infirm health all her life was brought to Durham, and so great was her misery that her condition excited the compassion of the most hard-hearted. Her feet and thighs were twisted backwards and dragged behind her, and she crept on her hands, and in this posture she dragged herself from place to place. It so happened that she conveyed herself to the spot aforementioned where the most holy body had rested for a few days, and there she suddenly began alternately to leap up (for the veins had resumed their natural position) and to fall again to the ground, and her cries disturbed the whole neighbourhood. After a little time the woman stood upon her feet, erect and strong, and she returned thanks to Christ, who had become her saviour through the intercession of the blessed Cuthbert. When this was noised abroad the whole

city hastened to the church, the bells were rung, the clergy sang the "Te Deum laudamus," the people joined their voices in celebrating the praises of God." Symeon.

The Community were settled at Durham by Uchtred of Bamburgh, the Bishop's son-in-law, who recruited men from the Coquet to the Tees to clear and defend the site. It is possible that Uchtred was looking for a base less exposed to Scottish pressure than Bamburgh.

The place was celebrated in Old English verse;

The city is celebrated
Throughout the kingdom of the Britons;
Placed on a steep eminence
Surrounded with cliffs,
Wonderfully large.
The Wear surrounds it,
A river strong in its current;
And therein reside
Various kinds of fish
In the midst of the floods.
And there grows
A great fortress of woods,
In the recesses of which dwell
Many wild animals.
In the deep dales there is
A countless number of beasts.
There is also in the town,
One, illustrious among men,
The honourable and blessed Cuthbert;
And the head of the pure king
Oswald, the lion of the English;
And Bishop Aidan,
Aedbercht, and Aedfrid,

Illustrious associates
Therein, along with them, is
Aethelwald, the bishop,
And the illustrious author, Beda;
And Boisil, the abbot,
Who taught the pure Cuthbert
Willingly in his youth;
And well did he receive his instruction.
There abide with that blessed one
Within that minster
Countless relics,
Where many persons honour them wonderfully,

As writers report.
Whilst they await
The just sentence of the Lord.   Simeon.p.785.

Had it not been already named Durham it might well have been called *Cuthbert's church* or in Northumbrian, *Kirkcudbright,* since Cuthbert is the reason for the city's existence.

As the poem says the shrine of St Cuthbert also contained other relics brought from Lindisfarne; the Head of Oswald, bones of Aidan and Eadberht; bones of Bishop Eadfrith who wrote the Lindisfarne gospels and bones of Aethelwold who bound the Gospels, and also his cross. Later were added relics of Bede, Boisil, Baltherus, Balfridus, the anchorite who decorated the Gospels, Bishop Acca and Aelchmund from Hexham, Ebba and Ethelgitha. Many of these bones were accumulated by a Durham priest called Alfred Westou. *"he was commanded by a vision to visit in succession the sites of the ancient monasteries and churches in the province of the Northumbrians; and he raised from the ground the bones of such of the saints as he knew were buried in these places; and he left them above ground, in order that they might be exhibited to the people and venerated. A portion of all these relics he conveyed with him to Durham."* But it was above all the presence of Cuthbert's uncorrupted body which made Durham the number one English site for pilgrims. The first church built of boughs, is usually taken to be St Mary-le-Bow. Later a large Anglo-Saxon Church of stone was constructed, the White Church. This was short lived, being replaced by the Norman cathedral. Graves of the community and cross heads were discovered in the 19th century when restoring the Norman chapter house.

The Community were a group of religious men described variously as secular canons or monks. They married and passed down their positions within their families. Those allowed to touch the shrine of St Cuthbert were the most prestigious. They claimed the right to choose their own bishop, a right they were to defend strongly in years to come. As devout, fearful or cunning nobles kept in with the Saint and the bishop, they offered grants of lands, so the Patrimony of St Cuthbert grew to encompass most of Durham, but also a large part of Northumberland; Norhamshire and Islandshire and Bedlingtonshire. The bishop was a major figure, politically, in the North and was to remain so for the next 500 years.

Durham

UCHTRED OF BAMBURGH, EARL OF NORTHUMBRIA.
    In 995 Uchtred, son of the English Lord of Bamburgh, Waltheof, settled the community of St Cuthbert at Durham and fortified the peninsula. He was powerful enough to conscript labour from an area stretching from Coquet to the Tees. He was also powerful enough to destroy an invading Scot's army. In 1006AD Malcolm II of Scotland raided the North; they were stopped and defeated at Durham by Uchtred, who had married the daughter of the Bishop, so no doubt felt obliged to protect his father-in-law.

        "he collected together into one body a considerable number of the men of Northumbria and Yorkshire, and cut to pieces nearly the entire multitude of the Scots; the king himself and a few others, escaping with

difficulty. He caused to be carried to Durham the best looking heads of the slain, ornamented (as the fashion of the times was) with braided locks ,and after they had been washed by four women,-to each of whom he gave a cow for her trouble,-he caused these heads to be fixed upon stakes, and placed around the walls." Simeon.

This success saw Uchtred promoted by King Aethelred not just to his father's position in Northumbria but also to York where Aethelred had just had the incumbent Aelfhelm murdered and his sons blinded. To appease the normally hostile Danish Yorkshiremen Uchtred married Sige the daughter of a local nobleman, Styr. Part of the wedding contract was that Uchtred should kill Styr's rival Thurbrand. It was deal that Uchtred, unwisely, did not immediately implement. Aldhun, bishop of Durham, his former father-in-law, does not appear to be put out by this marriage, and sent his daughter, Uhtred's former wife, Ecgthryth south to marry another Yorkshireman. Styr made a grant of land, including Darlington to the bishop which no doubt smoothed the deal.

This did not end Uchtred's upward mobility, or his marriage alliances. Pleased by his performance in the North, King Aethelred gave him his own daughter, Aelfgifu, in marriage.Unfortunately, Uchtred's fate was now bound up with that of the king Aethelred.

The Danish army had temporarily moved to Normandy in 1000AD; Aethelred used the lull to ravage the Cumbrian possessions of Strathclyde. Then in 1002 AD, on St Brice's Day, the unlucky 13th of November, Aethelred, ignoring counsel, ordered the butchering of all Danes in his kingdom. The dead included Gunhill, the sister of Sven Forkbeard the terrifying Danish leader. This slaughter led to the revival of Danish raids of increasing intensity backed by royal Danish power from organized army camps in Denmark.

Viking camp at Trelleborg, Denmark.

In 1007AD the Danegeld was 30,000 pounds. Eadric Streona, the newly created Earl of Mercia was, like Uchtred, married to one of Aethelred's daughters. He encouraged the payment of the geld as he appears to have benefited from raising it. He also treacherously betrayed the English army on a number of occasions. The hopelessness of the situation is captured in the chronicle,

"AD 1010. When the King's army should have gone out to meet them as they went up, then went they home; and when they were in the east, then was the army detained in the west; and when they were in the south, then was the army in the north." ASC

Wulfstan's sermon continued;

"the English for a long time now have been entirely devoid of victories and too greatly disheartened, through God's anger; and the Viking shipmen so strong, by God's consent, that often in battle one puts to flight ten...we pay them off constantly and they mortify us daily; they ravage and they burn, rob and plunder and cart off to their ships...."

In 1012 the Danegeld was 48,000 pounds. In the same year the Archbishop of Cantebury, Aelfeah who refused a separate ransom for himself was murdered;

"AD 1012 Then took they the bishop, and led him to their hustings, and there they shamefully killed him. They overwhelmed him with bones and horns of oxen; and one of them smote him with an axe-iron on the skull, so that he sank downwards with the blow; and his holy blood fell upon the earth." ASC.

Viking hall reconstruction, Trelleborg, Denmark.

These defeats forced Aethelred to flee abroad to Normandy, his second wife Emma being the sister of Duke Richard of Normandy. Sven claimed the kingship. Sven's death in 1014AD allowed Aethelred to return to contest the throne with Sven's son Cnut. Aethelred was invited back "if he would rule better than before", a pious hope. Cnut, a youth, withdrew to consolidate his resources, he left behind the English hostages given to Sven, minus their hands, ears and noses.

Uchtred in return for the king's favours, supported Aethelred even after he had been overthrown, despite offers of bribes from the Danes,

> **"So long as king Aethelred lives, I will be faithful to him, for he is my lord and my wife's father, and the abundant honours and riches which are mine, I possess by his gift. I will never he a traitor to him."** Simeon.

His defiance echoed that of Bryhnoth at Maldon;

"He grasped the shield; he brandished the slender spear of ash.
He uttered words; angry and resolute, he gave him answer:
'Dost thou hear, seafarer, what this people say?
They will give you darts for tribute,
Poisonous spears and ancient swords,
Gear which will profit you naught in the fight.
Messenger of the seamen, take word back again,
Say to thy people far more hateful tidings,
That here stands a noble Earl with his troop who will defend this land,
The home of Aethelred, my prince, the people, and the ground.
The heathen shall fall in the battle.
It seems to me too shameful
That ye should embark with our tribute with impunity,
Now that ye have come thus far hither to our land.
Nor shall ye win treasure so lightly;

*Point and edge shall reconcile us first,
    Grim battle-play, ere we yield tribute."* Battle of Maldon Gordon.

When Edmund Ironside, Aethelred's son, whose mother was a Northumbrian, raised an army Uchtred joined him. Together they ravaged the lands of Eadric Streona, the treacherous Mercian leader. Cnut in reply ravaged Northumbria along the line of the Roman road, Watling Street. Uchtred hurried north to make his peace. He went to submit on a safe conduct, but as he entered the Hall, a curtain was drawn back and armed men fell on him and his followers. Uchtred was murdered and a large number of Northumbrians fell with him. The murderers were Cnut's men led by Thurbrand Hold, a Dane of York, the man Uchtred should have killed. For the moment the Danes of Yorkshire had prevailed over the Bamburgh English. The murder "set in motion the most remarkable private feud in English History", (Stenton). The convoluted bloodlines formed by Uchtred's numerous marriages were to bedevil Northumbrian politics for generations.

Meanwhile the death of king Aethelred on 23 April 1016 allowed for Edmund and Cnut to divide the country, but suspiciously Edmund died a few months later, some said murdered by Eadric (using a crossbow fitted into a lavatory.) Cnut became king. He had married the daughter of the murdered Aelfhelm of Northumbria, now he appointed Eric of Norway as Earl in York, the man who with Thorkell the Tall, had helped him to the throne. But Eric's hold over Bernicia seems to have been slight.

THE LOSS OF LOTHIAN.

More importantly for the North, Uchtred was succeeded by his brother Eadulf Cudel . "A lazy and cowardly fellow." In 1016AD or 1018AD at Carham on Tweed, the Scots, defeated him. They had seized prosperous Lothian, the northern portion of the old kingdom of Northumbria, and effectively established the border on the Tweed. This was a disaster for Northumbria, Bishop Aldhun died when he heard the news.

"a comet appeared for 30 nights to the people of Northumbria, a terrible presage of the calamity by which that province was about to be desolated. **For shortly afterwards, nearly the whole population, from the river Tees to the Tweed and their borders were cut off in a conflict in which they were engaged with a countless multitude of Scots.** *When the bishop heard of the miserable destruction of the people of St Cuthbert, he was smitten to the heart with deep grief, and he sighed forth these words, "It is my miserable lot to be reserved to see such days as these are, Have I lived so long only to the witness of such destruction of my people as the present? The land will never recover its original condition. O most Holy St Cuthbert if ever at any time I have done aught that was well pleasing in your sight, make me now, some return for the same, and let this be my reward, that since my people have fallen, I may not survive them." a few days afterwards he was seized with a sickness, and died."* Simeon

The loss of these prosperous lands was an economic body blow to the power of the Northumbrian English. It also left large numbers of Northumbrians under Scots rule, people whose language tied them to Bamburgh rather than Dunadd. The position of the border and the reopening of the thousand year war between Scots and Northumbrians would separate the Northumbrians for centuries to come.

Lothian

Map showing Lost Northumbrian lands, featuring the rivers Whiteadder, Tweed, Till, Glen, Teviot, Kale, Berwick, The Border, and Dere Street.

Place names on both sides of the present border show many similarities, and in a few cases are identical.

The Northumbrian settlement endings, of -ingtun, -ingham, -botl, and -wic, -ham and -worth are common in the lands North of the Tweed. Isolated examples even exist in Ayrshire and north of the Forth. (see Nicholaisen.). The border remained permeable for the next 300 years, and Northumbrian settlement continued until the reign of Edward I. The lasting legacy of the Northumbrians is the language which is now called Scots, but which was called Inglis as late as the 15th century. Many of the claims made for Scots as a distinctive language by McClure in "Why Scots Matters" could be made for Northumbrian. The uses of grammar, such as "I done it, I didn't went, he's got the flu, the kye has come hame," the particular use of "yous", are common in Northumbria. Words such as "bairn, bide, byre, bield, blate, greet," are in frequent use. Even the imported words from gaelic, "bog, lough" and Norwegian, "gars, lass, gowk, lowse, lowp, lug," are found in Northumbrian. If McClure can say " the Scots language is a mark of the distinctive identity of the Scottish people" and "it is a language spoken

189

nowhere else in the world." Northumbrians can feel justified in putting forward the claims of their own distinctive language themselves.

"In effect the people of the Merse were English in their language, customs, method of land cultivation and way of life." Barrow.

There follows a list of the place names of this region which show many English names.

The Whiteadder

North side	**South Side**
Lilliestead	Gainslaw
Cocklaw	Paxton
Edrington	Broadmeadow
Greenlaw	Hutton
Foulden	Allanton
Edington	Todheugh
Broadhaugh	Edrom
Chirnside	
Blanerne	
Cruxfield	
Preston	
Cockburn	

Place Names in North Northumbria (Lothian)

River Tweed

North side	**South Side**
Letham	East Ord
Fairney	Loan End
Lilliestead	Horncliffe
Gainslaw	Norham
Paxton	West Newbiggin
Spital	Groat haugh
Nabdean	Twizel
Fishwick	St Cuthberts
Horndean	Melkington
Ladykirk	Cramond
Upsettlington	Cornhill
Lennelhill	Learmouth
Oxenrig	Wark
Lennel	Gallows Hill
Coldstream	Carham
Birgham	Reddon
Edenmouth	Whitmuirhaugh
Ednam hill	Sprouston
Kelso	Mellendean
Galalaw	Roxburgh barns
Stodrig	Rutherford
Sucklawridge	Littleden

190

Makerstoun
Mertoun
Clinthill
Bemersyde
Leaderfoot

Maxton
St Boswells
Eildon

River Teviot

Roxburgh
Ormiston
Nisbet
Copland
Ancrum
Chesters
Cleuchead

Heiton
Sunlaws
Kalemouth
Eckford
Crailing
Bonjedward

The River Kale

Kalemouth
Easter Wooden
Marlefield
Whinnyhouse
Otterburn
Morebattle
Wether Hill
Harrow Law
Deanbraelaw
Chester house.

Grahams law
Caverton
Morebattle
Grubbitlaw
Hownam

River Till. English.

Castle Heaton

Shellacres
Heaton Mill
Fadden Hill
Duddo Hill
Tindal
Berry Hill
Etal
Lethamhillhaugh

Crookham
Sandyford
Haugh
Whitton Hill
Milfield
Thirling
Ewart

Heatherslaw
Ford
Kimmerston
Fenton

The coast

Berwick, Redheugh, Ewe ford ,Fernyness, Lamberton, Greenheugh, Hedderwick, Longniddry, Ayton, Cockburnspath, Tyningham, Seton, Chester hill, Dunglass, Pefferside, Cockenzie, Ross, Bilsdean, Seacliff, Prestonpans, Burnmouth, Branxton, Dirleton, Musselburgh, Netherbyres, Thornton,

Muirfield, Edinburgh Eyemouth, Innerwick, Gullane, Cramond, Acredale, Oxwell, Craigie law, Coldingham, Broxburn, Aberlady, St Abbs, Dunbar, Gosford.

At this critical time there was no help from the Danes either in York or London. Uchtred's sons then succeeded in Bamburgh; first, Ealdred son of Ecgythryth. He avenged his father by killing Thurbrand. This led to a feud with Thurbrand's son Carl, which lasted sometime until they settled their differences and arranged to go on pilgrimage to Rome together. After feasting together in Carl's hall, Carl murdered Ealdred, in a wood called Risewude in 1038 AD. Ealdred was succeeded by his half-brother, Sige's son, Eadulf, who carried on the rivalry with the Yorkshire Danes. Unfortunately this isolated position of the Northumbrians was an invitation to the Scots who invaded under King Duncan. Once again the Northumbrians held them at Durham, and Eadulf even carried the fight across the border to the lands of the Galwegians who accompanied the Scots. However, his isolated position was untenable and he went south on safe conduct to negotiate with Cnut's son King Hardacnut.
Unfortunately the son was no more reliable than the father and Eadulf was murdered by the latest Danish Earl of York, Siward in 1041.

Siward had been made Earl of all of Northumbria, despite the existence of Cospatric another of Uchtred's sons. Siward established himself in the North by invading and laying it waste, a tactic that was to be followed by others over the next 50 years. He tried to solve the problem of Danish-Northumbrian rivalry by marrying the daughter of Ealdred, Aelffleda; their son was named Waltheof after his great grandfather. But he imposed a non-northerner, Aethelric of Peterborough, as Bishop of Durham, contrary to the usual practice of the community choosing their own bishop. When the new bishop promoted his brother Aethelwine above them, the clerks rebelled and drove him out. Siward restored him to his position, but the resentment bubbled under the surface. Siward's hostility to the Community was at variance with the King's actions. Cnut had visited the shrine of St Cuthbert at Durham, acknowledging the power of the saint. He dismounted at Trimdon, where he had his hair cut and then, "He walked barefoot from as far as the place which is called Garmundsway, a distance of nearly five miles."

In 1034 the powerful Scots king Malcolm II died. He was succeeded by his grandson Duncan. This king Duncan was a young headstrong ruler, the opposite of the wise old Duncan as portrayed by Shakespeare in "Macbeth". He had led his army to a crushing defeat when he attacked Durham,

"for a large proportion of his cavalry was slain by the besieged, and when he was put to disorderly flight, in which he lost all his foot soldiers, whose heads were collected in the market place and hung up on posts." Simeon.

On his return home Macbeth killed Duncan at Pitgavery near Elgin. Duncan's sons fled south to seek protection from Cnut's Earl, Siward. The stage was set for Siward's intervention in Scotland, somewhat inaccurately portrayed by Shakespeare.

> **"Macbeth shall never vanquished be, until Great Birnham wood to high Dunsinane hill, Shall come against him."** Shakespeare. Macbeth. IV.I.

Macbeth had recruited Norman knights who had been evicted from England by the rising Godwin family, but he was defeated by Siward on 27th July 1052, and the Normans were butchered. (A proof to many that a Norman victory 14 years later was not inevitable).

Macbeth was later killed by the new king Malcolm III, nicknamed "Canmore" or big-head. (the term probably means big-chief, it is unlikely that anyone would dare to insult Canmore to his face.) Siward also conquered Cumbria, so reducing the threat from that border.

Cnut makes a gift.

Both Siward's elder son, Osbeorn, and his nephew Siward were killed in Scotland, leaving only the son of his Bamburgh marriage. However, Waltheof was too young to succeed when Siward died at York in 1055. His death was romanticised by 19th century artists who portray him fully armed sitting awaiting death. Actually he died cursing "the cow's disease" that was killing him. He was buried in the minister of St Olaf, York, which he had founded himself. The church was dedicated to Olaf the Norwegian king who forcibly converted his country to Christianity. Olaf had been killed by Cnut in 1030AD. Olaf, the Viking's saint, is usually portrayed with a halo and a five foot long battle axe. A potent symbol of the type of Christianity followed by the Scandinavians.

Cnut's death, had been followed by that of his sons Harold and Hardacnut. A scheming power in the land was Emma, Aethelred's widow, who became Cnut's second wife. She was Hardacnut's mother. However;

"AD 1042 This year died King Hardacnut at Lambeth as he stood drinking; he suddenly fell to earth with a tremendous struggle, and spoke not a word afterwards but expired on the sixth day before the Ides of June." Anglo-Saxon Chronicle.

Edward the Confessor, ("a holy simpleton", Maitland,) son of Aethelred and Emma became king, French-speaking, with a Norman mother and relatives he knew little of England. But the real power in the land was Godwin, Earl of Wessex and his family. When Siward died in 1055, Harold Godwinson, who succeeded as Earl of Wessex ensured that Northumbria went to his brother Tosti. His brother Gyrth was soon to be Earl of East Anglia, Leofwine Earl of Kent and Essex, and his sister was the Confessor's wife. The Godwins were the power in Anglo-Saxon England's final decade.

THE ENGLISH SUCCESSION

AETHELRED II, THE UNREADY. Died 1016AD. Married first, Aelfgifu, daughter of Thorold of Northumbria. Their offspring did not rule. Their son EDMUND IRONSIDES, was murdered 1016AD. His son Edward the Exile Died 1057AD. His children were EDGAR AETHLING and MARGARET who married MALCOLM CANMORE of Scotland.

Aethelred married second, Emma, daughter of Richard Duke of Normandy. Their son Edward the Confessor succeeded, his brother Alfred was killed by Earl Godwin 1035AD.

EDWARD THE CONFESSOR, married Edith (Eadgyth) daughter of Earl Godwin. Died 1066AD.

THE DANES

SWEYN King of Denmark and Norway, and England 1013AD. Died 1014AD. Succeeded in Denmark by his son Harold, who was supplanted by Cnut who also seized England in 1016AD.

Sweyn's daughter Thyra was the first wife of Godwin Earl of Wessex.

CNUT (CANUTE) was succeeded by two sons. He married first Aelgifu, their son was Harold I ,Harefoot. Cnut married second Emma, widow of King Aethelred , their son was Canute II (Hardicanute) . Cnut died 1035AD
HAROLD I, Died 1040 AD.
HARDICANUTE. Died 1042AD. He was succeeded by Edward the Confessor.

THE GODWINS
Godwin, Earl of Wessex, married first Thyra King Sweyn's daughter, and second Gytha a relative of Cnut. Godwin's daughter married King Edward the successor. His son was,
HAROLD II. Died 1066 AD.

The appointment of Tosti marked an attempt to end Northumbria's autonomy. He was soon involved in the long dispute over who had the power to appoint the bishop of Durham. The Bishop of Durham was a powerful and rich man, the monks valued their right to appoint their own candidate as they had done when they chose Edmund in 1020AD.The king tried to extend his influence into the north by making the appointment, as Hardacnut did when he sold the position to Bishop Eadred. Tosti now appointed Aethelwine to succeed his unpopular brother Aethelric who had retired south. The Durham community had accused Aethelric of theft. When he had ordered the rebuilding of the wooden church at Chester-le-Street in stone, ("because Saint Cuthbert's body had once rested there." Simeon.) workers on the site, inside the old Roman fort, stumbled upon a store of treasure. Aethelric was accused of moving this south to Peterborough. Despite a fine gift of Countess Judith's gospels to Durham, the Earl had alienated the powerful community. At Chester-le-Street there was also a cenotaph marking where the body had lain. It was seen by Leland in the 16th century.

Bishops of Durham.

Aldhun –1018.Father-in-law of Earl Uhtred. Established the community at Durham
vacant
Edmund 1020-1040
Eadred 1040.The last Northumbrian-born Bishop.
Aethelric 1041, restored 1056
Aethelwine 1056 deprived 1071.The last Anglo-Saxon-born Bishop.

Tosti also appointed a new Archbishop of York, Aldred, and together they went on pilgrimage to Rome.
The Scots under the ungrateful Malcolm III, Canmore, had already attacked Northumbria in 1058, but he had made a peace treaty with the

English, Malcolm and Tosti became sworn brothers. Tosti relied on this to keep the peace. He should not have done. Malcolm was a restless, ravaging raider, who lived and died in harness. Once Tosti left, he fell upon Northumbria, and was also able to retake Cumbria, which was to prove a useful base for later raids. Failure to defend the country against the Scots was a powerful indictment of the Earl.

Tosti's unpopularity with the local Northumbrians increased when he had his sister, Queen Edith, murder the last of Uchtred's sons, Cospatric, at King Edward's Christmas court. This followed his own treachery by murdering Cospatric's relatives and supporters, including his nephew Gamel and Ulf, while on safe conduct at York. He had wiped out the main Bamburgh claimant and his support.

Tosti's unpopularity also stemmed from his attempts to introduce new taxes contrary to Northumbrian custom. The North paid much lighter taxes than elsewhere and they were determined to maintain this privilege.

THE NORTHUMBRIAN REBELLION 1065 AD.

Northumbria rebelled, led by Gamelbearn, Dunstan and others, both Bernicia and York joined forces to declare Tosti outlawed, kill his supporters, and march into Tosti's Mercian territory to plunder. They demanded the laws of Cnut, which would maintain their tax privileges. They also demanded the right to name their own Earl. For once, sinking the differences between York and Bernicia, they chose Morcar, brother of Edwin of Mercia; calculating correctly but perhaps shortsightedly that the young man would be a mere figurehead and power would remain in the hands of the local aristocracy.

"all the Thanes of Yorkshire and Northumberland gathered themselves together at York, and outlawed their Earl Tosti, slaying all the men of his clan that they could reach, both Danish and English; and took all his weapons in York, with gold and silver." ASC 1065 AD.

The rising was encouraged and abetted by the Durham clerks led by Elfred, who produced the bones of King Oswine murdered in the 7th century as a talisman. These had been fortuitously discovered at Tynemouth.

"The northernmen did much damage round Northampton in that they killed people and burned houses and corn and took all the cattle that they could get at, which was many thousands, and captured many hundred people and took them north with them."
AS 1065AD

"averring that they were a people free born and freely educated and unable to tolerate the cruelty of any prince, that they had been taught by their ancestors either to be free or die." William of Malmesbury

King Edward and Harold Godwinson backed down and accepted the rebel's demands. The north had established its right to approval of its ruler. The choice of a Mercian Morcar overcame the endemic rivalry between Yorkshire and the North, in any case Morcar ruled through Osulf of Bamburgh, and Waltheof of York was compensated with Tosti's lands further south. Tosti fled to his wife's country, Flanders. After his death his widow married Welf of Bavaria and seems to have been the reason for a cult of Oswald being introduced there. Tosti however was to play a vital part in the defeat of both his brother, Harold, and England.

This successful defence of Northumbrian autonomy was important.

"At a time when they were challenging the whole authority of the crown in order to remove a hated Earl, the Northumbrians showed no desire to choose a separate king. It is the combination of strong provincial feeling with respect for the unity of England which makes their behaviour interesting." (Stenton. p.571.)

"it enshrines Northumbrian perspectives concerning the role of their province within England."

"They were not appointed Earls of Northumbria by the king of England: they succeeded by hereditary right. And they appear to have paid no tribute to the English King." Lomas.

Unfortunately the recognition of this autonomy was to be short lived, within ten weeks King Edward was dead. The fate of Northumbria was now bound up in the struggle for the crown between Harold Godwinson, Harald Hardrada and Duke William of Normandy. It was 1066 AD.

CHAPTER 11.

THE ARRIVAL OF THE NORMANS

Harold Godwinson was crowned king on the same day that Edward the Confessor was buried, 6 Jan.1066. The ceremony was conducted by Archbishop Ealdred of York, not Stigand as the Bayeux tapestry claims. Stigand was considered unlawful as his predecessor, Robert of Jumieges, was still alive. The tapestry was Norman propaganda casting doubts on the legality of Harold`s coronation. The unseemly haste could be justified when the threats to Harold's position are considered, they came from his own brother Tosti, ex-Earl of Northumbria, the King of Norway, Harald Hardrada, and William, the Duke of Normandy.

The disgruntled Tosti first launched an attack on the Isle of Wight and later on the Humber but was driven off.

"he went north into the Humber with 60 ships; whence he plundered Lindsey, and there slew many good men. When the Earls Edwin and Morcar understood that, they came hither and drove him from the land." ASC

Abandoned by his Flemish allies he then fell in with Harald Hardrada, King of Norway. Hardrada was one of the most terrifying vikings of his day, with vast expericnce in war against the Swedes, Danes and also in Russia. He had led the Byzantine Emperor`s famous Varangian guard. Now he ravaged down the coast of Northumbria and brought his 300 ships into the Humber.

THE BATTLE OF FULFORD GATE 1066 AD.

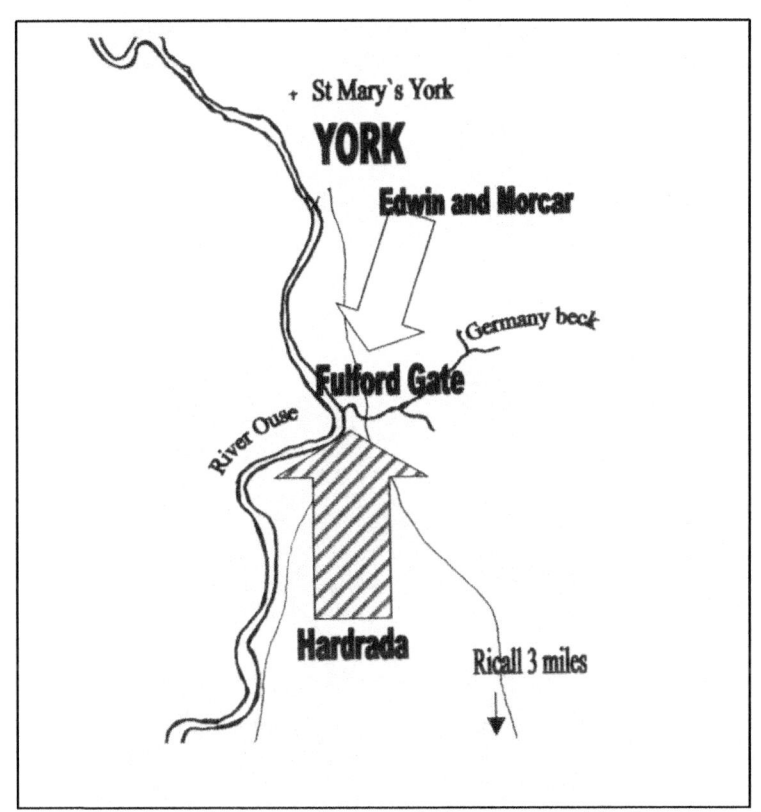

Edwin and Morcar drew up their army outside the gates of York at Fulford, on the 26th of Sep. 1066.AD . Hadrada's army drove them from the field. The population of York once more threw their support behind a Norse leader.

" the Earls Edwin and Morkar had gathered from their Earldoms as great a force as they could get, and fought with the enemy.' They made a great slaughter too; but there was a good number of the English people slain, and drowned, and put to flight: and the Northmen had possession of the field of battle. And this fight was on the eve of St. Matthew the apostle, which was Wednesday. Then after the fight went Harold, King of Norway, and Earl Tosty into York with as many followers as they thought fit; and having procured hostages and provisions from the city, they proceeded to their ships, and proclaimed full friendship, on condition that all would go southward with them, and gain this land." ASC

Charles Jones places the site of the battle at Fulford Gate, the Northumbrian and Mercians were drawn up along the Germany Beck protected by marshy ground and the beck itself. The fact that they chose not to defend York itself suggests they may have doubted the loyalty of its inhabitants.

"Thereafter the king (Hardrada) sailed to the Humber, and up along the river, and then he landed. Up in Jorvik were two Earls, Earl Morukare, and his brother, Earl Valthiof, and they had an immense army. While the army of the Earls was coming down from the upper part of the country, King Harald lay in the Usa (Ouse)".

The proposed site of the Battle of Fulford, the Germany Beck.

"King Harald now went on the land, and drew up his men. The one arm of this line stood at the outer edge of the river, the other turned up towards the land along a ditch; and there was also a morass, deep, broad, and full of water. The Earls let their army proceed slowly down along the ditch, with all their troops in line. The king's banner was next the river, where the line was thickest .It was thinnest at the ditch, where also the weakest of the men were. When the Earls advanced downwards along the ditch, the arm of the Northmen's line which was at the ditch gave way; and the Englishmen followed, thinking the Northmen would fly. The banner of Earl Morukare advanced then bravely."

"When King Harald saw that the English array had come to the ditch against him, he ordered the charge to be sounded, and urged on his men. He ordered the banner which was called the Land-ravager to be carried before him, and made so severe an assault that all had to give way before it; and there was a great loss among the men of the Earls, and they soon broke into flight, some running up the river, some down, and the most leaping into the ditch, which was so filled with dead that the Norsemen could go dry-foot over the fen. There Earl Morukare fell. Earl Valthiof, and the people who escaped, fled up to the castle of York; and there the greatest loss of men had been. This battle took place upon the Wednesday next Mathias."

"After the battle now told of, all people in the nearest districts submitted to Harald, but some fled. Then the king advanced to take the castle, and laid his army at Stanforda-bryggiur ; and as King Harald had gained so great a victory against so great chiefs and so great an army, the people were dismayed, and doubted if they could make any opposition. The men of the castle therefore determined, in a council, to send a message to King Harald, and deliver up the castle into his power." Snorri Sturlson.

This account has topographical details which fit the site. However he says Waltheof was Morcar's brother, and that Morcar was killed. Edwin was Morcar's brother and both survived. Waltheof's presence was noted by another Scandinavian source,

> *"Earl Valthiof's men*
> *Lay in the fen,*
> *By sword down hewed,*
> *So thickly strewed,*
> *That Norsemen say*
> *They paved the way*
> *Across the fen*
> *For the brave Norsemen"* "Harald's stave"

Harold Godwinson was hurrying North to aid his brothers-in-law. (He had married Edith, their sister, and repudiated his long time mistress Edith Swan neck.) He caught the Norwegians on the 25th of September at Stamford Bridge.

The Battle of Stamford Bridge

"Now the battle began. The Englishmen made a hot assault upon the Northmen, who sustained it bravely. It was no easy matter for the English to ride against the Northmen on account of their missiles; and so they rode in a circle around them. And the fight at first was but loose and light, as long as the Northmen kept their order of battle; for although the English rode hard against the Northmen, they gave way again immediately, as they could do nothing against them. Now when the northmen thought they perceived that the enemy were making but weak assaults, they set after them, and would drive them into flight; but when they had broken their shield rampart the Englishmen rode up from all sides, and threw arrows and spears at them. Now when king Harald Sigurdson saw this, he went into the fray where the greatest crash of weapons was; and there was a sharp conflict, in which many people fell on both sides. King Harald then was in a rage, and ran out in front of the array, and hewed down with both hands; so that neither helmet or armour could with stand him ,and all who were nearest gave way before him. It was then very near with the English that they had taken flight."

"King Harald Sigurdson was hit by an arrow in the windpipe, and that was his death wound. He fell, and all who had advanced with him, except those who retired with the banner. There was afterwards the warmest conflict, and Earl Toste had taken charge of the king's banner.

Then Eystein got King Harald's banner Landravager, and now was for the third time, one of the sharpest conflicts, in which many Englishmen fell, and they were near to taking flight. This conflict is called Orre's storm. Eystein and his men had hastened so fast from the ships that they were quite exhausted, and scarcely able to fight before they came into battle; but afterwards they became so furious, that they did not guard themselves with their shields so long as they could stand upright. At last they threw off their coats of ring mail, and then the Englishmen could easily lay their blows at them; and many fell from weariness, and died without a wound. Thus fell almost all the chief men among the Norway People". Snorri Sturlson, Heimskringla.

This account of the critical battle of Stamford Bridge is again from a later Scandinavian source. The battle bears some startling similarities to the later battle at Hastings with which Snorri may have confused it. Here it is the Northmen who hold the shield wall against the mounted English and their arrows. It is the Northmen who break ranks when they think the English are weakening. It is the Norwegian King who is killed by an arrow, and whose army is eventually destroyed. This all suggests that Snorri's poetry was more impressive than his history. All of these events were to be replayed 19 days later at Senlac Hill, Hastings, only at this time the English were defending with the shield wall and the Normans launching mounted attacks assisted by archers.

The Anglo-Saxon Chronicle account is the one that has been handed down as nearer the truth, it calls the Norwegians, Normans:

"There was slain Harold the Fair-hair'd, King of Norway and Earl Tosty, and a multitude of people with them, both Normans and English; and the Normans that were left fled from the English, who slew them hotly behind; until some came to their ships, some were drowned, some burned to death, and thus variously destroyed, so that there was little left: and the English gained possession of the field. But there was one of the Norwegians who withstood the English folk, so they could not pass over the bridge, nor complete the victory. An Englishman aimed at him with a javelin, but it availed nothing. Then came another under the bridge, who pierced him terribly inwards under the coat of mail. Then Harold, king of the English, then came over the bridge, followed by his army; and there they made great slaughter, both of the Norwegians and of the Flemings."

This was a tremendous victory for the English and says a lot for Harold Godwinson's generalship, but it was all to be thrown away. Harold rushed south from Stamford Bridge to meet the threat from William of Normandy. He ignored pleas to regroup at London and pressed on towards Hastings provoked by William's calculated ravaging of Harold's own people of Wessex.

By the end of the day Harold, his brothers and his house carles were dead, as was the English monarchy. **"*From the third hour of daylight right until the dusk of nightfall King Harold resisted his enemies with the utmost*** *bravery..he himself fell-alas-at dusk, and with him the more noble of the men of all England."* Liber Eliensis.

William the Bastard, became William the Conqueror. Although the Witan recognized the young Aethling, Edgar, grandson of Edmund Ironside as king, the nobility including Edwin and Morcar recognized William. The Archbishop of York, Ealdred, crowned him on Christmas Day. *"this was the first of the Normans to rule England-of those, I mean, who were Norman on both sides of their family-and brought up in Normandy."* Liber Eliensis. The writer knew well that Edward the Confessor was more Norman than English.

THE BATTLE FOR NORTHUMBRIA

An English axeman. BT

William's first dealings with the North show either an ignorance or a disdain for the sensibilities of the locals. William appointed Copsi as Earl of Northumbria in Feb 1067. He was Tosti's lieutenant, this was the man who had imposed Tosti's rule in the North, then raided the coastline with Tosti and Hardrada. The Northumbrians beheaded him in March. The Northumbrians believing that assassination was the most persuasive form of criticism, surprised him at a banquet at Newburn. He fled into the church, which was set alight, and Osulf of Bamburgh, hacked off his head when he emerged. Again it appears that an underlying cause of opposition was William's attempt to raise taxes from the North. Osulf did not live long to enjoy his victory, he was killed by a robber towards the end of the year.

William then sold the Earldom to Cospatric, grandson of Uhtred and Aelfgifu, Aethelred the Unready's daughter.

The Earls of Northumbria. 1000-1100 AD.
Waltheof.
Uhtred Earl of York and Northumberland.1006-16 murdered by Thurbrand of York on King Cnut's orders.
Eadulf Cudel, his brother, defeated at Carham 1018,lost Lothian.
Ealdred, son of Uhtred, killed Thurbrand. Murdered by Carl, son of Thurbrand. 1038.
Eadulf, son of Uhtred, 1033-55.Murdered by Siward Earl of York, on orders of Hardacnut, 1041.AD
<u>Siward</u> of York, Earl of Northumberland 1041-1055,marry daughter of Ealdred.
Tosti Godwinson. Earl l055-65.With Queen Edith murder Cospatric son of Uhtred .Removed by
rebellion.
Morcar of Mercia chosen by Northumbrian nobles, ruled through Osulf, son of Eadulf.
Copsi, lieutenant of Tosti, appointed by William I, murdered at Newburn by Osulf.1067.Osulf
killed by bandits.
Cospatric grandson of Uhtred buy the Earldom.1068-72.Cospatric rebelled. Became Earl of Dunbar.
Waltheof ,son of Siward, grandson of Ealdred. Appointed by William I. 1072AD. He murdered the sons of Carl. Rebelled. Executed by William 1075.
Walcher Bishop of Durham buys the Earldom.1075.His relatives murdered Ligulf, Ealdred's son in-law 1080.Walcher was murdered by Eadulf Rus. Uhtred's grandson.
Aubrey de Coucy appointed by William I. Resigned.
Robert Mowbray appointed. Rebelled against William II. Imprisoned for 30 years.
William II, Rufus, ruled Northumberland through sheriffs.
 Key. **Northumbrian**. <u>Danish</u>. *Anglo-Saxon,* **French.**

The Northumbrian Rising
William's demands for increased taxes in 1068 caused both Northumbria and Mercia to rise up. This was a dangerous rising against the Normans. It was led by Edgar the Atheling, the Saxon claimant to the throne, the Earls Edwin and Morcar, Cospatric and Arkill the Thane. This time the rising failed as the Normans threw up castles in Mercia, and the Northumbrian leaders fled north to Canmore's Scotland where they witnessed his marriage to Margaret the

Atheling's sister. The ambitious Scottish king was now allied to the main claimant of the English throne.

William also built a castle at York then returned south. He then sent Robert Commines, north as Earl to subdue the land north of the Tees. The Earl was warned by the Bishop Aethelwine of plots against him but,
"He was one of those persons who paid the wages of their followers by licensing their ravagings and murders, and he had already killed many rustics of the church. So the Earl entered Durham with 700 men, and they treated the householders as if they had been enemies. Very early in the morning, the Northumbrians having collected themselves together, broke in through all the gates, and running through the city, hither and thither they slew the Earl's associates. So great at last was the multitude of the slain that the very street was covered with blood and filled with dead bodies." Simeon.

Normans

The failure of a Norman counter attack, attributed to a mist sent by St Cuthbert, encouraged the rebels, as did the arrival of Edgar Aetheling. Robert Fitz Richard was caught and killed outside York, and the Northerners laid siege to the castle with a force which included the ancient enemies Cospatric and the sons of Carl. However William came north once more, defeated the rebels and sacked York. This time he left two castles and a bigger garrison. In September Sweyn of Denmark arrived in the Humber with 240 ships and joined with Edgar, Waltheof and Cospatric, so combining most of the claimants to Northumbria, as well as two claimants, Edgar and Sweyn to the throne of England.

"A council was now held of the chiefs of both people, at which universal complaints were made of the outrages and tyranny to which the English were exposed from the Normans and their adherents, and messages were dispatched to all parts of Britain to arouse the natives against their enemies. All joined in a firm league and bold conspiracy for the recovery of their ancient liberties, and the rebellion broke out with great violence in the provinces beyond the Humber. The insurgents fortified themselves in the woods and marshes, and near the estuaries of the tidal rivers, and some also in the towns. York was in a state of utmost excitement, which the Archbishop in vain attempted to allay. Many of the citizens lived in tents, disdaining the shelter of houses, as tending to enervate them, and these the Normans stigmatized as savages."

The Normans in York tried to protect themselves by burning the houses around their castles but lost control of the blaze and succeeded in burning down the city including St Peter's church. They were killed or made prisoner. Waltheof was at the forefront of the attack;

"The warrior caused a hundred of the king`s retainers to burn in the heat of the fire:
that was a night of burning for the men.
It is told that the warriors had to lie beneath the wolf's claws;
By death spear food was got for the dusky wolf.
It is certain that William, the reddener of weapons,
He who clove foamy sea from the south, has kept bad faith with valiant Waltheof.
Truly it will be long before slaying of men ceases in England.
But my lord was gallant.
No more famous chief than he shall die in England." Thorkell son of Thord. Skalli. In AA 1952

However the Danes could not hold the burnt town and were grateful to be allowed to withdraw in front of the furious Conqueror. William could therefore deal with the rebellious Northumbrians at his leisure

"When the news was brought to William, (the destruction of York and massacre of 3,000 Normans by the Danes.) he assembled an army and hastened into Northumberland where he spent the whole winter laying waste the country, slaughtering the inhabitants, and inflicting on them, without intermission, every sort of evil. Meanwhile he sent envoys to Osborn, promising to pay him secretly a large sum of money, besides giving him free leave to plunder the whole coast throughout the winter provided he would abandon his enterprise and return home in the spring. This proposal to his utter disgrace, he accepted. In consequence of the ravages of the Normans, so severe a famine prevailed throughout the kingdom, but chiefly in Northumberland and the adjacent provinces, that men were driven to feed on the carcasses of horses, dogs and cats, and even on human flesh. Ordericus Vitalis.

This was the systematic destruction of the north. **The Harrying of the North** would also make it less attractive to Danish settlement. (Musgrove.) Yorkshire bore the brunt of the Norman's fury, but Durham was not spared, William himself led an army through Durham, but does not seem to have gone further north than the Tyne.(despite the above comments of the chronicler, who seems to confuse Northumberland and Northumbria.) The community once more fled with St Cuthbert's body to Lindisfarne, via Jarrow, Bedlington and Tughall, it took them five days. They returned in March 1070 AD.

"It was dreadful to behold human corpses, rotting in the houses, streets and highways, reeking with putrefaction, swarming with worms, and contaminating the air with daily exhalations; for all the people being cut off by the sword or by famine, there was none left to bury them. For nine years was the land, deprived of its cultivators, a dreary waste. Between York and Durham there was not one inhabited town or village; dens of wild beasts, and the haunts of robbers were alone to be seen." Florence of Worcester.

"Thus were the resources of a once flourishing provinces cut off by fire, slaughter and devastation, and the ground for more than sixty miles, (about the distance from York to Durham) totally uncultivated and unproductive, remains bare to this day." William of Malmesbury.

"I fell on the English in the northern counties like a raging lion. I commanded their houses and their barns, with all their corn, their implements, and their furniture, to be burnt without distinction, and their horses and cattle to be destroyed wherever they were found. Thus did I wreak my vengeance on multitudes of both sexes by subjecting them to the horrors of cruel famine." William I, in Ordericus Vitalis.

Normans attacking a town, (with God on their side.)

Despite all that had happened William reinstated Cospatric as Earl. William was not of an unduly forgiving nature, so this suggests that he was unable at this time to control the lands north of the Tees without local cooperation. Cospatric's problem was that the devastation of Yorkshire and parts of Durham meant that he had fewer resources and less chance of support in the event of an attack from Scotland. In 1070 AD Canmore once more invaded, this time from Cumbria with an army including undisciplined Galwegians,

"On five occasions Canmore had afflicted Northumberland with dreadful ravages and carried off its wretched inhabitants into slavery."

"Amidst these pillagings and depredations of the Scots, Earl Gospatric who had obtained the Earldom of Northumbria from William for money made a furious plundering attack on Cumberland, for Cumberland was at that time under the dominion of King Malcolm, not held by right, but subjugated by force. Having heard what Gospatric had committed against his people, scarcely able to contain his fury, he ordered his troops no longer to

209

spare any of the English nation, but either to smite all to the earth, or to carry them off captives under the yoke of perpetual slavery. It was misery even to witness the deeds against the English. Some aged men and women were beheaded with the sword; others were thrust through with pikes, like swine destined for food, infants snatched from their mothers breasts were thrown high into the air, and in their fall were received on the points of lances and pikes placed in the ground. The Scots, more savage than wild animals, delighted in this cruelty, as an amusing spectacle. Young men also and maidens, and whosoever seemed fit for toil and labour, were bound and driven before the face of their enemies. Some of these females, worn out by running in front of their drivers further than their strength would bear, falling to the earth, perished even where they fell." Simeon of Durham.

The invasion by Canmore and his brother-in-law Edgar reached Wearmouth where they burned St Peter's Church.

William meanwhile, had to deal with the rising in the Isle of Ely led by Hereward the Wake, which some of the Northumbrian rebels including Siward Barn supported.

> **"Wulf is on an island, I on another.**
> **Fen fast is that island,**
> **Cruel men defend it."**   Wulf and Eadwacer.

Morcar was also amongst the rebels, but his brother Edwin had been slain by his own men. The Worcester chronicle says because he was trying to do a deal with Canmore. A plausible explanation. Hereward had seized the arm of Saint Oswald from Peterborough where his uncle Brand had been Abbot. (The previous abbot had died at Hastings, which raises the possibility that Oswald's arm was taken to that battle). More spiritual assistance came from the Ely community of St Aethelthryth (the wife of Ecgfrith of Northumbria). Also among the rebels, though perhaps unwillingly, was Aethelwine Bishop of Durham who had abandoned his bishopric,

" seeing the affairs of the English in turmoil on every side and fearing the severe lordship of a foreign people whose language and customs he did not know, he decided to give up his bishopric and provide for himself wherever he could as a stranger." HRA

He headed for Germany but ended up in Scotland and then Ely with Siward Barn, perhaps he was trying to join his brother Aelric. Neither had been too popular in the North as outsiders and plunderers of St Cuthbert's shrine, but Aethelwine's capture and subsequent death allowed William to bring his own man to the Bishopric.

The Ely rising was put down, William then launched a combined naval and land attack on Scotland which he no doubt saw as the source of the trouble. He gained Canmore's submission, and perhaps his vassalage, and the expulsion of the rebels. He also replaced Cospatric with Waltheof, son of Earl Siward. Cospatric was compensated by Malcolm who gave him lands in Lothian and Allerdale in Cumberland. His son Dolphin was described as ruler of Carlisle until driven out by William Rufus in 1092.Cospatric's line were to become Earls of Dunbar and the most powerful men in Scotland.

An English Housecarle, BT.

THE LAST ENGLISH EARL OF NORTHUMBRIA

Waltheof, the new Earl, was also a grandson of Uchtred, son of Siward and more importantly married to the Conqueror's half-sister, Judith. However he had also played an important point in the rising at York;

"His arms were muscular, his chest brawny, his whole person tall and robust, resembling in this his father Siward. He had slain many of the Normans with his own hand during the conflict at York, striking off their heads one after another as they entered the gate." Simeon.

Waltheof proved unreliable. He apparently opposed Williams attempt at raising taxes in 1074AD. He had also moved against the offspring of Carl, who had killed his grandfather Ealdred, and had them murdered at a Banquet. So ending the feud that had run on since the murder of Uchtred in 1014AD. Then he became involved with a rebellion when Roger, Earl of Hereford, and Ralph FitzOsbern, Earl of East Anglia, plotted against William. Waltheof's part was unclear, he had attended a wedding between the Earls families and became aware of the plot.

"there was that bride-ale
The source of man's bale." ASC 1075

Waltheof informed the Archbishop of Cantebury of the plot who in turn advised him to inform the King. Waltheof submitted , no doubt expecting clemency, he was to be quickly disillusioned. William had him imprisoned. Expected assistance from the Danes came too late, and the rebellion was defeated in detail. The Norman penalty for treason was life imprisonment, the English penalty was death. Waltheof was executed in 1075. It is said that his wife`s evidence counted against him.

After his death a cult grew up at Crowland Abbey where he was buried and where his relative and namesake was Abbot. Different versions of his death were given.

"Later Waltheof went to the king's presence; he had already obtained the king's peace for himself; two knights rode with him. King William received him well and at parting granted him an Earldom in Northumberland over which he had been Earl previously. When the Earl had received writ and seafaring he went away and came to a certain moor. There twelve fully armed knights with many attendants came against him; these knights king William had sent after him to have him killed. The Earl leapt from his horse, as he had no armour; he drew his sword and defended himself for a while. But because many men turned on him the Earl was captured and one of the knights prepared to kill him. And when the Earl knew which one was going to kill him, he fully surrendered to that knight and thus to the king and to all the others who had come after him. And as a remembrance he gave his silk kirtle to knight who was about to kill him. Then he lay down on the ground and crossed himself, stretching out both his arms, and then his neck was severed. And many men are healed through his blood; Waltheof is a true saint."

The second version shows the Earl as less robust:

"Waltheof. It is said, was led to the spot early in the morning, before the citizens awoke, for fear that they would try to prevent his death. There the Earl distributed his clothes to the poor and the clergy. Then lying on the ground began to weep and pray. The executioners, growing impatient and fearing the people, begged him to rise and let them finish the king's work.

"Wait a little while." He said, "so that I may say the Lord's Prayer myself and for you." This was granted but so great was emotion that his tears prevented his proceeding beyond "Lead us not into temptation "... and the executioner, growing impatient, drew his sword and cut off his head. And then, goes the story, in the hearing of all, the head, in a clear voice, finished the prayer, "But deliver us from evil. Amen."
The men and Yeomen of Winchester, when they heard the news, set up a great lamentation for the fallen Earl." AA 1952.

So on 31st of May, the mass day of St Petronilla,1076 AD, on St Giles Hill, Winchester, died Waltheof, the last English Earl of Northumbria, and the last Englishman in a position of power in the land.

NORMAN CONTROL OF THE CHURCH

William tried to control Northumbria through the church. He had ensured that the new Norman bishop of York, Thomas of Bayeux, admitted the primacy of Lanfranc at Cantebury, so reducing the powers of the North, and as Lanfranc pointed out lessening the chance of a claimant to the throne gaining credibility by being crowned in the North. He had also appointed a Lotharingian (from Lorraine) Walcher to Durham. In 1072 he and Earl Waltheof had built a castle for Walcher at Durham, so moving the Norman presence north to the Wear. William himself visited the shrine of St Cuthbert and left gifts there as his Danish and Anglo-Saxon predecessors had done. According to Simeon, William, in Conqueror mode, demanded to see the body of the saint, but was struck down and fled Durham and the Patrimony on horseback. On the death of Waltheof William sold the Earldom to Walcher, so uniting the offices of Earl and Bishop.

Again the Northumbrians showed their distaste for foreigners imposed upon them. Walcher had failed to defend Northumberland during a 3 week raid by Canmore in 1079.Failure to defend Northumbria from the Scot had already cost Tosti his Earldom. Walcher seems also to have increased the burdens on peasants on his lands. His men also were accused of highhanded and brutal treatment of the locals including theft and murder. Opposition was expressed by Ligulf one of his own advisers. Ligulf's wife, Ealdgyth, was a daughter of Earl Ealdred, so he was linked to the Bamburgh line, so Walcher had been trying to rule with some local approval which he had now lost.

"Of a truth, he was a man worthily beloved by all for the honesty of his life and the sobriety and gentleness of his disposition; but yet he displeased the natives by permitting his followers unrestrainedly to do whatever they pleased, nor did he curb them when they even acted wrongfully. And further his archdeacon swept away from the church many of its ornaments and much of its money, and distributed them amongst his own friends and relations. And again his soldiers carried themselves with excessive insolence towards the people, frequently plundering them by force, and they even killed some of the more influential of them." Simeon.

Simeon does not condemn Walcher outright because he saw him as responsible for encouraging the return of Monks to Jarrow/Wearmouth.

However it is plain that he was presiding over the dispossession and murder of the native Northumbrian aristocracy.

Matters came to a head with the night-time murder of Ligulf and his household. The murderers were Gilebert, the Bishop`s relative, and Leobwine, Walcher's chaplain. Walcher tried to defuse the situation by meeting the Northumbrians at the traditional spot in Gateshead. It is suggested that Bottle bank in Gateshead opposite St Mary's church was the site of a lord's hall or botl. (Barrow in Aird.97n)

St. Mary's church ,Gateshead, scene of the last stand of the English.

The enraged Northumbrians cornered the accused along with Walcher in St Mary's church . Gilebert was surrendered to placate the mob and quickly executed. The church was then fired, and the Bishop and his chaplain along with 100 Frenchmen were killed by the English chanting, "Short rede is good rede." (Quick counsel is good counsel).The Northumbrians were led by Eadulf Rus the grandson of Uchtred.

"The bishop and his retainers assembled at a place called Gateshead, where all the elders, and a very large concourse of the people who dwell beyond the Tyne, had met together. In order to avoid the crowd the bishop entered the little church, where he summoned the chief men among the people to him. Shortly after this, the riotous crowd raised a shout, and then all on a sudden the work of death was begun, without the least regard being paid to humanity. Some of the bishops soldiers, entirely unsuspicious of evil, sitting or reclining apart from each other, were quickly surrounded and killed, others coming up set fire to the church, others with drawn swords and brandished spears, stood at the door in knots, and suffered none to go out

alive: for those who were within, being unable any longer to endure the violence of the flames, having humbly confessed their sins and received the bishops benediction before going out, were immediately put to death while they were in the act of crossing the threshold." Simeon.

The English flee. BT
The monks of Jarrow rowed up the river and after finding the corpse of the bishop transported it back to Durham. An attempt by the Northumbrians to capture the castle at Durham was abandoned after three days.

Retribution was to be swift, violent, and for English Northumbria all but final. William sent North his half-brother Odo, Bishop of Bayeux. He in accordance with the rule that clerics should not shed blood, went into battle armed with a large club. Odo harried and murdered his way through Northumberland. Most of the Northumbrian nobility was killed.

> *"they reduced nearly the whole land to a wilderness. The miserable inhabitants who, trusting their innocence, had remained in their homes, were either beheaded as criminals, or mutilated by the loss of some of their members. False accusations were brought against them, in order that they might purchase their safety and their life by money."* Simeon

"Desolate through the ancient devastation of the Danes or the more recent of the Normans presents but little to allure the mind." William of Malmesbury on The North.

The extent of the waste created by the Conqueror in Yorkshire can be gauged by reference to the entries in Domesday book; the impact on Durham and Northumberland is more difficult to assess as they do not appear in that survey. However parts of Durham seem to have been devastated when the Conqueror crossed the Tees, after the 1069 rising. He entered Durham and destroyed Jarrow. He then progressed towards Hexham and then returned south, probably by the Roman road through Ebchester and Lanchester. There is little evidence for waste by William north of the Tyne at that time, but activities by the Scots may have been as devastating. Odo`s raid carried Norman tactics across the Tyne. The Normans killed and drove out the peasants in the areas they harried and refugees are recorded far to the south in Evesham. Crops would be burnt, seed corn destroyed, ploughs destroyed and animals killed or driven off. The legacy of the Normans was a deliberately induced famine, the people starved or fled. Canmore's raids carried many off into slavery, possibly since there was little else left to steal but the peasants themselves.

After Odo's raid, a Norman Aubrey de Coucy, was made Earl. In 1080 after an
incursion into Scotland William's eldest son, Robert ,built a New-castle on the North side of the Tyne, in the area of the old Roman fort. The Norman presence had moved up to Newcastle-upon-Tyne.

The end of the community of St Cuthbert.

Important ecclesiastical changes, which were to diminish Northumbrian particularism, also were taking place at the time. Under Bishop Walcher monks had returned to Durham:

> "Not long after this, certain meek-spirited monks, belonging to the southern part of England, having been admonished from heaven that they should go upon a pilgrimage for God's service into the province of Northumberland, came to Bishop Walcher, and entreated him that he would assign them a place to reside. He dispatched them to Jarrow and Wearmouth, which had formerly been the habitations of holy men. Having rebuilt the ancient dwellings of the saints, several persons profited so far by their life and example, that renouncing the world, they attached themselves to the originators of this design." Symeon.

Aldwin, Prior of Winchcombe in Gloucester and Aelfwig a priest of Evesham sought to follow a simple monastic life in the ruins of the ancient English monasteries of Northumbria. Reinfrid a Norman knight in the service of William de Percy joined them; he had been converted to a more Christian life when viewing the ruins of Whitby. They were settled firstly at Monkchester (Newcastle) by Earl Waltheof. The fact that Waltheof supported them by placing his nephew Morcar in their care and offering them land at Tynemouth may have led Walcher to see the monks as supporters of English Northumbrian identity. Walcher's sponsorship of the monks then may not have been disinterested. Newcastle was in the territory of the Earl of Northumberland. Walcher offered them the Church at Jarrow which placed them under the Bishop's jurisdiction. Jarrow certainly had a greater cachet, as home to Aldwin's hero, Bede; but it was in ruins following William's raids of 1069-70AD.Aldwin and a follower, Turgot, soon moved on to the site of Melrose. But Walcher threatened them with excommunication if they did not return. Persecution by Malcolm Canmore hurried their reluctant return. Reinfrid moved to his beloved Whitby and later part of his community moved on to York, St Mary's. It appears that the founders of the English Northumbrian monastic revival were seeking the simple life of Cuthbert and

Bede and were keen to avoid the control of the Norman Bishops. If so they were to be disappointed

William de St Calais now became Bishop of Durham. Unlike Walcher, he was a monk, Abbot of Saint-Vincent at Le Mans. He had links with Odo's Bayeux, and had been a monk at St Calais in Maine, as had his father. He was a skillful politician who had thrived in the turbulent Norman-Angevin borderlands. This may have prompted William to send him to Durham. Bishop William was responsible for the destruction of the community of St Cuthbert and their replacement with Benedictine monks.23 monks were brought from Jarrow to Durham, many appear to have been local Northumbrian recruits.

The first Monks of Durham.

Aldwin, Elfwy, Willelmus, Leofwin, Wulmar, Turgot, Edwin, Turkill, Columbanus, Elfwin, Godwin, Elmar, Helias, Swartebrand, Gamel, Godwin, Wiking, Godwin, Egelric, Seulfus, Gregorius, Edmund, Rotbert. Aird.137n.

In 1083 the remnants of the community minus their saint were moved to Darlington.

> "and as for those individuals who had hitherto resided therein,(canons by name, but men who in no one respect followed the canonical rule,) them he commanded henceforth to lead a monastic life along with the monks ,if they had any wish to continue their residence within the church. All of them preferred abandoning the church to retaining it upon such a condition, except one of their number, the dean, whose son, a monk, had difficulty in persuading him to follow his own example." Simeon

One of the Community, Eilaf, moved to Hexham where he set up a house for canons which he passed on to his son. Another descendant, Ailred, was to become a famous abbot of Rievaulx. (see volume 2.) The absorption and dispersal of the community meant that the native families lost control over the lands of the Patrimony of St Cuthbert, these lands now fell under the control of the Bishop and the Prior of Durham.

The Durham Benedictines who replaced the secular clergy of the Community of St Cuthbert encouraged the idea of Cuthbert's misogyny, possibly to justify their replacement of the married clergy. Women were excluded from the cathedral until the building of the Galilee chapel, this despite the fact that the first miracle at Durham had been the curing of a Scots woman, and Cuthbert himself was often in the company of women. Otherwise the monks stressed their continuity with the past.

Bishop William also began the building of the great stone Cathedral at Durham. This was to replace the Anglo-Saxon cathedral which itself was fairly new. The first stones were laid by the bishop, Prior Turgot and (some chronicles claim) Malcolm Canmore on 11 August 1093.It was ready to receive the body of St Cuthbert in 1104.Ever the opportunist, when Aubrey gave up his Earldom in frustration, the Bishop, already abbot of Durham as well, bought it from the King. William of St Calais, Bishop, Abbot and Earl has been seen as one of the organisers of the Domesday Book, William`s inventory of his possessions. Certainly his value as an administrator kept him away from Durham for long periods. This allowed Prior and Archdeacon Turgot to exercise power.

WILLIAM II, RUFUS, AND THE END OF NORTHUMBRIA

In 1087 William I died leaving a disputed succession between his sons. Rufus became king of England, and his elder brother Robert, Duke of Normandy. The youngest, Henry, the only son of a king, since the others were born before l066, gained the least.

Within a year of taking the throne William Rufus was at war with his brother Robert, his uncle Odo, and the Bishop of Durham. Rufus displaying the energy of his father came North to dealt with the rebellion. He invested Durham and forced the Bishop into exile for 3 years.

Rufus carried on his father`s policy of blocking the Pennine passes with castles. He ringed Cumbria in the south provoking Malcolm Canmore to attack, which he duly did in 1091 reaching as far as Durham before withdrawing in the face of Rufus' advance.

Rufus then conquered Cumbria, driving out Dolphin and brought north English peasants from the south to colonise it. They were to be protected by the new castle at Carlisle. This move also protected Northumbria's flank. This was a blow to the Scots king who claimed the area and led to Canmore's last invasion in 1093.

He was surprised at Alnwick on St Brice's day by Earl Robert Mowbray's men and killed by Arkle Morel, who was described as Malcolm's "gesith, or companion". The Arkles were amongst those families who had fled to Scotland in the face of the Conqueror. The story goes that Arkle Morel was pretending to betray the castle and was offering the keys to Canmore on a spear when he ran him through, considering Arkle Morels later history this treachery seems quite likely. Canmore`s eldest son Edward was also wounded but died three days later at Edward's Isle, Jedwood. He was buried at Dunfermline on the 15th November and his mother, the sainted Margaret died of a broken heart the following day in 1093.Canmore's body was buried at Tynemouth. In later years the Scots demanded the body back, and according to legend the monks substituted another, though how they produced a skeleton of the height and of Canmore is problematic. So Canmore may still lie at Tynemouth.

Malcolm's death and that of his son, was followed by a disputed succession. Canmore had tried to pass over his brother Donald Bane, who had the best claim according to the scottish custom. This allowed Rufus to play kingmaker. First he supported Duncan, Malcolm's son who had been a hostage in England. They stopped at Durham for St Cuthbert`s blessing and

Duncan paid with the grant of Tyningham to the monks. Duncan was temporarily successful and overthrew his uncle, but Donald Bane fought back, killed Duncan and became king again.

Malcolm's Cross, Alnwick, Northumberland.

In 1095 the Norman Earl of Northumberland, Robert de Mowbray revolted. He had plotted with the Welsh Marcher lords, but they dropped out when the Welsh rebelled. Mowbray and Arkle Morel, (now described as his kinsman,) had also been accused of plundering Norwegian vessels and Rufus ordered restitution. When Mowbray refused to come to court, Rufus headed North once more, he avoided an ambush and caught up with Mowbray who was holed up in Bamburgh, the ancient centre of the Bernician Kings, this was to be the conclusion of the conflict between southern kings and Northumbrian independence. It was fitting that it took place at Bamburgh. The event was marked by the heavens:

"numerous and manifold stars were seen to fall from heaven, not by one or two, but so thick in succession, that no man could tell it." ASC

"Rufus arriving at Bamburgh saw that he could not win it, then ordered his men to make a castle before Bamburgh ,and called it in his speech, "Malveisin", that is in English, "Evil Neighbour". And he fortified it strongly with his men." ASC

Mowbray however escaped to Tynemouth but was followed, wounded and captured. He was then taken before the castle at Bamburgh which was still holding out. There they threatened to put out both his eyes unless the castle was given up. The defenders, Robert's wife and Arkle gave in. The latter then turned king's evidence and many Northumbrians were imprisoned. Mowbray was imprisoned at Windsor for 30 years. Arkle Morel was exiled and died abroad. His lands came into the hands of the Durham Monks.

Rufus then established Edgar, Canmore's third son as King in Scotland, using Edgar the Aethling and an army to overthrow Donald Bane. In this battle the Banner of St Cuthbert was carried by the Anglo-Norman troops. With a client king holding Scotland, the military importance of Northumberland disappeared. Rufus did not replace Earl Robert, henceforth he ruled Northumberland with sheriffs. The first 100 years of the new millennium had seen the English of Northumbria fight an unequal battle to maintain the right to choose their own rulers of both state and church, against the threats of Scots, Danes, and English and Norman kings.

Normans attack a Motte and Bailey Castle.

"No Englishman today is an Earl or bishop or abbot, the newcomers gnaw at the wealth and guts of England, nor is there a hope of ending this misery". ASC

The Liber Eliensis agreed, "What he(William I) did to the leaders of the English who were able to survive this very great battle-not one of them in the whole realm was permitted to enjoy his former power, but that all were driven into a woeful state of poverty or deprived of their inheritance and exiled from their homeland, or made the object of men's scorn by the gouging out of their eyes or the amputation of other parts of the body, or, indeed being tortured most wretchedly and deprived of life. I reckon it no good purpose to speak of what was done to lesser folk not only by William but by his followers, given that we know that this is difficult to speak of and perhaps because of its monstrous cruelty, beyond belief."

The once great Kingdom of Northumbria had been reduced to a shire, the people divided into those under a Scottish King and those under a Norman King. What remained? A common language, a common history, a common religious heritage.

Whither has gone the man?

Whither has gone the giver of treasure?
Whither has gone the place of feasting?
Where are the joys of hall?
Alas, the bright cup!
Alas, the warrior in his corslet
Alas, the glory of the prince!
How that time has passed away,
Has grown dark under the shadow of night, as if it had never been!
Now in the place of the dear warriors stands a wall,
Wondrous high, covered with serpent shapes;
The might of the ash-wood spears has carried off the Earls,
The weapon greedy for slaughter—a glorious fate;
and storms beat upon these rocky slopes;
the falling storm binds the earth,
The terror of winter.
Then comes darkness, the night shadow casts gloom,
Sends from the north fierce hailstorms to the terror of men.
Everything is full of hardship in the kingdom of earth;
The decree of fate changes the world under the heavens.
Here possessions are transient, here friends are transient,
Here man is transient, here woman is transient;
All this firm-set earth becomes empty"   Wanderer. Gordon.

The separate identity of Northumbrians had been obliterated…..or had it?

BIBLIOGRAPHY

Adomnan of Iona. Life of St Columba. Penguin 1995.
Bede.The Ecclesiastical History of the English Nation ed. E Rhys. 1910.
Bede Life and Miracles of St Cuthbert.
The Anglo-Saxon Chronicle. Tr. J Ingram.1912.
Simeon. History of the Church of Durham. Llanerch reprint 1993.
Simeon A History of the Kings of England.1987.
Wulfstan Sermon to the English people. Trans. Bradley SAJ.

Northern History. NH 1991 Higham N. Cavalry in Bernicia. NH 1993 Cessford. C. Cavalry. Hooper NJ Aberlemno Stone.
NH 94 Cessford C, Death of Aethelfrith. NH 93 Palliser DM .The Harrying of the north.NH1. 1966 Barrow Anglo-Scottish border.NH4 1969 .
Barrow North English Society. NH XLI 2004.Woolf A Caedulla.
Surtees Society; SS 75 The Rites of Durham. SS 1841 Oswine.
AA; Archealogiae Aeliana. AA.NSxvi.1894.Craster.Place names.
Aa 4s xxvi 1948 Hunter Blair P .The Northumbrian and their southern frontier. AA 1952 Waltheof. AA 5s5.1977. Northumbrian and Viking settlement.
Peritia. V 2. Moisil.H.1983.The Bernician royal dynasty and the Irish.

Aird W M St Cuthbert and the Normans.
Alexander M The earliest English poems .Penguin 1966
Appleby JC &Dalton P Government, Religion, and Society in Northern England 1000-1700 AD.
Backhouse J The Lindisfarne Gospels. Phaidon Oxford 1981
Basset S.The origins of the Anglo-Saxon Kingdoms. Leic.
Beckensall S. Durham place names.
Blair PH Northumbria in the days of Bede.L.1976.
Bonner St Cuthbert, his cult and Community to AD 1200.Woodbridge Boydell press.
Bonner G Saint Cuthbert at Chester-le-Street.
Bradley SAJ Anglo-Saxon Poetry.
Bradley, SAJ, Anglo-Saxon Poetry .L 1982.
Brown W St Cuthbert`s remains. Ushaw.1909
Brown K et al Treasures from Durham Cathedral.
Campbell J The Anglo-Saxons. 1982
Chadwick N et al. Celt and Saxon.
Clack and Ivy The Borders.
Clemoes. The Anglo-Saxons.
Colgrave B Lives of St Cuthbert. Reprint 1985.CUP

Cramp R.J. studies in Anglo-Saxon sculpture. 1992.
Crossley Holland K, The Anglo-Saxon world.
Cummins WA The age of the Picts. Stroud 1995
Ellis PB Celt and Saxon 1994
Fairweather. J. Liber Eliensis.
Fletcher R Who's Who in Roman Britain and Anglo-Saxon England. Shepheard-Walwyn 1989.
Fisher. DJV. The Anglo-Saxon Age.
Fraser JE. From Caledonia to Pictland. Scotland to 795.
Gallyon M The early church in Northumbria. Dalton.1977
Godfrey CJ The church in Anglo-Saxon Engand.1962.
Gordon RK Anglo-Saxon Poetry. Everyman 1926.
Hall RA. Ed. The Viking Age. York and the North. London. Council of British Archaeology Research report 27.
Hawkes J & Mills Northumbria's Golden Age Sutton 1999
Higham N Northern counties to AD 1000. L 1986.
Higham N. The kingdom of Northumbria. Sutton 1993.
Hindley G. The Anglo-Saxons.
Humble R The Saxon Kings.
Hunter Blair P. The world of Bede.
Hutchinson History of Durham. 1785.
Jackson K Hurlstone. A celtic Miscellany. Penguin 1951.
Jackson K. Language and history in Early Britain.
Kirby DP Ed. St Wilfrid at Hexham. Oriel 1976.
Kirby DP The earliest English kings. London. Unwin and Hyman. 1991
Kramer E. Ed et al. Kings of the North Sea .Ad 250-850.
Mayr-Harting HMRE The coming of Christianity to Anglo-Saxon England.
Marsden J. Northanhymbre Saga. BCA 1992.
Marsden J The fury of the Northmen.
Mawer ,A. The place names of Northumberland and Durham .CUP.1920
Morris CJ Marriage and Murder in IIth Century Northumbria. Borthwick paper. 82.
Myers JNL The English settlements .1986
Nicolaisen. WFH. Scottish Place names.
Omand D The Borders Book Birlinn Edinburgh 1995
Page RJ Life in Anglo-Saxon England.
Pevsner, N. The buildings of England. Northumberland. Penguin 1957.
Ritchie A. Picts. Edin. HMSO.
Rollason D et al. Anglo-Norman Durham.
Rollason D. Northumbria, 500-1100. camb.
Rollason D. Cuthbert. Saint and Patron.
Sawyer PH From Roman Britain to Norman England. 1978
Stancliffe C. Ed, & E Cambridge Oswald Northumbrian king to European saint. 1995
Stenton FM. Anglo-Saxon England.

Swanton M. English Literature before Chaucer. Longman 1987
Rowland TH. Anglo-Saxon Northumbria. 1973 Sandhill.
Thomas C. Britain and Ireland in early Christian Times.1971.
Thomas C. The early Christian architecture of North Britain, 1971.
Tomlinson. WW. Comprehensive Guide to Northumberland.
Watson, G. Goodwife Hot and other places. Sandhill 1970
Whitelock D.The beginnings of English Society. Pelican. 1952.
Wormald. P. The Times of Bede.
Woolf A From Pictland to Alba, 789-1070 AD.
Wrenn CL. A study of Old English Literature.
Yorke B. Kings and Kingdoms in early Anglo-Saxon England. L. Seaby.

More Northumbrian Books from Chris Kilkenny,

Available now; More volumes in this series, following the History of the Northumbrian people to the present day.

Vol.2. Knights and Bishops.
Vol.3. Reivers and Recusants.
Vol.4. Royalists, Roundheads and Recusants.
Vol.5. Gentlemen and Scholars, and The lesser Sort.
Vol.6. The North East Powerhouse. Northumbrians in the 19th Century.
Vol.7. pending, see Amazon books.

Also;
Northumbrian Songs; "Singin' Hinnies", the story of traditional song in the North East.
Northumbrian icons. "The Lindisfarne Gospels and Cuthbert, The body, book and banner" The story of the patron saint of the North, his book the Lindisfarne Gospels and his banner carried in wars against the Scots."

All the above available as ebooks; as are;
Northumbrian Pub signs; "The Inn Sign Story", the story behind pub signs in the North East.
Cuthbert Coffin Trails. Walks following the travels of Cuthbert's coffin around the North of England.

And also in print;
Northumbria-on this day, historical events for every day of the year.

X 2018

Printed in Great Britain
by Amazon